The PRESENT *as* HISTORY

> The un- and anti-historical core of bourgeois thought appears in its most glaring form when we consider the *problem of the present as a historical problem*.
>
> GEORG LUKACS

BOOKS BY PAUL M. SWEEZY

Monopoly and Competition in the English Coal Trade, 1550-1850

The Theory of Capitalist Development

Socialism

Cuba: Anatomy of a Revolution (with Leo Huberman)

BOOKS EDITED BY PAUL M. SWEEZY

F. O. Matthiessen (1902-1950): A Collective Portrait, edited with Leo Huberman

Karl Marx and the Close of His System by Eugen von Böhm-Bawerk, and *Böhm-Bawerk's Criticism of Marx* by Rudolf Hilferding

Imperialism and Social Classes by Joseph A. Schumpeter

The PRESENT as HISTORY

Essays and Reviews on Capitalism and Socialism

by
PAUL M. SWEEZY

MONTHLY REVIEW PRESS
New York

Copyright, 1953, by Paul M. Sweezy

Library of Congress catalog card number: 53-12728

ACKNOWLEDGMENT is gratefully made to the editors or publishers of the following periodicals for permission to reprint: *The American Economic Review, The Antioch Review, The Economic Review* (Tokyo), *The Journal of Economic History, The Journal of Political Economy, Monthly Review, The Nation, The New Republic, The New Statesman and Nation, Plan Age, The Review of Economics and Statistics,* and *Science & Society.*

Second Printing 1962

MANUFACTURED IN THE UNITED STATES OF AMERICA

Preface

This volume brings together essays and reviews written over a period of some fifteen years and covering a wide range of topics and books. The title is not an attempt to define the subject matter but rather to suggest the angle of vision from which the various pieces were written. Everyone knows that the present will some day be history. I believe that the most important task of the social scientist is to try to comprehend it as history now, while it is still the present and while we still have the power to influence its shape and outcome. I hope that collecting these essays and reviews in a single volume will make a contribution to that end.

Three of these papers are here published for the first time: "Science, Marxism, and Democracy," "A Crucial Difference Between Capitalism and Socialism," and "Peace and Prosperity." For the rest, place and date of earlier publication are given in introductory notes which in some cases add comments that have seemed necessary or helpful on the occasion of republication. I have edited the entire volume as though it were an original manuscript, cutting unnecessary verbiage, improving the formulation here and there, inserting an occasional cross reference, and imposing consistency in matters of punctuation, capitalization, and the like. But I have not added or eliminated or changed anything of any substance.

The quotation which I have chosen as an epigraph is taken from Georg Lukacs, *Geschichte und Klassenbewusstsein* (Berlin, 1923, page 173).

I want to thank John Rackliffe for encouragement and assistance at all stages in the planning and production of the book.

P. M. S.

TO LEO

With Gratitude and Affection

CONTENTS

Preface   v

PART I - *The Character of Our Epoch*

1. The Communist Manifesto After 100 Years   3
2. Toynbee's Universal History   30
3. The Illusion of the Managerial Revolution   39
4. The Marshall Plan and the Crisis of Western Europe   67
5. Marxism in the East: Decomposition or Enrichment?   74

PART II - *Imperialism*

6. A Marxist View of Imperialism   79
7. Three Works on Imperialism   93

PART III - *American Capitalism*

8. Recent Developments in American Capitalism   111
9. The American Ruling Class   120
10. Capitalism and Race Relations   139
11. The Heyday of the Investment Banker   153
12. Interest Groups in the American Economy   158
13. The Decline of the Investment Banker   189
14. Critics and Crusaders   197
15. Socialist Humanitarianism   202
16. An Economic Program for America   205

PART IV - *German Capitalism*

17. The German Problem   223
18. National Socialism   233

19. Post Mortem 242
20. Resurrection? 244

PART V - *Thinkers and Theories*

21. John Maynard Keynes 253
22. Pigou and the Case for Socialism 263
23. Hansen and the Crisis of Capitalism 267
24. Schumpeter's Theory of Innovation 274
25. Hayek's Road to Serfdom 283
26. Rosa Luxemburg and the Theory of Capitalism 291
27. Thorstein Veblen: Strengths and Weaknesses 295

PART VI - *Some Problems in Political Economy*

28. Marxian and Orthodox Economics 305
29. Fabian Political Economy 317
30. Science, Marxism, and Democracy 330
31. Strategy for Socialism 338
32. A Crucial Difference Between Capitalism and Socialism 341
33. A Reply to Critics 352
34. Peace and Prosperity 363

Index 370

Part I

The Character of Our Epoch

1

The Communist Manifesto After 100 Years

This essay was written in close collaboration with my fellow editor of Monthly Review, *Leo Huberman, and was first published as an editorial in the issue of August 1949.*

THE *Communist Manifesto*, the most famous document in the history of the socialist movement, was written by Karl Marx and Friedrich Engels during the latter part of 1847 and the first month of 1848. It was published in February 1848. This appreciation of the *Manifesto* at the end of its first century is thus more than a year late. This is a case, however, in which we hope our readers will agree with us: better late than never.

THE HISTORICAL IMPORTANCE OF THE MANIFESTO

What gives the *Manifesto* its unique importance? In order to answer this question it is necessary to see clearly its place in the history of socialism.

Despite a frequently encountered opinion to the contrary, there was no socialism in ancient or medieval times. There were movements and doctrines of social reform which were radical in the sense that they sought greater equality or even complete community of consumer goods, but none even approached the modern socialist conception of a society in which the means of production are publicly owned and managed. This is, of course, not surprising. Production actually took place on a primitive level in scattered workshops and agricultural strips — conditions under which public ownership and management were not only impossible but even unthinkable.

The first theoretical expression of a genuinely socialist position came in Thomas More's *Utopia*, written in the early years of the sixteenth century — in other words, at the very threshold of what we call the modern period. But *Utopia* was the work of an individual genius and not the reflection of a social movement. It was not until the English Civil War, in the middle of the seventeenth century, that socialism first began to assume the shape of a social movement. Gerrard Winstanley (born 1609, died sometime after 1660) was probably the greatest socialist thinker that the English-speaking countries have yet produced, and the Digger movement which he led was certainly the first practical expression of socialism. But it lasted only a very short time, and the same was true of the movement led by Babeuf during the French Revolution a century and a half later. Meanwhile, quite a number of writers had formulated views of a more or less definitely socialist character.

But it was not until the nineteenth century that socialism became an important public issue and socialists began to play a significant role in the political life of the most advanced European countries. The Utopian socialists (Owen, Fourier, St. Simon) were key figures in this period of emergence; and the Chartist movement in Britain, which flourished during the late 1830s and early 1840s, showed that the new factory working class formed a potentially powerful base for a socialist political party.

Thus we see that socialism is strictly a modern phenomenon, a child of the industrial revolution which got under way in England in the seventeenth century and decisively altered the economic and social structure of all of western Europe during the eighteenth and early nineteenth centuries. By 1840 or so, socialism had arrived in the sense that it was already widely discussed and politically promising.

But socialism was still shapeless and inchoate — a collection of brilliant insights and perceptions, of more or less fanciful projects, of passionate beliefs and hopes. There was an urgent need for systematization; for a careful review picking out what was sound, dropping what was unsound, integrating into the socialist outlook the most progressive elements of bourgeois philosophy and social science.

It was the historical mission of Karl Marx and Friedrich Engels to perform this task. They appeared on the scene at just the right time; they were admirably prepared by background and training; they seized upon their opportunity with a remarkably clear estimate of its crucial importance to the future of mankind.

Marx and Engels began their work of transforming socialism "from Utopia to science" in the early 1840s. In the next few years of profound study and intense discussion they worked out their own new socialist synthesis. The *Manifesto* for the first time broadcast this new synthesis to the world — in briefest compass and in arrestingly brilliant prose.

The *Manifesto* thus marks a decisive watershed in the history of socialism. Previous thought and experience lead up to it; subsequent developments start from it. It is this fact which stamps the *Manifesto* as the most important document in the history of socialism. And the steady growth of socialism as a world force since 1848 has raised the *Manifesto* to the status of one of the most important documents in the entire history of the human race.

HOW SHOULD WE EVALUATE THE MANIFESTO TODAY?

How has the *Manifesto* stood up during its first hundred years? The answer we give to this question will depend largely on the criteria by which — consciously or unconsciously — we form our judgments.

Some who consider themselves Marxists approach the *Manifesto* in the spirit of a religious fundamentalist approaching the Bible — every word and every proposition were literally true when written and remain sacrosanct and untouchable after the most eventful century in world history. It is, of course, not difficult to demonstrate to the satisfaction of any reasonable person that this is an untenable position. For this very reason, no doubt, a favorite procedure of enemies of Marxism is to assume that all Marxists take this view of the *Manifesto*. If the *Manifesto* is judged by the criterion of one-hundred-percent infallibility it can be readily disposed of by any second-rate hack who thus convinces himself that he is a greater man than the founders of scientific socialism. The American academic community, it may be noted in passing, is full of such great men today. But theirs is a hollow victory which, though repeated thousands of times every year, leaves the *Manifesto* untouched and the stature of its authors undiminished.

Much more relevant and significant are the criteria which Marx and Engels themselves, in later years, used in judging the *Manifesto*. For this reason the prefaces which they wrote to various reprints and translations are both revealing and important (especially the prefaces to the German edition of 1872, the Russian edition of 1882, the German edition of 1883, and the English edition of 1888). Let us sum up what seem to us to be the main points which emerge from a study of these prefaces:

(1) In certain respects, Marx and Engels regarded the *Manifesto* as clearly dated. This is particularly the case as regards the programmatic section and the section dealing with socialist literature (end of Part II and all of Part III).

(2) The general principles set forth in the *Manifesto* were, in their view, "on the whole as correct today as ever" (first written in 1872, repeated in 1888).

(3) The experience of the Paris Commune caused them to add a principle of great importance which was absent from the original, namely, that "the working class cannot simply lay hold of the ready-made state machinery and wield it for its own purposes." In other words, the "ready-made state machinery" had been created by and for the existing ruling classes and would have to be replaced by new state

machinery after the conquest of power by the working class.

(4) Finally — and this is perhaps the most important point of all — in their last joint preface (to the Russian edition of 1882), Marx and Engels brought out clearly the fact that the *Manifesto* was based on the historical experience of western and central Europe. But by 1882 Russia, in their opinion, formed "the vanguard of revolutionary action in Europe," and this development inevitably gave rise to new questions and problems which did not and could not arise within the framework of the original *Manifesto*.

It is thus quite obvious from these later prefaces that Marx and Engels never for a moment entertained the notion that they were blueprinting the future course of history or laying down a set of dogmas which would be binding on future generations of socialists. In particular, they implicitly recognized that as capitalism spread and drew new countries and regions into the mainstream of modern history, problems and forms of development not considered in the *Manifesto* must necessarily be encountered.

On the other hand, Marx and Engels never wavered in their conviction that the *general principles* set forth in the *Manifesto* were sound and valid. Neither the events of the succeeding decades nor their own subsequent studies, profound and wide-ranging as they were, caused them to alter or question its central theoretical framework.

It seems clear to us that in judging the *Manifesto* today, a century after its publication, we should be guided by the same criteria that the authors themselves used twenty-five, thirty, and forty years after its publication. We should not concern ourselves with details but should go straight to the general principles and examine them in the light of the changed conditions of the mid-twentieth century.

THE GENERAL PRINCIPLES OF THE MANIFESTO

The general principles of the *Manifesto* can be grouped under the following headings: (a) historical materialism, (b) class struggle, (c) the nature of capitalism, (d) the inevitability of socialism, and (e) the road to socialism. Let us review these principles as briefly and concisely as we can.

HISTORICAL MATERIALISM. This is the theory of history which runs through the *Manifesto* as it does through all the mature writings of Marx and Engels. It holds that the way people act and think is determined in the final analysis by the way they get their living; hence the foundation of any society is its economic system; and therefore economic change is the driving force of history. Part I of the *Manifesto* is essentially a brilliant and amazingly compact application of this theory to the rise and development of capitalism from its earliest beginnings in the Middle Ages to its full-fledged mid-nineteenth-century form. Part II contains a passage which puts the case for historical materialism as against historical idealism with unexampled clarity:

> Does it require deep intuition to comprehend that man's ideas, views, and conceptions, in one word, man's consciousness, changes with every change in the conditions of his material existence, in his social relations and in his social life?
>
> What else does the history of ideas prove, than that intellectual production changes its character in proportion as material production is changed? The ruling ideas of each age have ever been the ideas of its ruling class.
>
> When people speak of ideas that revolutionize society, they do but express the fact, that within the old society, the elements of a new one have been created, and that the dissolution of the old ideas keeps even pace with the dissolution of the old conditions of existence.

CLASS STRUGGLE. The *Manifesto* opens with the famous sentence: "The history of all hitherto existing society is the history of class struggles." This is in no sense a contradiction of the theory of historical materialism but rather an essential part of it. "Hitherto existing society" (Engels explained in a footnote to the 1888 edition that this term should not be interpreted to include preliterate societies) had always been based on an economic system in which some people did the work and others appropriated the social surplus. Fundamental differences in the method of securing a livelihood — some by working, some by owning — must, according to historical materialism, create groups with fundamentally different and in many respects antagonistic interests, attitudes, aspirations. These groups are the classes of Marxian theory. They, and not individuals, are the chief actors on the stage of history. Their activities and strivings — above all, their conflicts—underlie the social movements, the wars and revolutions, which trace out the pattern of human progress.

THE NATURE OF CAPITALISM. The *Manifesto* contains the bold outlines of the theory of capitalism which Marx was to spend most of the remainder of his life perfecting and elaborating. (It is interesting to note that the term "capitalism" does not occur in the *Manifesto;* instead, Marx and Engels use a variety of expressions, such as "existing society," "bourgeois society," "the rule of the bourgeoisie," and so forth.) Capitalism is pre-eminently a market, or commodity-producing, economy, which "has left no other nexus between man and man than naked self-interest, than callous 'cash payment.'" Even the laborer is a commodity and must sell himself piecemeal to the capitalist. The capitalist purchases labor (later Marx would have substituted "labor power" for "labor" in this context) in order to make profits, and he makes profits in order to expand his capital. Thus the laborers form a class "who live only so long as they find work, and who find work only so long as their labor increases capital."

It follows that capitalism, in contrast to all earlier forms of society, is a restlessly expanding system which "cannot exist without constantly revolutionizing the instruments of production, and thereby the relations of production, and with them the whole relations of society." Moreover, "the need of a constantly expanding market for its products chases the bourgeoisie over the whole surface of the globe. It must nestle everywhere, settle everywhere, establish connections everywhere." Thanks to these qualities, "the bourgeoisie, during its rule of scarce one hundred years, has created more massive and more colossal productive forces than have all preceding generations together." But, by a peculiar irony, its enormous productivity turns out to be the nemesis of capitalism. In one of the great passages of the *Manifesto*, which is worth quoting in full, Marx and Engels lay bare the inner contradictions which are driving capitalism to certain shipwreck:

Modern bourgeois society with its relations of production, of exchange and of property, a society that has conjured up such gigantic means of production and of exchange, is like the sorcerer who is no longer able to control the powers of the nether world whom he has called up by his spells. For many a decade past the history of industry and commerce is but the history of the revolt of modern productive forces against modern conditions of production, against the property relations that are the conditions for the existence of the bourgeoisie and of its rule. It is enough to mention the commercial crises that by their periodical return put the existence of the entire bourgeois society on its trial, each time more threateningly. In these crises a great part not only of the existing products, but also of the previously created productive forces, are periodically destroyed. In these crises there breaks out an epidemic that, in all earlier epochs, would have seemed an absurdity — the epidemic of overproduction. Society suddenly finds itself put back into a state of momentary barbarism; it appears as if a famine, a universal war of devastation had cut off the supply of every means of subsistence; industry and commerce seem to be destroyed. And why? Because there is too much civilization, too much means of subsistence, too much industry, too much commerce. The productive forces at the disposal of society no longer tend to further the development of the conditions of bourgeois property; on the contrary, they have become too powerful for these conditions, by which they are fettered, and so soon as they overcome these fetters, they bring disorder into the whole of bourgeois society, endanger the existence of bourgeois property. The conditions of bourgeois society are too narrow to comprise the wealth created by them. And how does the bourgeoisie get over these crises? On the one hand, by enforced destruction of a mass of productive forces; on the other, by the conquest of new markets, and by the more thorough exploitation of the old ones. That is to say, by paving the way for more extensive and more destructive crises, and by diminishing the means whereby crises are prevented.

THE INEVITABILITY OF SOCIALISM. The mere fact that capitalism is doomed is not enough to ensure the triumph of socialism. History is full of examples which show that the dissolution of a society can lead to chaos and retrogression as well as to a new and more progressive system. Hence it is of greatest importance that capitalism by its very nature creates and trains the force which at a certain stage of development must overthrow it and replace it by socialism. The reasoning is concisely summed up in the last paragraph of Part I:

The essential condition for the existence and for the sway of the bourgeois class, is the formation and augmentation of capital; the condition for capital is wage labor. Wage labor rests exclusively on competition between the laborers. The advance of industry, whose involuntary promoter is the bourgeoisie, replaces the isolation of the laborers, due to competition, by their revolutionary combination, due to association. The development of modern industry, therefore, cuts from under its feet the very foundation on which the bourgeoisie produces and appropriates products. What the bourgeoisie therefore produces, above all, are its own grave-diggers. Its fall and the victory of the proletariat are equally inevitable.

THE ROAD TO SOCIALISM. There are two aspects to this question as it appears in the *Manifesto:* first, the general character of the socialist revolution; and, second, the course of the revolution on an international scale.

The socialist revolution must be essentially a working-class revolution, though Marx and Engels were far from denying a role to elements of other classes. As pointed out above, the development of capitalism itself requires more and more wage workers; moreover, as industry grows and the transport network is extended and improved, the workers are increasingly unified and trained for collective action. At a certain stage this results in the "organization of the proletarians into a class, and consequently into a political party." The contradictions of capitalism will sooner or later give rise to a situation from which there is no escape except through revolution. What Marx and Engels call the "first step" in this revolution is the conquest of power, "to raise the proletariat to the position of ruling class, to win the battle of democracy." It is important to note — because it has been so often overlooked — that basic social changes come only after the working class has acquired power:

> The proletariat will use its political supremacy to wrest, by degrees, all capital from the bourgeoisie, to centralize all instruments of production in the hands of the state, i.e. of the proletariat organized as the ruling class; and to increase the total of productive powers as rapidly as possible.

This will be a transition period during which the working class "sweeps away by force the old conditions of production." (In view of present-day misrepresentations of Marxism, it may be as well to point out that "sweeping away by force" in this connection implies the orderly use of state power and not the indiscriminate use of violence.) Finally, along with these conditions, the working class will

> have swept away the conditions for the existence of class antagonisms and of classes generally, and will thereby have abolished its own supremacy as a class.
>
> In place of the old bourgeois society, with its classes and class antagonisms, we shall have an association, in which the free development of each is the condition for the free development of all.

So much for the general character of the socialist revolution. There remains the question of the international course of the revolution. Here it was clear to Marx and Engels that though the modern working-class movement is essentially an international movement directed against a system which knows no national boundaries, "yet in form, the struggle of the proletariat with the bourgeoisie is at first a national struggle." And from this it follows that "the proletariat of each country must, of course, first of all settle matters with its own bourgeoisie." At the same time, Marx and Engels were well aware of the international character of the counter-revolutionary forces which would certainly attempt to crush an isolated workers' revolution. Hence, "united action of the leading civilized countries at least, is one of the first conditions for the emancipation of the proletariat." Thus the various national revolutions must reinforce and protect one another and eventually merge into a new society from which international exploitation and hostility will have vanished. For, as Marx and Engels point out:

In proportion as the exploitation of one individual by another is put an end to, the exploitation of one nation by another will also be put an end to. In proportion as the antagonism between classes within the nation vanishes, the hostility of one nation to another will come to an end.

As to the actual geography of the revolution, Marx and Engels took it for granted that it would start and spread from the most advanced capitalist countries of western and central Europe. At the time of writing the *Manifesto*, they correctly judged that Europe was on the verge of a new revolutionary upheaval, and they expected that Germany would be the cockpit:

The Communists turn their attention chiefly to Germany, because that country is on the eve of a bourgeois revolution that is bound to be carried out under more advanced conditions of European civilization and with a much more developed proletariat than that of England was in the seventeenth, and of France in the eighteenth century, and because the bourgeois revolution in Germany will be but the prelude to an immediately following proletarian revolution.

This prediction, of course, turned out to be overoptimistic. Not the revolution but the counter-revolution won the day in Germany, and indeed in all of Europe. But at no time in their later lives did Marx and Engels revise the view of the *Manifesto* that the proletarian, or socialist, revolution would come first in one or more of the most advanced capitalist countries of western and central Europe. In the 1870s and 1880s they became increasingly interested in Russia, convinced that that country must soon be the scene of a revolution similar in scope and character to the great French Revolution of a hundred years earlier. No small part of their interest in Russia derived from a conviction that the Russian revolution, though it would be essentially a bourgeois revolution, would flash the signal for the final showdown in the West. As Gustav Mayer says in his biography of Engels, speaking of the later years, "his speculations about the future always centered on the approaching Russian revolution, the revolution which was to clear the way for the proletarian revolution in the West." (English translation, p. 278.) But "he never imagined that his ideas might triumph, in that Empire lying on the very edge of European civilization, before capitalism was overthrown in western Europe." (P. 286.)

THE GENERAL PRINCIPLES OF THE MANIFESTO A HUNDRED YEARS LATER

What are we to say of the theoretical framework of the *Manifesto* after a hundred years? Can we say, as Marx and Engels said, that the general principles are "on the whole as correct today as ever"? Or have the events of the last five or six decades been such as to force us to abandon or revise these principles? Let us review our list item by item.

HISTORICAL MATERIALISM. The last half century has certainly provided no grounds whatever to question the validity of historical materialism. Rather the contrary. There has probably never been a period in which it was more obvious that the prime mover of history is economic change; and certainly the thesis has never been so widely recognized as at present. This recognition is by no means confined to Marxists or socialists; one can even say that it provides the starting point for an increasingly large proportion of all serious historical scholarship. Moreover, the point of view of historical materialism — that "man's ideas, views, and conceptions, in one word, man's consciousness, changes with every change in the conditions of his material existence, in his social relations and in his social life" — has been taken over (ordinarily without acknowledgment, and perhaps frequently without even knowledge, of its source) by nearly all social scientists worthy of the name. It is, of course, true that the world-wide crisis of the capitalist system, along with the wars and depressions and catastrophes to which it has given rise, has produced a vast outpouring of mystical, irrational theories in recent years, and that such theories are increasingly characteristic of bourgeois thought as a whole. But wherever sanity and reason prevail, both inside and outside the socialist movement, there the truth of historical materialism is ever more clearly perceived as a beacon lighting up the path to an understanding of human society and its history.

CLASS STRUGGLE. The theory of class struggle, like the theory of historical materialism, has been strengthened rather than weakened by the events of the last half century. Not only is it increasingly clear that internal events in the leading nations of the world are dominated by class conflicts, but also the crucial role of class conflict in international affairs is much nearer the surface and hence more easily visible today than ever before. Above all, the rise and spread of fascism in the interwar period did more than anything else possibly could have done to educate millions of people all over the world to the class character of capitalism and the lengths to which the ruling class will go to preserve its privileges against any threat from below. Moreover, here, as in the case of historical materialism, serious social scientists have been forced to pay Marx and Engels the compliment of imitation. The study of such diverse phenomena as social psychology, the development of Chinese society, the caste system in India, and racial discrimination in the United States South, is being transformed by a recognition of the central role of class and class struggle. Honest enemies of Marxism are no longer able to pooh-pooh the theory of class struggle as they once did; they now leave the pooh-poohing to the dupes and paid propagandists of the ruling class. They must admit, with H. G. Wells, that "Marx, who did not so much advocate the class war, the war of the expropriated mass against the appropriating few, as foretell it, is being more and more justified by events" (*The Outline of History*, Vol. II, p. 399); or, with Professor Talcott Parsons, Chairman of the Social Relations Department at Harvard, that "the Marxian view of the importance of class structure has in a broad way been vindicated." (*Papers and Proceedings of the 61st Annual Meeting of the American Economic Association*, May 1949, p. 26.)

THE NATURE OF CAPITALISM. In political economy, bourgeois social science has borrowed less from, and made fewer concessions to, the Marxian position than in historiography and sociology. The reason is not far to seek. Historical materialism and class struggle are general theories which apply to many different societies and epochs. It is not difficult, with the help of circumlocutions and evasions, to make use of them in relatively "safe" ways and at the same time to obtain results incomparably more valuable than anything yielded by the traditional bourgeois idealist and individualist approaches. When it comes to political economy, however, the case is very different. Marxian political economy applies specifically to capitalism, to the system under which the bourgeois social scientist lives (and makes his living) here and now; its conclusions are clear-cut, difficult to evade, and absolutely unacceptable to the ruling class. The result is that for bourgeois economists Marxian political economy scarcely exists, and it is rare to find in their writings an admission of Marx's greatness as an economist stated so specifically as in the following: "He was the first economist of top rank to see and to teach systematically how economic theory may be turned into historical analysis and how the historical narrative may be turned into *histoire raisonnée*." (J. A. Schumpeter, *Capitalism, Socialism, and Democracy*, 1st edition, p. 44.)

Does the neglect of Marx as an economist indicate the failure of the ideas of the *Manifesto*? On the contrary; the correlation is an inverse one. What idea has been more completely confirmed by the last century than the conception of capitalism's restless need to expand, of the capitalist's irresistible urge to "nestle everywhere, settle everywhere, establish connections everywhere"? Who can deny today that the periodical return of crises is a fact which puts the "existence of the entire bourgeois society on its trial, each time more threateningly"? Who can fail to see that "the conditions of bourgeois society are too narrow to comprise the wealth created by them"? In short, who can any longer be blind to the fact that capitalism is riddled with contradictions which make its continued existence — at least in anything like its traditional form — impossible and unthinkable?

THE INEVITABILITY OF SOCIALISM. There are, of course, many who, recognizing the dire straits to which the capitalist world has come, believe that it is possible to patch up and reform the system in such a way as to make it serve the real interests of society. But their number is diminishing every day, and conversely the great international army of socialism is growing in strength and confidence. Its members have every reason for confidence.

When the *Manifesto* was written, socialism was composed of "little sects," as Engels told the Zurich Congress of the Second International in 1893; by that time, two years before his death, it "had developed into a powerful party before which the world of officialdom trembles."

Twenty-five years later, after World War I, one sixth of the land surface of the globe had passed through a proletarian revolution and was, as subsequent events showed, securely on the path to socialism.

Three decades later, after World War II, more than a quarter of the human race, in eastern Europe and China, had followed suit.

If capitalism could not prevent the growth of socialism when it was healthy and in sole possession of the field, what reason is there to suppose that it can now perform the feat when it is sick to death and challenged by an actually functioning socialist system which grows in strength and vigor with every year that passes? The central message of the *Manifesto* was the impending doom of capitalism and its replacement by a new, socialist order. Has anything else in the whole document been more brilliantly verified by the intervening hundred years?

THE ROAD TO SOCIALISM. Much of what Marx and Engels said in the *Manifesto* about the general character of the socialist revolution has been amply confirmed by the experience of Russia. The working class did lead the way and play the decisive role. The first step was "to raise the proletariat to the position of ruling class." The proletariat did "use its political supremacy to wrest, by degrees, all capital from the bourgeoisie, to centralize all instruments of production in the hands of the state, . . . and to increase the total of productive powers as rapidly as possible." The conditions for the existence of class antagonisms have been "swept away." On the other hand, the relative backwardness of Russia and the aggravation of class and international conflicts on a world scale have combined to bring about the intensification rather than the dismantling of state power in the USSR. The achievement of "an association in which the free development of each is the condition for the free development of all" remains what it was a century ago, a goal for the future.

It is also true that an important part of what is said in the *Manifesto* about the international course of the revolution has been corroborated by subsequent experience. The socialist revolution has not taken the form of a simultaneous international uprising; rather it has taken, and gives every prospect of continuing to take, the form of a series of national revolutions which differ from one another in many respects. Such differences, however, do not alter the fact that in content all these socialist revolutions, like the bourgeois revolutions of an earlier period, are international in character and are contributing to the building of a new world order. We cannot yet state as a fact that this new world order will be one from which international enmity will have vanished, and the quarrel between Yugoslavia and the other socialist countries of eastern Europe may seem to point to an opposite conclusion. The present status of international relations, however, is so dominated by the division of the world into two systems and the preparation of both sides for a possible "final" conflict, and the existence of more than one socialist country is such a recent phenomenon, that we shall do well to reserve judgment on the import of the Yugoslav case. In the meantime, the reasons for expecting the gradual disappearance of international exploitation and hostility from a *predominantly* socialist world are just as strong as they were a hundred years ago.

We now come to our last topic, the geography of the socialist revolution. Here there can be no question that Marx and Engels were mistaken, not only when they wrote the *Manifesto* but in their later writings as well. The socialist revolution did not come first in the most advanced capitalist countries of Europe; nor did it come first in America after the United States had displaced Great Britain as the world's leading capitalist country. Further, the socialist revolution is not spreading first to these regions from its country of origin; on the contrary, it is spreading first to comparatively backward countries which are relatively inaccessible to the economic and military power of the most advanced capitalist countries. The first country to pass through a successful socialist revolution was Russia, and this was not only not anticipated by Marx and Engels but would have been impossible under conditions which existed during the lifetime of their generation.

Why were Marx and Engels mistaken on this issue? We must examine this question carefully, both because it is an important issue in its own right and because it is the source of many misconceptions.

At first sight, it might appear that the mistake of Marx and Engels consisted in not providing explanatory principles adequate to account for the Russian Revolution. But we do not believe that this reaches the heart of the problem. It is, of course, true, as we pointed out above, that during the 1870s and 1880s Marx and Engels denied the possibility of a *socialist* revolution in Russia. But at that time they were perfectly right, and it is not inconsistent to record this fact and at the same time to assert that the pattern and timing of the Russian Revolution were in accord with the principles of the *Manifesto*. What is too often forgotten is that between 1880 and World War I capitalism developed extremely rapidly in the empire of the tsars. In 1917 Russia was still, *on the whole*, a relatively backward country; but she also possessed some of the largest factories in Europe and a working class which, in terms of numbers, degree of organization, and quality of leadership, was almost entirely a product of the preceding three decades. Capitalism was certainly more highly developed in Russia in 1917 than it had been in Germany in 1848. Bearing this in mind, let us substitute "Russia" for "Germany" in a passage from the *Manifesto* already quoted above:

> The Communists turn their attention chiefly to Russia, because that country is on the eve of a bourgeois revolution that is bound to be carried out under more advanced conditions of European civilization and with a more developed proletariat than that of England was in the seventeenth, and of France in the eighteenth century, and because the bourgeois revolution in Russia will be but the prelude to an immediately following proletarian revolution.

Clearly, what Marx and Engels had overoptimistically predicted for Germany in 1848 actually occurred in Russia seventy years later. What this means is that, *given the fact that the socialist revolution had failed to materialize in the West,* Russia was, even according to the theory of the *Manifesto*, a logical starting point.

Furthermore, there is no contradiction between Marxian theory and the fact that the socialist revolution, having once taken place in Russia, spread first to relatively backward countries. For Marx and Engels fully recognized what might be called the possibility of historical borrowing. One consequence of the triumph of socialism anywhere would be the opening up of new paths to socialism elsewhere. Or, to put the matter differently, not all countries need go through the same stages of development; once one country has achieved socialism, other countries will have the possibility of abbreviating or skipping certain stages which the pioneer country had to pass through. There was obviously no occasion to discuss this question in the *Manifesto,* but it arose later on in connection with the debate among Russian socialists as to whether Russia would necessarily have to pass through capitalism on the way to socialism. In 1877 Marx sharply criticized a Russian writer who

> felt obliged to metamorphose my historical sketch [in *Capital*] of the genesis of capitalism in Western Europe into an historico-

philosophical theory of the *marche générale* imposed by fate upon every people, whatever the historic circumstances in which it finds itself, in order that it may ultimately arrive at the form of economy which will ensure, together with the greatest expansion of the productive powers of social labour, the most complete development of man. (Marx and Engels, *Selected Correspondence*, p. 354.)

And Engels, in 1893, dealt with the specific point at issue in the Russian debate in the following terms:

... no more in Russia than anywhere else would it have been possible to develop a higher social form out of primitive agrarian communism unless — that higher form was *already in existence* in another country, so as to serve as a model. That higher form being, wherever it is historically possible, the necessary consequence of the capitalistic form of production and of the social dualistic antagonism created by it, it could not be developed directly out of the agrarian commune, unless in imitation of an example already in existence somewhere else. Had the West of Europe been ripe, 1860-70, for such a transformation, had that transformation then been taken in hand in England, France, etc., then the Russians would have been called upon to show what could have been made out of their commune, which was then more or less intact. (*Selected Correspondence*, p. 515.)

While this argument is developed in a particular context, it is clear that the general principle involved — the possibility of historical borrowing — applies to, say, China today. Unless both the theory and the actual practice of socialism had been developed elsewhere it is hardly likely that China would now be actually tackling the problem of transforming itself into a socialist society. But given the experience of western Europe (in theory) and of Russia (in both theory and practice), this is a logical and feasible course for the Chinese Revolution to take.

Thus we must conclude that while of course Marx and Engels did not expect Russia to be the scene of the first socialist revolution, and still less could they look beyond and foretell that the next countries would be relatively backward ones, nevertheless both of these developments, coming as and when they did, are consistent with Marxian theory as worked out by the founders themselves. What, then, was the nature of their mistake?

The answer, clearly, is that Marx and Engels were wrong in expecting an early socialist revolution in western Europe. What needs explaining is why the advanced capitalist countries did not go ahead, so to speak, "on schedule" but stubbornly remained capitalist until, and indeed long after, Russia, a latecomer to the family of capitalist nations, had passed through its own socialist revolution. In other words, how are we to explain the apparent paradox that, though in a broad historical sense socialism is undeniably the product of capitalism, nevertheless the most fully developed capitalist countries not only were not the first to go socialist but, as it now seems, may turn out to be the last? The *Manifesto* does not help us to answer this question; never in their own lifetime did Marx and Engels imagine that such a question might arise.

THE PROBLEM OF THE ADVANCED CAPITALIST COUNTRIES

To explain why the advanced capitalist countries have failed to go socialist in the hundred years since the publication of the *Manifesto* is certainly not easy, and we know of no satisfactory analysis which is specifically concerned with this problem. But it would be a poor compliment to the authors of the *Manifesto*, who have given us all the basic tools for an understanding of the nature of capitalism and hence for an understanding of our own epoch, to evade a problem because they themselves did not pose and solve it. Let us therefore indicate — as a stimulus to study and discussion rather than as an attempt at a definitive answer — what seem to us to be the main factors which have to be taken into account.

If we consider the chief countries of Europe, certain things seem clear. First, even under conditions prevailing in the middle of the nineteenth century, Marx and Engels underestimated the extent to which capitalism could still continue to expand in these countries. Second, and much more important, this "margin of expansibility" was vastly extended in the three or four decades preceding World War I by the development of a new pattern of imperialism which enabled the advanced countries to exploit the resources and manpower of the backward regions of the world to a previously unheard-of degree. As Lenin concisely put it in 1920: "Capitalism has grown into a world system of colonial oppression and of the financial strangulation of the overwhelming majority of the people of the world by a handful of 'advanced' countries." (*Collected Works*, Vol. XIX, p. 87.) (This development only began to take place toward the end of Marx's and Engels' lives, and it would have been little short of a miracle if they had been able to foresee all its momentous consequences.) Third, it was this new system of imperialism which brought western Europe out of the long depression of the 1870s and 1880s, gave capitalism a new lease on life, and enabled the ruling class to secure — by means of an astute policy of social reforms and concessions to the working class — widespread support from all sections of society.

The other side of the imperialist coin was the awakening of the backward peoples, the putting into their hands of the moral, psychological, and material means by which they could begin the struggle for their political independence and their economic advancement.

In all this development, it should be noted, Russia occupied a special place. The Russian bourgeoisie, or at least certain sections of it, participated in the expansion of imperialism, especially in the Middle and Far East. But on balance Russia was more an object than a beneficiary of imperialism. Hence few, if any, of the effects which imperialism produced in the West — amelioration of internal social conflicts, widespread class collaboration, and the like — appeared in Russia.

To sum up: imperialism prolonged the life of capitalism in the West and turned what was a revolutionary working-class movement (as in Germany) or what might have become one (as in England) into reformist and collaborationist channels. It intensified the contradictions of capitalism in Russia. And it laid the foundations of a revolutionary movement in the exploited colonial and semicolonial countries. Here, it seems to us, is the basic reason why the advanced capitalist countries of western Europe failed to fulfill the revolutionary expectations of the *Manifesto*. Here also is to be found an important part of the explanation of the role which Russia and the backward regions of the world have played and are playing in the world transition from capitalism to socialism.

But, it may be objected, by the beginning of the twentieth century the United States was already the most advanced capitalist country, and the United States did not really become enmeshed in the imperialist system until World War I. Why did the United States not lead the way to socialism?

Generally speaking, the answer to this question is well known. North America offered unique opportunities for the development of capitalism; the "margin of expansibility" in the late nineteenth century was much greater than that enjoyed by the European countries even when account is taken of the new system of imperialism which was only then beginning to be put into operation. There is no space to enumerate and analyze the advantages enjoyed by this continent; the following list, compiled and commented upon by William Z. Foster in a recent article ("Marxism and American Exceptionalism," *Political Affairs*, September 1947), certainly includes the most important: (1) absence of a feudal political national past, (2) tremendous natural resources, (3) a vast unified land area, (4) insatiable demand for labor power, (5) highly strategic location, and (6) freedom from the ravages of war.

American capitalism, making the most of these advantages, developed a degree of productivity and wealth far surpassing that of any other capitalist country or region; and it offered opportunities for advancement to members of the working class which — at least up until the Great Depression of the 1930s — were without parallel in the history of capitalism or, for that matter, of any class society that ever existed. (On this point, see the article on "Socialism and American Labor," by Leo Huberman, in the May 1949 issue of *Monthly Review*.) This does not mean, of course, that the United States economy was at any time free from the contradictions of capitalism; it merely means that American capitalism, *in spite of these contradictions,* has been able to reach a much higher level than the capitalist system of other countries. It also means that capitalism in this country could go — and actually has gone — further than in the European imperialist countries toward winning support for the system from all sections of the population, including the working class. It is thus not surprising that the United States, far from taking the place of western Europe as the leader of the world socialist revolution, has actually had a weaker socialist movement than any other developed capitalist country.

We see that, for reasons which could hardly have been uncovered a hundred years ago, capitalism has been able to dig in deep in the advanced countries of western Europe and America and to resist the rising tide of socialism much longer than Marx and Engels ever thought possible.

Before we leave the problem of the advanced countries, however, a word of caution seems necessary. It ought to be obvious, though it often seems to be anything but, that to say that capitalism has enjoyed an unexpectedly long life in the most advanced countries is very different from saying that it will live forever. Similarly, to say that the western European and American working classes have so far failed to fulfill the role of "grave-diggers" of capitalism is not equivalent to asserting that they never will do so. Marx and Engels were certainly wrong in their timing, but we believe that their basic theory of capitalism and of the manner of its transformation into socialism remains valid and is no less applicable to western Europe and America than to other parts of the world.

Present-day indications all point to this conclusion. Two world wars and the growth of the revolutionary movement in the backward areas have irrevocably undermined the system of imperialism which formerly pumped lifeblood into western European capitalism. The ruling class of the United States, threatened as never before by the peculiar capitalist disease of overproduction, is struggling, Atlas-like, to carry the whole capitalist world on its shoulders — and is showing more clearly every day that it has no idea how the miracle is to be accomplished. Are we to assume that the western European and American working classes are so thoroughly bemused by the past that they will never learn the lessons of the present and turn their eyes to the future? Are we to assume that, because capitalism was able to offer them concessions in its period of good fortune, they will be content to sink (or be blown up) with a doomed system?

We refuse to make any such assumptions. We believe that the time is not distant when the working man of the most advanced, as well as of the most backward, countries will be compelled, in the words of the *Manifesto*, "to face with sober senses his real conditions of life and his relations with his kind." And when he does, we have no doubt that he will choose to live under socialism rather than die under capitalism.

CONCLUSION

On the whole, the *Manifesto* has stood up amazingly well during its first hundred years. The theory of history, the analysis of capitalism, the prognosis of socialism, have all been brilliantly confirmed. Only in one respect — the view that socialism would come first in the most advanced capitalist countries — has the *Manifesto* been proved mistaken by experience. This mistake, moreover, is one which could hardly have been avoided in the conditions of a hundred years ago. It is in no sense a reflection on the authors; it only shows that Engels was right when he insisted in his celebrated critique of Dühring that "each mental image of the world system is and remains in actual fact limited, objectively through the historical stage and subjectively through the physical and mental constitution of its maker."

How fortunate it would have been for mankind if the world socialist revolution had proceeded in accordance with the expectations of the authors of the *Manifesto!* How much more rapid and less painful the crossing would be if Britain or Germany or — best of all — the United States had been the first to set foot on the road! Only imagine what we in this country could do to lead the world into the promised land of peace and abundance if we could but control, instead of being dominated by, our vast powers of production!

But, as Engels once remarked, "history is about the most cruel of all goddesses." She has decreed that the world transition from capitalism to socialism, instead of being relatively quick and smooth, as it might have been if the most productive and civilized nations had led the way, is to be a long-drawn-out period of intense suffering and bitter conflict. There is even a danger that in the heat of the struggle some of the finest fruits of the bourgeois epoch will be temporarily lost to mankind, instead of being extended and universalized by the spread of the socialist revolution. Intellectual freedom and personal security guaranteed by law — to name only the most precious — have been virtually unknown to the peoples who are now blazing the trail to socialism; in the advanced countries, they are seriously jeopardized by the fierce onslaughts of reaction and counter-revolution. No one can say whether they will survive the period of tension and strife through which we are now passing, or whether they will have to be rediscovered and recaptured in a more rational world of the future.

The passage is dangerous and difficult, the worst may be yet to come. But there is no escape for the disillusioned, the timid, or the weary. Those who have mastered the message of the *Manifesto* and caught the spirit of its authors will understand that the clock cannot be turned back, that capitalism is surely doomed, and that the only hope of mankind lies in completing the journey to socialism with maximum speed and minimum violence.

2

Toynbee's Universal History

This review of the first six volumes of Toynbee's *A Study of History* (Vols. I-III, London and New York, 1934, Vols. IV-VI, 1939) appeared under the title "Signs of the Times" in *The Nation*, October 19, 1946.

AN INCREASING number of American intellectuals are reading — and being influenced by — Professor Arnold J. Toynbee's monumental work *A Study of History*, of which six volumes, of a projected nine, have so far been published. This is not surprising. The work has many solid merits, and its very scope and form are stimulating and exciting to a generation of historians brought up in an arid tradition of academic specialization. Moreover, in a time when the interconnectedness of the world's continents and cultures is both more real and more apparent than ever before, and when serious scholars leave the larger problems of history and politics to quacks and columnists, it is altogether natural that so distinguished a work on universal history as Toynbee's should be eagerly read and deeply pondered.

The merits of Toynbee will be immediately obvious to the reader, so much so, indeed, that they may entirely blind him to his weaknesses. For the benefit of those who are unacquainted with his work, I should like to quote a distinguished scholar whose opinion carries more weight than mine possibly could. Reviewing the first three volumes of *A Study of History*, M. M. Postan, professor of economic history at Cambridge University, had the following to say:

The infinite wealth of fact and allusion creates a pattern as intricate and a texture as rich as those of an Oriental carpet. There is no subject in history which it does not touch, and for every subject it touches it gives a complete summary of the present position in scientific discussion. . . . Professor Toynbee possesses the gifts of a truly great encyclopedist, of a Diderot or a D'Alembert, for he is capable of holding and giving out essential information while pursuing an argument. It matters not that on some topics the information is slightly out of focus, or that on others the present state of knowledge is too nebulous and too yielding to be even summarized with impunity by men with a philosophical purpose. What is important is that for the first time the essentials of modern knowledge in every imaginable field of history and archaeology have been set out by a man capable of comprehending and handling them. (*Sociological Review*, January 1936.)

This is high praise indeed, but it is amply justified. It is astonishing how much information Toynbee has packed into the six volumes which have so far been published. Professional historians will be delighted with the range and accuracy of his scholarship, while the layman will find that almost every page contributes to the enrichment of knowledge and understanding. Nearly everyone has at one time or another heard about or read references to a great number of historical figures and events without having more than the vaguest idea of their background and significance. It is this fact more than anything else, I suppose, which makes Toynbee such fascinating and rewarding reading. Time and again one feels that these odd bits of half-knowledge suddenly emerge from obscurity, assume a lifelike form, and fall into their proper historical frame of reference. The reader of *A Study of History* experiences all the satisfactions of the traveler who finally visits cities and countries which have hitherto remained unreal abstractions. Moreover, the work is written in so graceful a style and with such a wealth of metaphor and allusion that it deserves to rank high as a literary product in its own right.

Dwelling on the merits of such a work as this, however, is not particularly useful except in so far as it induces people to read it, and I hope I have made it quite clear that *A Study of History* is well worth all the time and attention which it requires. The rest of this article, therefore, will be devoted to a critical analysis of the work, which I hope may assist those who are persuaded to read it to a just appreciation of Toynbee's contribution as a whole.

Toynbee's method, reduced to its barest essentials, is to treat Hellenic (Graeco-Roman) "civilization" as an archetype to which all other civilizations, past and present, are assumed to conform with more or less fidelity. This results in the establishment of a theoretical schema — expressed in such concepts as birth, growth, breakdown, disintegration, creative and dominant minorities, internal and external proletariats, universal states, universal churches, and so forth — which is used for the purpose of bringing form and meaning into a vast collection of data from all lands and all ages.

There are numerous objections to this procedure, of which only the most important can be mentioned in a brief review. Toynbee nowhere defines a civilization, and his practice in delimiting particular civilizations is essentially arbitrary. It follows that the historical uniformities which he believes he has discovered by empirical means are in reality imposed upon his materials from without. If he had sought to define a social system — using the term in the scientific sense of a whole of which the parts are interrelated in a definite and ascertainable way — and if he had tried to identify a number of historical social systems, he would have discovered much more diversity than uniformity. It is this lack of appreciation of historical diversity, with its roots in different social systems existing in different environments and with different means at their disposal, which constitutes the cardinal weakness of Toynbee's work.

This weakness comes out most clearly when we consider the present as history, as Toynbee frequently does. Looking at the world around us through the spectacles provided by Toynbee's theory, we see a Western civilization, which has already spread its tentacles into the farthest corners of the earth and is in the process of overcoming or absorbing its surviving rivals, tearing itself to pieces in a crescendo of fratricidal strife. Will this process lead to a knockout blow by which one great power, emulating the example of Rome, will vanquish its enemies and establish a Western universal state? Such an outcome, in Toynbee's view, would be but a temporary respite. No more than in the days of the Roman Empire could a world conqueror of our time save civilization from disintegration and dissolution. Since the theory allows of no alternative course, however, Toynbee is impelled by logic and emotion alike to look to divine intervention for salvation. He hopes and prays for "Western Christendom" to be "given grace to be born again as the *Respublica Christiana* which is its own earlier and better ideal of what it should strive to be." (Vol. V, p. 194.) The last two volumes, written as the storm clouds of war gathered on the horizon, are increasingly occupied with this theme.

The flaw in Toynbee's reasoning is not hard to discover. A prisoner of his own theory, he is quite unable to appreciate the vast changes which capitalism — a scientifically accurate designation for our dominant Western social system — has wrought during the last four hundred years, or to understand the significance of the emergence of socialism as an actually functioning rival social system. Under present-day conditions a theory distilled from the experience of the ancient Mediterranean world is for the most part irrelevant and therefore entirely misleading.

Capitalism's achievements in the realm of science and industry have laid the foundation for an integration into one body social of all existing "civilizations" and of all remaining barbarians as well. Nomadism, once such a powerful historical force, is rapidly disappearing and with it the "external proletariats" which play an important role in all Toynbee's dramas. Science and industry, once again, have altered the social basis of religion. There is no longer any ground on which to build Universal Churches preaching new Higher Religions; nor, sad to relate, is there any prospect that *organized* Christianity will ever play a constructive role again. Higher Religions and Universal Churches were proletarian — in Toynbee's sense of the word — creations at a time when the objective possibility of abolishing the proletarian status did not exist. Today, for the first time in history, that possibility does exist, and the proletariat has reacted by building a socialist movement which is secular in both spirit and aim. It is highly significant that precisely in those parts of the world where the proletarian status of the masses is most extreme and least endurable, people turn to socialism, not to religion, for salvation. Finally, the burning question which we face today is not whether "Western civilization" can be saved from its own suicidal folly, but whether a capitalist social system which has lost its creative power and is rapidly barbarizing its own children can be replaced by a rational socialist order in time to save the fruits of all the civilizations which have flourished on the face of the earth in the past six thousand years.

When we see that Toynbee's theory fails when applied to the present, we are naturally led to ask whether he has not, after all, been off on a false trail in dealing with the past; and the answer is surely Yes. The true purpose of a study of history should be to discover and analyze and illustrate the inner laws of social change and development. Had Toynbee been pursuing this purpose he must have rejected from the outset the disastrous doctrine of the "philosophic contemporaneity" of all civilizations, and he must have concentrated on problems of variety and development rather than on the supposedly uniform life cycle of members of a single unchanging species. What we want to know from the historian — as distinct from the antiquarian — is how we came to be where we are and what we are today; and Toynbee's contributions to the solution of this problem, however substantial in volume, are essentially incidental.

If space were available, it would be worth while to examine in detail Toynbee's treatment of a number of important historical topics in order to demonstrate how his failure to identify and analyze specific social systems gives rise to false problems and leads to erroneous conclusions. The bare mention of two examples, however, will have to suffice.

One of the most important — and also most neglected — problems in the history of the entire civilized world right up to the opening of the modern period is the repeated eruptions of nomads from the Eurasian and Afrasian steppes into the territories of the surrounding agricultural societies. It is altogether to Toynbee's credit that he fully recognizes the importance of the problem, and his catalogue of nomad eruptions (presented in an annex to the third volume) is a magnificent piece of historical research. But his treatment of the causes of the phenomenon is vitiated by a failure to analyze (a) the social structure of nomadism, and (b) the normal relations between nomad and neighboring sedentary societies. As a result he is driven to adopt the quite unsubstantiated and equally unnecessary hypothesis of periodic climatic changes as the cause of nomad eruptions. His procedure is like that of those economists who, having described the wholly social phenomena of the business cycle, sought an explanation in the wholly nonsocial realm of sunspots. Toynbee adopts this course because he believes that nomadism is really a "society without a history," which is incapable of internal development and change. Anyone wishing to convince himself of the untenability of this view need only consult the brilliant studies of nomadism contained in Owen Lattimore's *Inner Asian Frontiers of China*.

In an entirely different field, we find Toynbee categorically rejecting what he calls the "customary" view that "in the eastern portion of the Theodosian heritage the Roman Empire survived until A.D. 1453" (Vol. IV, p. 328) and building up instead the theory that a new Orthodox Christian civilization came into being side by side with a Western Christian civilization in the main European domains of the Roman Empire, and that the two societies "are sister growths whose relation to the Hellenic Society is manifestly identical." (Vol. V, p. 6.) This theory, however, poses a great riddle: how account for the glaring contrast between a powerful centralized empire in the East, which never lost its firm grip on the Orthodox church, and the flimsy Holy Roman Empire in the West, which was actually the creature of the church and which committed suicide in the process of trying to win its independence? Toynbee explains the paradox by saying that Leo the Syrian, in turning back the onslaughts of the Arabs, successfully evoked a "ghost of the Roman Empire" in the East; while Charlemagne's attempt to perform the same political feat two generations later in the West proved to be a fiasco. The explanation is unquestionably ingenious, but even a slight acquaintance with the economic and social history of the period is sufficient to reveal its superficiality. The political and administrative structure of the Roman Empire rested upon an urban trading economy with the Mediterranean as its axis and lifeline. The decline of the empire in the West meant the decay of the inland provincial cities; and the interruption of Mediterranean trade, first by the Vandal pirates and finally by the Arabs, gave the *coup de grâce* to trade and urban life alike. By the time of Charlemagne the objective conditions necessary for a strong centralized state simply did not exist in the West, and they did not again appear until the revival of commerce and cities in the twelfth and thirteenth centuries. By contrast, Constantinople remained throughout the entire period a large city even by present-day standards and the hub of a flourishing eastern Mediterranean and Black Sea trade. The continuity of the Roman Empire in the East is indeed more than a dynastic will-o'-the-wisp.

If Toynbee had taken account of such simple facts of economic and social structure as these, he could have often saved himself much unnecessary effort; and his theories would have gained in solidity what they lost in novelty.

I have tried to point out what are, from a scientific standpoint, the chief defects of *A Study of History*. It is equally appropriate, and perhaps no less rewarding, to examine the work as a manifestation of the intellectual climate of which it is a product. Really valuable works on universal history are not an everyday occurrence, and those rare groups or individuals who achieve success in this exacting field seem to exemplify and express to an altogether unusual degree the significant intellectual trends of their own milieu and period. Thus the Encyclopedists have come to be regarded as the archrepresentatives of the eighteenth-century Enlightenment; Buckle's *History of Civilization*, incomplete as it is, is a monument to the strengths and weaknesses of British liberalism in the heyday of the Manchester school; while H. G. Wells's *Outline of History* catches the spirit of men-of-goodwill in the early twentieth century as perhaps no other work does. If we analyze *A Study of History* from this angle, what do we find?

Toynbee himself is a highly civilized person whose learning is matched by an unflagging sensitivity to suffering and injustice and evil. One of the most sympathetic aspects of his work, in fact, is its unconcealed contempt for intolerance and discrimination in all their many forms. He is manifestly a product of exactly the same Christian-humanitarian tradition as Wells. But what a gulf separates the outlook of the *Study* from that of the *Outline!* Wells was an evolutionist who saw history as a continuous process of adaptation and growth, an optimist who was confident that the catastrophes of his own time were but the birth pangs of a new and higher society, a rationalist who, believing in the sovereign virtues of science and knowledge, confidently assumed that education is the key to salvation. Toynbee, on the other hand, is at bottom a mystic who believes that man is inherently incapable of shaping his own development and that therefore the only way to make life meaningful is to abandon the effort and embrace religion. From this standpoint history is a series of "philosophically contemporaneous" tragedies; the world we live in is a "City of Destruction"; and concern to know its ways — that is, to study science and economics and politics — is vulgar and superficial: the only worth-while goal of human aspirations is the attainment of the Kingdom of God.

The difference between these two outlooks is a great deal more than the difference between two individuals, important though that may be. Wells, though he wrote in the twentieth century, was essentially a child of the nineteenth; he spoke for an expanding society and a self-confident ruling class. Toynbee, coming on the scene a scant generation later, reflects a society in full decline and a class which has lost its grip and forfeited its claim to the respect and admiration it once regarded as its birthright. As a sensitive member of that class who is at the same time incapable of transcending its outlook and values, Toynbee can only look forward to the future with despair in his heart.

Toynbee's tragedy is, of course, a personal one; but it is more than that, for it is shared by many of the noblest spirits of our time. Knowing this, it is impossible to hear his cry of anguish and remain unmoved. But one must not allow oneself to be carried away. If the times are hard, they are also full of hope and promise for those who retain their faith in the human race and its ability to control its own destiny. It is, after all, to the good sense and steadfastness of ordinary people that we must look for salvation; and the invocation of religion and God amounts at best to abdication of one's responsibilities and at worst to bringing aid and comfort to those who, under cover of the Catholic Church, are backing the "barbarians from within" who have no use for either religion or God and who are bent on saving their own privileges at the cost of destroying everything that civilized men have learned to value.

3

The Illusion of the Managerial Revolution

James Burnham's widely publicized book, *The Managerial Revolution* (New York, 1941), appeared before either the Soviet Union or the United States had entered World War II. Its subtitle, "What Is Happening in the World," reads ironically today. If a theory is to be judged by its fruits, no commentary on *The Managerial Revolution* is required, beyond Burnham's own pontification: "I have predicted the division of the new world among three super-states. The nuclei of these three super-states are, whatever may be their future names, the previously existing nations, Japan, Germany, and the United States." (P. 178.)

Nevertheless, what may be called "managerial thinking," even if not its incarnation in Burnham's book, is very much alive today. In fact, it is probably more widespread than ever and has penetrated into what at one time would have been thought unlikely quarters. For example, the *New Fabian Essays* (1952), collective work of a group of British Labor Party intellectuals, is permeated with managerial thinking. A detailed factual and theoretical refutation of Burnham, which this essay attempts, is thus as timely now as it was when it was first published more than a decade ago (in the Winter 1942 issue of *Science & Society*).

THE events of the 1930s have created a healthy demand for explanations which go below the level of appearances and uncover the fundamental historical forces at work. Traditional academic social science has little to offer, not because its theorists are not able men but because the methodology which they adopt denies the possibility of a coherent and comprehensive theory of social change. Marxism, because it is wholly unacceptable to those who control the main channels of publicity, is able to reach only a small minority of those who are eager for intellectual guidance. Under these circumstances it is not surprising that there should appear a varied assortment of theories to account for what is going on in the world.

Generally speaking, it is not difficult to classify and analyze these theories in terms of the subjective position of their authors. James Burnham's theory of the "managerial revolution" is no exception. Burnham is an ex-follower of Leon Trotsky whose disillusionment with political activity is matched only by his despair of any genuine improvement in social conditions. So far as Burnham can see, the contemporary situation is hopeless, and he wants nothing more than to wash his hands of the whole mess. But for an intellectual of Burnham's type, matters are not so easily arranged. If one is to retire to the ivory tower, *au-dessus de la mêlée*, one must have an elaborate justification. *The Managerial Revolution*, with its superobjective tone of fatalistic inevitability, provides just such a justification.

If Burnham's book were significant only as a symptom of the psychological defeatism which recent events have induced in a certain small group of intellectuals, it would scarcely warrant extended criticism. But the work has acquired a wider significance. It has received extensive and on the whole enthusiastic reviews in the public prints; among businessmen it has aroused so much interest that *Fortune* has published a full-length article by Burnham setting forth a summary of his theory.[1] The reasons for this are fairly obvious. Burnham has posed a series of really fundamental problems, problems which no one who reads the daily press and listens to the radio can avoid. Moreover, his solutions are

---

[1] In presenting this article to its readers, *Fortune* (November 1941) goes so far as to express the view that "by all odds the most debated book published so far this year has been James Burnham's *The Managerial Revolution*."

sufficiently plausible to attract the attention, if not the agreement, of a large number of intelligent people whose intellectual and political background has little in common with that of Burnham himself. A theory, whatever its source, which attracts the interest and attention of a significant number of people, must be subjected to a thorough criticism from a Marxist standpoint.

SUMMARY OF BURNHAM'S THEORY

Let us first summarize Burnham's theory in such a way as to bring out the crucial issues on which its validity can reasonably be judged. According to Burnham, the world is now going through a period of transition analogous to that which it passed through in the early modern period, say, from the fifteenth through the eighteenth centuries: in the earlier period the change was from feudalism to capitalism; now it is from capitalism to what Burnham calls "managerial society." The managerial revolution, he asserts, may be dated from 1914, and it is already well on the way to completion. Burnham maintains that in two countries, Germany and Russia, a managerial regime is already firmly established, while in a third, the United States, the process of transition has been going forward at an accelerating tempo since the beginning of the New Deal. The effect of World War II, he believes, will be to complete the process in all key sectors of the world economy, including the United States. Eventually three managerial superstates, based respectively on the western European, the North American, and the eastern Asian centers of heavy industry, will rise to world dominance, but no one of these superstates will be powerful enough to conquer the other two. The prospect seen is for an indefinitely long period of rivalry and war among the essentially stable managerial superstates. Presumably, although Burnham does not say this, a sufficient advance in the technology of transport and warfare might upset the balance and lead to the conquest of the whole world by one superstate. Such an outcome would be in keeping with the general tenor of his reasoning.

According to Burnham, the essence of the managerial revolution is, as in the case of the bourgeois revolution, the rise to power of a new ruling class, the class of managers. "Managers" are not to be confused with engineers and technicians, although they may be both; their specific function is that of "direction and coordination" of industrial production. (P. 80.) This function is said to be no longer performed, as it once was, by capitalists. Burnham argues that the growth of large-scale industry and the giant corporation has brought into being a separate class of managers who are becoming the *de facto* controllers of the means of production. He maintains that the managers, like the bourgeoisie before them, are moving to acquire the *de jure* recognition to which their power entitles them. The specific and developed form of managerial society is state ownership of the means of production and managerial control of the state. He concludes that Russia is the only complete managerial society so far, but that Germany is not far behind, and that the United States gives every sign of catching up in the relatively near future.

The dynamics of the managerial revolution is said to comprise three analytically distinct stages which may, however, overlap in practice: first, the seizure of political power from the capitalists and the reduction of the latter to a position of impotence; second, the curbing of the masses and their indoctrination with managerial ideologies; third, the struggle for dominance against rival sections of the world managers. It is Burnham's contention that in Russia the process unfolded in the order named; that in Germany the curbing of the masses came first, the reduction of the capitalists second; and that in the United States the decisive shift in all three respects will take place simultaneously under war conditions.

Burnham has a simple explanation as to why the theory of the managerial revolution has not hitherto been advanced:

political thought has been dominated by some variant of the theory that *either* capitalism must continue *or* socialism must take its place. But this "either-or" theory, he avers, has become in increasing measure at variance with the facts. In Burnham's eyes, Germany is not capitalist; Russia is not socialist; the New Deal has been anticapitalist, and the present drift of events is overwhelmingly in the same direction. He concludes that the only theory capable of integrating these diverse "facts" into a single coherent pattern is the theory of the managerial revolution.

The above summary is not, of course, complete, but it is, I think, adequate to bring into sharp relief four crucial theses by which to test Burnham's theory. These are: first, the alleged *de facto* control over the means of production by the managers; second, the alleged noncapitalist character of German fascism; third, the alleged nonsocialist character of the Soviet Union; and, finally, the alleged anticapitalism of the New Deal. If Burnham fails to offer convincing evidence and arguments in support of any one of these contentions, his theory will have suffered a severe blow; but if he fails in respect to all four there will be little left of the managerial revolution.

CONTROL OVER THE MEANS OF PRODUCTION

Burnham argues that on a world scale decisive control over the means of production has already shifted to the managers. In the United States the process is far from complete; the capitalists are still dominant. Nevertheless, he rests his case primarily on the United States, contending that here the trend is strongly away from capitalist control and toward managerial control. (Chapters 7 and 8.) Let us therefore examine the United States from this point of view, leaving Germany and Russia for later consideration.

If we disregard Burnham's frequent assertions of a trend toward managerial control, which are in themselves surely entitled to little weight, and look for proof of such a trend, we shall find little that is not derived from Berle and Means, *The Modern Corporation and Private Property*, published in 1931. As is well known, Berle and Means argued that the typical large corporation, which may be taken as the dominant institutional feature of the American economy, is controlled by "management" without benefit of substantial ownership interest. This conclusion was backed up by conscientious research into such data on ownership as were available at the time the book was published, and it has become widely accepted among scholars and the reading public at large. More specifically, Burnham cites Berle and Means to the effect that, in 1929, 65 percent of the 200 largest nonfinancial corporations, with 80 percent of their total assets, were "management-controlled." Burnham's concept of management is not the same as that of Berle and Means; nevertheless Burnham adduces these figures as strong, if not decisive, support for his argument that capitalist ownership is on the way out as a significant factor in control.

Now *The Modern Corporation and Private Property* was unquestionably a pioneer study at the time of its publication, and I have no desire to criticize it here. But it is equally unquestionable that in respect to the facts of ownership in the large corporation it has been superseded by the researches of the Securities and Exchange Commission undertaken on behalf of the Temporary National Economic Committee.[2] These reveal that in the vast majority of even the 200 largest nonfinancial corporations a few large stockholders occupy a dominant position. According to the SEC: "In about 140 of the 200 corporations the blocks of stock in the hands of one

---

[2] Particularly Raymond W. Goldsmith, Rexford C. Parmelee, and others, *The Distribution of Ownership in the 200 Largest Non-financial Corporations* (Washington, Government Printing Office, 1940), TNEC Investigation of Concentration of Economic Power, Monograph No. 29. Also Helene Granby, *Survey of Shareholdings in 1,710 Corporations With Securities Listed on a National Securities Exchange* (Washington, Government Printing Office, 1941), TNEC Investigation of Concentration of Economic Power, Monograph No. 30.

THE ILLUSION OF THE MANAGERIAL REVOLUTION

interest group were large enough to justify, together with other indications such as representation in the management, the classification of these companies as more or less definitely under ownership control."[3] What is true of the largest corporations unquestionably applies with even greater force to smaller corporations — many of which are neither so small nor so unimportant as is sometimes implied. Moreover, in companies where ownership plays little part in selecting top management, those who constitute the latter group, although owning an inconsequential *proportion* of stock, are nearly always owners of *absolutely* large amounts of stock, so that their interests are largely identical with the interests of the body of owners. The 2500-odd officers and directors of the 200 largest nonfinancial corporations jointly own more than $2 billion of stock in their respective companies. This amount is heavily concentrated in the hands of about 250 men who occupy the decisive executive positions. To speak of these men as "separated" from ownership in any practically important sense is clearly fallacious. *Fortune* magazine, summarizing the SEC findings in a recent issue, put the matter neatly when it said that "it is clear that the idea of absentee ownership as usually interpreted is largely a fiction."

So much for management control in the Berle and Means sense. Unfortunately for Burnham, management control in his sense is a concept with even less substance. It will be recalled that he identifies managers with those who perform the function of "direction and coordination" — plant managers, production engineers, top foremen and the like. Very few of these people hold the rank of officer or director, that is to say, belong to management in the more usual meaning of the term. By definition, of course, they "direct and coordinate"; they may have limited power to choose their subordinates. But beyond that their actions are completely subject to the dictates of the top executives who fall altogether outside Burnham's managerial category.

When it suits him to do so, Burnham equates control over

---
[3] TNEC Monograph No. 29, p. 104.

the means of production with control over access to the means of production and the latter in turn with the ultimate power to hire and fire. (E.g., pp. 100 ff.) This is undoubtedly correct. But judged by this standard his managers are certainly not controllers of the means of production, *de jure* or *de facto*. Burnham continually insists that we should be guided in our thinking not by emotion or preconception but by "the evidence." In theorizing about the economic status of the managers, he would do well to practice what he preaches.

THE NATURE OF GERMAN FASCISM

Burnham is very sure that Nazi Germany is a noncapitalist managerial state. Ten years ago, he says, it was reasonable to accept the Marxist view that Nazism is a form of "decadent capitalism." "There was no way to decide the problem with confidence beforehand," but "by now it has been decided," and in a sense unfavorable to the Marxist interpretation. (P. 232.) What has happened to convince Burnham of the noncapitalist character of the Nazi economy?

In the first place, mass unemployment has been eliminated, and "this is, in and by itself, a sufficient proof that Germany has left the basis of capitalism and entered the road of a new form of society." (P. 233.) While it is true that mass unemployment has been eliminated, we are entitled to ask why this supports Burnham's conclusion. His answer is simplicity itself: because "the great capitalist powers have proved that they cannot get rid of mass unemployment under capitalist institutions." (P. 233.) We might have expected more from a teacher of logic! Actually, of course, the elimination of mass unemployment is not only not a refutation of Marxist theory; rather it is a confirmation. Marxists are not content to assert that Nazism is merely a form of "decadent capitalism." They are more specific: Nazism is an extreme form of aggressive imperialism which from the outset has concentrated the energies of the nation on enlarging the *Lebensraum* of German capital. The uninterrupted continuation of mass unemployment would clearly be inconsistent with this theory. This is not to say, however, that Nazism has "solved" the economic problems of capitalism. The belief that it has simply betrays a misunderstanding of the nature of these problems. Mass unemployment is itself a symptom of the basic contradiction between the forces of production and the restrictive character of capitalist property relations. Under Nazism this contradiction takes on the more open and obvious form of exploitation of weaker peoples and interimperialist conflict, to which must now be added conflict with the socialist society of the Soviet Union. If we assume, although it seems most unlikely, a relative stabilization in the international sphere, the contradiction will assert itself *either* in a re-emergence of mass unemployment *or* in a rapidly declining rate of profit. In either case the Nazi leadership would be driven on to new imperialist adventures. Certainly we can find here no basis for the achievement of that relatively stable "managerial" society which Burnham foresees.

Secondly, according to Burnham, the role of the state in the economy has been steadily expanding at the expense of private enterprise; this process has included an extension of both direct state ownership and state intervention in all phases of economic life. So far as state ownership is concerned, the precise opposite is the case. Burnham dismisses as insignificant the so-called "reprivatization" of state-owned enterprises which characterized the first three or four years of the Nazi regime. Actually it was an extensive and highly important movement which, among other things, returned the bulk of the banking system, acquired by the state in the preceding period of financial crisis, to private ownership.[4]

---

[4] That reprivatization is still the policy of the Nazis is shown by the recent transfer to private ownership of the North German Lloyd and the Hamburg-America shipping lines (*Business Week*, September 27, 1941).

At the same time municipally owned utilities were for the first time subjected to the same taxation as private corporations, and the law allowing further socialization of power production was repealed. Since the beginning of the all-out armament effort in 1936, the state has put up large amounts of capital for the construction of new plants and the like. This has not, however, resulted, as Burnham believes, in "state ownership and operation . . . in the extensive areas of new enterprise opened up during the Nazi rule." (P. 236.) It has usually taken the form of so-called mixed enterprises, long familiar on the Continent, which are essentially a method of preserving private operation in spite of a heavy risk factor.[5] The *Bergwerkszeitung*, mouthpiece of heavy industry, expressing surprise that the creation of the Goering combine should be interpreted abroad as a step toward nationalization, commented significantly: "The state spares private industry the risk of investing capital and leaves it the responsibility of sharing voluntarily in the execution of great new projects."[6]

Burnham is undoubtedly correct in holding that state intervention in the economy, in the form of wage, price, and foreign exchange controls, and the like, has been extended, though it is to be remembered that this process had already gone far before the Nazis came to power. He is also correct

---

[5] The same problem has arisen in this country in connection with the production of armaments. It is both interesting and significant that it has been solved in much the same way as in Germany. Contracts for about $4.5 billion in new facilities related to the defense program had been let up to September 1941. Of this amount $3.6 billion (80 percent) was financed in one form or another by the government. Unqualified government ownership and operation, however, have been much more restricted, being largely confined to the production of finished munitions for which the demand can be expected to decline most sharply when hostilities cease. See John D. Wilson, "The New Defense Facilities," *Survey of Current Business* (United States Department of Commerce), November 1941.

[6] Maxine Sweezy, *The Structure of the Nazi Economy* (Cambridge, Massachusetts, 1941), p. 34. This work contains a careful review of the relations of the Nazi state to private enterprise.

in believing that these controls have frequently worked to the detriment of some branches of industry and in favor of others, that losses in some lines have been subsidized by taxes on others. But do these interventions into the economic process prove the noncapitalist character of Germany? To convince ourselves that they do not we need only note two of the general effects of government policy: suppression of labor unions and freezing of wage rates at depression levels on the one hand; recovery of profits for all corporations to very nearly the previous prosperity level, and for heavy industry to well above the 1929 level, on the other hand.[7] It is only Burnham's dogmatic conviction that under capitalism the state must strictly limit its economic activities that prevents him from seeing that Nazi policy has been beneficial *to capital as a whole*. This conviction arises in turn from an identification of capitalism as an historical mode of production with liberal capitalism, its specific nineteenth-century form. This error will be considered below.

A third proof that Nazism is noncapitalist, according to Burnham, is to be found in the virtual elimination of the capitalists' share of the national income. This is important because he holds, and we agree, that in the long run control over the means of production goes hand in hand with preferential treatment in the distribution of the fruits of industry. His sole "evidence" in this connection is, to say the least, curious. "A recent estimate by a New York statistician gives as a mere 5 percent the share of the German national income going to profits and interest. This is a substantial reduction from the 1933 figures. . . . Moreover, of the German capitalists' 5 percent, the greater part is appropriated by the state as taxes and 'contributions.'" (P. 238.) We may feel not altogether satisfied with Burnham's anonymous

---

[7] Maxine Sweezy, *op. cit.*, pp. 70 ff. With some qualifications, the recovery of profits has followed a pattern typical of a "normal" period of capitalist prosperity. This fact does not refute the point made earlier that in the long run — assuming the relevance of such a perspective — the Nazis will be faced with the problem of a falling rate of profit.

source. If so we can turn to a compilation based on official German statistics where quite a different story is told. Total income from property, before deduction of taxes, in 1938, accounted for 28 percent of the national income as against 20.9 percent in 1933 and 22.1 percent in 1929 at the top of the previous prosperity.[8] Further comment on the alleged sad plight to which the German capitalists have been reduced by the Nazis seems unnecessary — at least until Burnham deigns to reveal the source of his amazing information.

Burnham brings forth various further "proofs" that Nazism is noncapitalist, but they are all essentially subordinate to the three main contentions which have just been analyzed. Here again, as in the case of managerial "control," if evidence is to outweigh assertion it seems clear that Burnham has failed to make his point.

THE CHARACTER OF THE SOVIET UNION

According to Burnham, the Soviet Union is neither capitalist nor socialist but rather a highly developed managerial state. Since very few are likely to argue that the Soviet Union is capitalist, it follows that the real problem facing Burnham is to demonstrate that it is not socialist. His attempt to do so turns less on evidence — for he adduces little which is relevant to the question — than upon a misrepresentation of the historic meaning and significance of socialism.

Burnham alleges that there are three fundamental characteristics by which we may judge whether a society is socialist or not. It must be *"classless,* fully *democratic,* and *international."* (P. 39.) On this, he says, all kinds of socialists, including the various wings of the Marxist movement, are in agreement. Since the Soviet Union is found wanting on all three counts it is adjudged not a socialist state. Let us examine the Soviet Union in connection with Burnham's three criteria of socialism.

By classlessness Burnham says he means simply the ab-

---
[8] Maxine Sweezy, *op. cit.*, p. 208.

sence of all property rights in the instruments of production (p. 39), and it might seem that in this respect the Soviet Union rates a clean bill of health. But it soon turns out that what he *really* demands is something approaching a condition of complete equality of income distribution. By *this* standard the Soviet Union is certainly not a socialist society.[9] But, as is well known, ever since Marx's *Critique of the Gotha Program* (1875), socialists have rejected equality of incomes as a criterion of socialism. Marx insisted that in the earlier phases of socialist society incomes would be determined on a productivity basis. Even the principle of income distribution which would obtain in the highest stage of socialism ("from each according to his ability, to each according to his need") certainly does not imply equality. Naturally Burnham has the right to set up whatever criteria of socialism he pleases, but he is being something less than aboveboard when he tries to palm off his own notions as the historic theory of the socialist movement.

Without entering into a discussion of the precise meaning of the term "democracy," we may agree with Burnham that socialism has been historically thought of as "fully democratic . . . in all spheres — political, economic, and social." (P. 39.) We may also agree that this does not apply to the Soviet Union in the political sphere, where there is a single-party system and certain restrictions on civil liberty. At the same time, however, we should note there is much evidence from reliable observers that there is more genuine democracy in the economic and social spheres in the Soviet Union

---

[9] Although the fact of inequality in incomes in the Soviet Union is universally admitted, there is no reason to accept Burnham's opinion on the relative degrees of inequality in the United States and the USSR. For his "evidence" on this point consists solely of an article by Trotsky and Burnham's "personal knowledge based on a careful collation and analysis of statistics published in the Soviet press." (P. 46.) The field of income distribution, particularly in Russia, where accumulation is taken care of entirely by the state, is beset with serious conceptual and statistical problems of which no account is taken in *The Managerial Revolution*.

than anywhere else in the world. Does this support Burnham's contention that the Soviet Union is not socialist? Only in the sense that it indicates that the Soviet Union has *not yet* developed into a completely socialist society in the historic meaning of the term. But what Burnham forgets, or at least relegates to a single passing sentence, is that socialists, and particularly Marxists, never expected socialism to come into the world full-blown, like Minerva from the head of Jove. Their theory makes specific allowance for a period of transition, significantly called "the dictatorship of the proletariat." Engels once remarked that "as long as the proletariat still *needs* the state, it needs it not in the interests of freedom but for the purpose of crushing its antagonists." That suppression has been used to this end in the Soviet Union is not open to question. But does socialism have to commit suicide in order to prove its "socialist" character? Perhaps Burnham would interpose that twenty-five years have passed since the Revolution and that the transition period ought to be over by now. It would, of course, simplify the problem of analysis if history unfolded according to a timetable, but a student of the past like Burnham should know that it does not. Moreover, there are solid reasons for the prolongation of the transition period. Russia at the time of the Revolution was a technically backward, largely illiterate, agricultural country, tyrannically oppressed by a semifeudal ruling class and ravaged by war. Since the Revolution she has not been free from the actuality or threat of invasion by surrounding imperialist powers which have never scrupled to use any weapons at their disposal to undermine the Soviet regime. At the same time she has been literally forced — as who can now deny? — to reorganize her economy completely and at breakneck speed in order to create the means of survival. These facts are, of course, well known, but we cannot remind ourselves of them too often if we are to avoid the mechanical application of abstract criteria, like "full democracy," in judging the Soviet Union.

Mention of the hostile international environment surrounding the Soviet Union brings us to the last of Burnham's three major criteria of socialism, namely that it must be international. Here he relaxes the strictness of his standards a little by conceding that if socialist society cannot be organized "completely" on an international scale "in the first stages, at least this is to be the *tendency* of socialism." (P. 39.) Even so, he finds that the Soviet Union has not met the test, but supporting evidence is entirely lacking. If he means no more than that the Soviet system has not been extended beyond its national borders, this is of course true, but also irrelevant since it has been due to factors outside Soviet control. If, on the other hand, he means that the Soviet Union has failed to pursue a foreign policy consistent with the ideals of internationalism, the record belies him. In respect to disarmament and collective security, the Soviet Union followed a consistently internationalist policy until it became overwhelmingly clear that the democratic capitalist powers were building up German imperialism in the hope of using it to crush the Soviet Union. Fortunately the significance of the nonaggression pact with Germany has become clear since the launching of the Nazi invasion in June 1941, so that there is no need to go into the question here. In the Spanish Civil War, and again in the Sino-Japanese War, there can be no question of the genuinely international character of Soviet policy. To be sure, in all these cases, Soviet policy corresponded with Soviet interests, but this is strong confirmation of the view that we are dealing with a socialist state. Finally, in this connection there is a fact of overwhelming importance which Burnham fails even to mention, and that is the complete equality of treatment which has from the outset been accorded the several dozen nationalities which compose the Soviet Union. It is, to use a phrase of Burnham's, "a historical law which knows no exceptions" that domestic policy toward national and racial minorities is strictly correlated with foreign policy toward other nations and races. Is Burnham really unaware of this, or is it so inconvenient for his theory that he finds it better to suppress it altogether?

We shall return later to the so-called new ruling class of managers, considering Germany and Russia together. In the meantime we have shown that Burnham completely fails in his effort to prove that the Soviet Union is nonsocialist according to the historic criteria of socialist thought.

THE SIGNIFICANCE OF THE NEW DEAL

According to Burnham the New Deal is an embryonic form of managerialism and, as such, anticapitalist to the core. This he deduces from two sets of facts which are, generally speaking, indisputable: first, that the state has greatly extended the scope of its activities in the economic sphere; and, second, that capitalists, by and large, are vehemently opposed to the New Deal.

In connection with the extension of state activity, we meet again the same reasoning that Burnham applied in his analysis of Nazi Germany. He holds that the state under capitalism must confine its economic activities primarily to the negative function of policing the field of private enterprise. Any move toward greater participation in economic affairs is to him *ipso facto* a move away from capitalism. (P. 106.) As we shall show more specifically below, this theory has absolutely nothing in common with Marxism and is, in fact, a superficial form of economic liberalism. Capitalist relations are frozen into a mold abstracted largely from mid-nineteenth-century English experience, or from *The Wealth of Nations*, and any departure from this rigid pattern is declared to be a move away from capitalism. This method of argument has only one virtue: it makes it possible to pass judgment on historical processes without going to the bother of analyzing their content. One wonders how Burnham would interpret the age of mercantilism, that period of two centuries in which the state played the dominant role in economic life.

If he says that it was anticapitalist, as this particular theory would seem to require, then he would have to explain the curious paradox of an anticapitalist state busily engaged in fostering the accumulation of capital. If, on the other hand, he admits that mercantilism was a form of capitalism, then we are entitled to ask what is left of the theory. For Marxists the crucial question is precisely "who runs the government" and "for what." The extension of government activity in economic affairs, taken by itself, proves nothing for or against the capitalist character of the society in which it occurs.

But, Burnham would claim, the anticapitalism of the New Deal is proved by the fact that capitalists have been overwhelmingly opposed to it.

Orthodox Marxists [he writes] are very hard put to it to explain this simple and undoubted fact. They are compelled by their theory to say that Roosevelt and the New Deal represent capitalism and the capitalist class. . . . This, apparently, must be partly hypocrisy and partly because the capitalists "do not understand their own interests." What a pitiful way out of a theoretical difficulty! And what a weak insult to the capitalists, who number among themselves not a few very intelligent persons! (P. 260.)

It may be remarked that Burnham himself is not above such pitiful ways out of theoretical difficulties, since he assumes without hesitation that the German capitalists were thoroughly duped by the Nazis; this is, however, hardly a sufficient excuse for attributing a similar shortcoming to Marxism. The truth of the matter is that Burnham seriously distorts the Marxist position.

Roosevelt and the New Deal represent capitalism if by that is meant that they stand ready to protect the general structure of capitalist property relations. This is so commonly taken for granted that it is rarely explicitly mentioned. But within the limits imposed by this obligation, Roosevelt and the New Deal represent a great deal more than capitalists;

they also represent workers, farmers, professionals, intellectuals. In short, the United States is a democracy — a capitalist democracy, to be sure, but nevertheless a democracy. The masses have the vote, and they can use it to influence the policies of the government and to bring pressure on the administration in power. If their circumstances become sufficiently desperate they do so in no uncertain terms — this is hardly a new phenomenon in American history. The year 1932 found the masses in just such a state. Roosevelt, an astute man, realized, probably more intuitively than rationally, that the situation called for a program of extensive concessions, a program which would have the double effect of consolidating his own popular position and of directing the discontent of the masses into relatively safe reformist channels. What had been done in England and Germany, over a long period of time, was to be accomplished in this country in little more than five years. Naturally the interests of the capitalists were not neglected, although Burnham characteristically ignores those features of the New Deal which were sponsored and approved by capitalists. Nevertheless the main impact of the New Deal was inevitably that of a program of widespread and unprecedentedly rapid reform. The capitalists sensed certain very real dangers in the situation; their traditional habits of mind received a rude shock; they reacted by conceiving a profound animosity against the symbol of the things they feared, against Roosevelt and his circle of immediate advisers. This, however, is not in the least a sign that the capitalists were disturbed by the growing power of Burnham's production managers (whom they know how to handle well enough), but rather that they saw behind the New Deal that specter which they have good reason to dread, an awakened and militant working class.

As to the larger historical problem whether the New Deal is serving the long-run interests of the capitalist class, there seems to be little doubt that it is; but the question certainly cannot be settled by asking them if they like it. Burnham knows this well enough when he is not engaged in scoring points favorable to his own theory. Social Democracy he refers to as a "defender of capitalism." (P. 195.) Quite so, but can Burnham tell us how many capitalists ever voted for Social Democrats?

A complete Marxist account of the New Deal has yet to be written; when it is, I think it is safe to predict that it will bear little resemblance to Burnham's straw-man version and that it will have to take small account of the "managerial" interpretation.

THE NATURE OF A RULING CLASS

So far we have concentrated on four specific contentions of Burnham: that the managers are acquiring actual control over the instruments of production in the United States; that Nazi Germany is noncapitalist; that the Soviet Union is nonsocialist; and that the New Deal is anticapitalist and pro-managerial in its tendencies. But underlying Burnham's position on these and related issues there are certain more general theoretical problems which it is particularly appropriate to discuss in a theoretical organ like *Science & Society*. For reasons of space we shall have to confine our attention to a brief consideration of two of these: first, the meaning of the concept of a "ruling class";[10] and, second, the outstanding characteristics and tendencies of present-day capitalism.

Class affiliation is not a question of social origins. One who is born a worker can become a capitalist and vice versa. Common social origins are important to the thinking and cohesiveness of a class, but they do not determine its composition. This is a matter of the position which individuals actually occupy in society, that is to say, their relations to others and to society as a whole. For Marxists this means,

---

[10] On this subject, see also the article below on "The American Ruling Class," pp. 120-138.

primarily, position in the structure of economic relations which, for reasons which cannot be gone into here, dominate the totality of social relations. It is by this path that we arrive at the definition of the ruling class as comprising those persons who individually or in combination own the means of production, ownership implying effective control.

This is a *general* definition which is unobjectionable as far as it goes, but it is important to realize that it does not go very far and that its uncritical application can be misleading. While it is correct that the ruling class is made up of those who control the means of production, the converse is not necessarily true. Control over the means of production is by no means synonymous with exploitation of one part of society by another. If the relation of exploitation does not exist, the concept of a ruling class is inapplicable; the society is said to be classless. The most unambiguous example of a classless society is provided by what Marx called "simple commodity production," in which each producer owns and works with his own means of production. Because of its nature as a general definition applying to all class societies, the definition in question furnishes no clue to the differences between them and hence no criteria for telling one ruling class from another. When a new set of individuals acquires control over the means of production, one must ask whether it is a new ruling class or just a new personnel for the old ruling class. The general definition is of no assistance in answering this question.

This example should serve to warn us of the impossibility of treating the problem of the ruling class as an abstract problem of society in general. We must be *historically specific* if we are to make the concept a useful tool of social analysis. This means that in the case of every particular ruling class we must carefully specify the character of the social relations in which it occupies the dominant position, and the form of control which it exercises over the means of production. It is these factors, *and these factors alone*, which determine the all-important motives and objectives of the ruling class. In this way we can distinguish between ruling classes; we shall, in short, have a method of separating genuine social revolutions (shifts in class rule) from mere substitutions, more or less thorough, of new faces for old.

Let us now apply these considerations to the case of capitalism. Here we have two basic classes, apart from intermediate groups and remnants of earlier social forms, namely, the bourgeoisie who own the means of production and the class of free wage laborers who own nothing but their own capacity to work. The importance of the *form* of control exercised by the bourgeoisie over the means of production cannot be overemphasized. This form is the ownership of *capital*, from which, of course, capitalism derives its designation. Exploitation takes the form of the production of surplus value. "Capital" is not simply another name for means of production; it is means of production reduced to a qualitatively homogeneous and quantitatively measurable fund of value. The concern of the capitalist is not with means of production as such, but with capital, and this necessarily means capital regarded as a quantity, for capital has only one dimension, the dimension of magnitude.

For several reasons this concern of the capitalist with the quantity of capital must have the result that the expansion of capital becomes his primary and dominant objective. In the first place, his social status is decided, and can only be decided, by the quantity of capital under his control; and in the second place, even if the capitalist as an individual were content to "maintain his capital intact" without increase, he could rationally pursue this end only by striving to expand. Capital "naturally" tends to contract — the forces of competition and technological change work wholly in this direction — and this tendency can be defeated only by a continuous effort to expand. Fundamentally, profit is an increment to capital, a point of view which saturates the theory and practice of corporate finance. The fact that the capitalist consumes a part of his profit is an altogether secondary phenomenon.[11]

The objective of expanding capital is thus not one which capitalists are free to take or leave as they choose; they *must* pursue it on pain of elimination from the ruling class. This holds equally for actual owners of capital and for those who, though not themselves substantial owners, come into the "management" of capital.[12] Neither is in any sense a free agent. The ruling class under capitalism is made up of the *functionaries of capital,* those whose motives and objectives are prescribed for them by the specific historical form of their control over the means of production.

This analysis assists us in solving the "riddle" of the Nazis. The Nazi movement was a product of the ills of postwar German capitalism (ills which were both capitalist and specifically German), chief of which was the extremely limited opportunity for capital to expand in a "normal" way. The aggressively nationalist and antisocialist ideology of the

---

[11] For reasons of space we must limit ourselves to suggesting a few important points which arise in this connection. (1) The abandonment of the view that the expansion of capital (i.e. accumulation) is the central characteristic of capitalism, more than anything else, differentiates vulgar from classical political economy. (2) The reasoning outlined in the text lies at the heart of Marx's theoretical economics. His insistence on the importance of M-C-M' as the specific form of capitalist circulation, and his repeated reference to capitalism as a process of "self-expansion of value" (*Verwertungsprozess*), are merely two among many indications of this. (3) A correct theory of capitalists' consumption is clearly suggested by Marx but is more fully treated by Veblen in *The Theory of the Leisure Class*. Basically, capitalists' consumption, beyond a certain modest minimum, is the method of displaying success in the field of accumulation. This accounts for the pecuniary and emulative standards of taste which are such a marked characteristic of bourgeois society.

[12] "Management" is here used in the Berle and Means sense. That something of this sort does happen in not a few giant corporations is unquestionable. Our earlier discussion of the subject was primarily designed to demonstrate that the phenomenon has been greatly exaggerated. Now, however, we can see that even if this were not the case there would be little justification for extreme conclusions.

Nazis grew out of and corresponded to the objective needs of German capital, which complained both of "foreign encirclement" and of "excessive demands" of the masses. Hence not only the capitalists but also the whole bourgeois state apparatus boosted the Nazis into the position of political dominance. Once in power they set out to do what they always said they were going to do and exactly what German capital needed to have done. It is clearly naive to say that the Nazis didn't have to act as they did, and that whenever they choose they can turn to increasing the living standards of the masses. They are not simply paying off a debt to the capitalists; politics doesn't recognize valid debts. *They never had any idea of doing anything else.* They accept the imperatives of capitalist society unquestioningly and uncritically, as even a modest acquaintance with their less propagandistic literature shows. To be sure, those capitalists who are Jewish and also those who have opposed Nazi policy have been unceremoniously suppressed. But their place has been taken by others, many from the ranks of the Nazi Party (Goering and Ley are outstanding examples), whose objectives are not their own but rather those of the ruling-class position which they have come to occupy. Ultimately the proof that Nazism is capitalist and that the ruling class in Germany, despite certain (easily exaggerated) shifts in personnel, is still the capitalist class is to be found in the simple and undoubted fact that the Nazis *have* retained all the essential forms of capitalism. It is a bad joke to maintain, as Burnham and others do, that the "mere" retention of the forms of capitalism is an incidental phenomenon devoid of historical meaning.

We can analyze the problem of the ruling class in relation to the Soviet Union more briefly. In the Soviet Union not only were the capitalists virtually wiped out by the Revolution (which, in itself, would not be decisive) but the entire structure of capitalist property relations was smashed. In the Soviet Union practically the worst crime is the ownership of capital, that is, the hiring of wage labor with a view to selling the product. In other words not only the capitalists but also the capitalist class has been eliminated. Has a new ruling class risen to take the place of the capitalist class? It is indeed true that a small political leadership (not at all Burnham's managers) exercises directive control over the means of production at the present time. But to stop there is, as we know, to be extremely superficial. We must ask the further question: what are the objectives of this political group and what social forces determine its status? Political leaders are not able to generate "their own" outlook and aims. In the Soviet economy, the task of the leadership is that of planning the production of use values; this corresponds to the objectives of the only class in capitalism which by its position is forced to combat the accumulation of capital and to favor the expansion of consumption, the working class. From the standpoint of economic science, the political leadership in the Soviet Union is acting as the agent of the working class. No relation of exploitation exists between controllers and workers. To say this is not at all to deny that there are among those in authority in the Soviet Union cases of individuals who are selfish, greedy, and who misuse their power for their own private ends; if this were not the case in a country with Russia's history it would indeed be a miracle. The real issue is one of general interests and objectives, which are prescribed by the structure and form of social relations as a whole. In this sense the objective of those who direct the Soviet economy can only be production of use values which corresponds in every way to the interests of the working class. We might, therefore, say that the working class is the ruling class in the Soviet Union. But clearly, as other classes with objectives at variance with those of the working class dwindle in importance, this becomes a less and less meaningful statement. Actually there is no longer a ruling class in the proper sense of the term in the Soviet Union: it is evolving toward the condition of a classless society.

Finally, before leaving the subject of the ruling class, we may notice the basic fallacy in Burnham's conception of the managers as a new ruling class arising out of the present-day structure of capitalism. Managers are the best-kept salaried workers under capitalism. Their outlook and objectives are entirely bound up with those of their superiors; their greatest ambition is to become genuine functionaries of capital, whether as owners or as executives. They are, in short, utterly unsuited by training and social status to adopt an independent historical position. They do not in fact control the means of production, but even if they did they would be quite incapable of transcending the limits of the capitalist order. It is not without significance that Burnham, in thinking up a set of objectives for his managers, gets no further than the most obvious tendencies of capitalism in its imperialist phase. The managers will repress the masses and fight among themselves for world dominance. It never even occurs to him that the Soviet Union, which he imagines to be a managerial state, is headed in quite a different direction.

We now turn to the question of the main characteristics of present-day capitalism, with particular reference to the role of the state. A negative state policy in economic matters and a liberal, individualistic ideology are in no sense intrinsic to capitalism. Burnham's contrary belief, which is shared by many, is pure dogma which finds no support in the historical record. *Laissez faire* and liberalism grew out of a special phase of capitalist development. It was clearly marked in the Anglo-Saxon countries and France during the greater part of the nineteenth century, was present for a considerably shorter time in a seriously modified and weakened form in Germany, and was virtually nonexistent in Russia and Japan. This phase of capitalism has two fundamental features which are closely interdependent: competition and relatively unlimited opportunities for capital to expand. Both of these features tend to disappear, not accidentally but as a consequence of the working of the capitalist process itself. Monopoly replaces competition, and the limits of accumulation narrow relatively to the needs of capital. *Laissez faire* and liberalism, which shielded the onward march of capital in the earlier period, are inapplicable in the new phase. Just as in the formative days of bourgeois society, capital once again requires the active assistance of the state in smoothing the way for its own expansion. A new state policy and a changed ideology are developed, and more readily so in direct proportion to the weakness of the liberal phase. Generally speaking, the effectuation of the new state policy requires considerable change in political institutions (often erroneously interpreted as a "social revolution"). The liberal period fostered the growth of political democracy which enabled the masses to pursue aims of their own and to hamstring those policies which had become desirable from a capitalist standpoint. Hence the ideology of the new period is not only antiliberal in a cultural sense but also politically antidemocratic. In economics, the new capitalist ideology now stresses "planning," by which is meant state intervention to foster the accumulation of capital. The leitmotif of this ideology is the idea of *domination*, which in turn implies an entirely different ethical outlook from that which characterized the liberal epoch. The whole movement reaches its culminating point, materially and ideologically, in the present-day fascist state.

It may be objected that this theory is a *post hoc* rationalization designed to square Marxist theory with the latest social and economic trends. Such a view reveals a profound although all too common ignorance of the literature of Marxism. All the essentials of the theory were developed long before the Great Depression and the rise of Nazism, for the most part even before World War I. The realization that bourgeois society was entering a new stage of its life history — generally called the stage of "imperialism," since the publication in 1917 of Lenin's book of that name — dates back to the 1890s. Strong traces of it can already be found in the last works of Engels. After Engels' death in 1895,

THE ILLUSION OF THE MANAGERIAL REVOLUTION

Marxist theorists including Rosa Luxemburg, Kautsky, Hilferding, and Lenin all wrote on the theory of imperialism.

If space permitted, it would be worth while to reproduce passages from each of these writers to show how clearly they, as Marxists, recognized the basic characteristics of the new period: the predominance of monopoly, the growing restrictions to the further expansion of capital, the prevalence of state interventionism, and the advance of a thoroughly antiliberal ideology. We shall, however, have to be content with a passage from Hilferding's *Finanzkapital* (1909):

As an ideal there now appears the conquest of world mastery for one's own nation, a striving as unlimited as capital's striving for profit from which it springs. Capital becomes the conqueror of the world and, with every new land conquered, sets a new border which must be overstepped. This striving becomes an economic necessity, since any holding back lowers the profit of finance capital, reduces its ability to compete, and finally can turn a smaller economic region into a mere tributary of a larger one. Economically grounded, it is ideologically justified by that remarkable twisting of the national idea, which no longer recognizes the right of every nation to political self-determination and independence, and which is no longer an expression of the democratic belief in the equality of all nationalities. Rather, the economic advantage of monopoly is mirrored in the favored place which must be ascribed to one's own nation. The latter appears chosen above all others. Since the subordination of foreign nations proceeds by force, that is to say in a very natural way, it appears to the dominant nation that it owes its mastery to its special natural qualities, in other words to its racial characteristics. Thus in racial ideology there emerges a scientifically cloaked foundation for the power lust of finance capital, which in this way demonstrates the cause and necessity of its operations. In place of the democratic ideal of equality there arises an oligarchical ideal of mastery.

If in the field of foreign policy this ideal seems to include the whole nation, in internal affairs it stresses the standpoint of mastery as against the working class. At the same time, the growing power of the workers increases the effort of capital to enhance the state power as security against the demands of the proletariat. (P. 427.)

This remarkable passage strikes the present-day reader as uncanny in its prophetic accuracy. But what is really important is that it was neither a lucky guess nor a unique pronouncement. It was the product of Marxism, to which many others beside Hilferding had contributed.

Marxists are entitled to a feeling of pride in the great intellectual traditions of their movements. Their theory of what is happening in the world is not an *ad hoc* invention, conceived on the spur of the moment to account for something unexpected; it is rather the living application of the principles of scientific socialism which, from the time of Marx himself, has never lost touch with the rich variety and continuous development of social realities. By comparison, theories such as those of Burnham reveal themselves for what they are, hasty improvisations devoid alike of scientific validity and historical significance.

4

The Marshall Plan and the Crisis of Western Europe

This is a revision of a speech delivered at the famous Waldorf-Astoria Peace Conference in March 1949; it was published under the title "Is The Marshall Plan an Instrument of Peace?" in Monthly Review, *July 1949.*

The essay starts with the proposition that the Marshall Plan could not create an economically independent western Europe and goes on to inquire why. The proposition has stood the test of four years of experience and is, I believe, as true of the present and prospective successors to the Marshall Plan as it was of the Marshall Plan itself. The reasons remain basically the same, and so do the conclusions regarding continued efforts to create a viable western Europe by infusions of outside aid.

THE Marshall Plan was sold to the American people as a program of aid to the countries of western Europe which would enable them to achieve, within the space of about five years, full economic independence. That is certainly a praiseworthy aim. Economically independent countries can also afford to be politically independent. A politically independent western Europe, tied to no blocs and defending its own interests in the arena of international politics, would be a powerful force for peace. If the Marshall Plan were really calculated to create an independent western Europe, it should receive support.

It is for precisely this reason that by far the most important fact about the Marshall Plan is that it is not creating an economically independent western Europe. There is not the slightest prospect that it will create an economically independent western Europe.

Official analyses of the Marshall Plan reveal this fact even though they dare not admit it. Honest evaluations of the Marshall Plan say it frankly and unequivocally.

Here, for example, is what Walter Lippmann had to say in his column in the *New York Herald Tribune* of June 13, 1949:

> There is current a good deal of pretense and propaganda about how well in hand everything is. Yet ever since the report of the Marshall Plan countries which was made available at the end of 1948 it has been known to the relatively few who studied it that the goal of European recovery, in the official and popular sense of the words, was unattainable by 1952 — during the period set by Congress and agreed to by the Marshall Plan countries. It was certain that even with almost unlimited wishful thinking the leading industrial countries of Europe could not become self-supporting and still achieve and maintain a tolerable standard of life by 1952, or in fact at any foreseeable date.

I believe this is a sober statement of the truth — the bedrock from which any rational evaluation of the Marshall Plan must start.

Why is the Marshall Plan failing to achieve its announced goals? Many theories are currently being put forward to explain this. Some say that it is because the United States is perverting the Marshall Plan into an instrument of American imperialism. Some say that it is because the British are selfishly looking out for their own recovery and neglecting the interests of western Europe as a whole. Some say that it is because of the maze of regulations and restrictions which are choking trade among the Marshall Plan countries themselves.

There is, of course, something to each one of these theories. But they are all essentially superficial, and even if the conditions to which they call attention were remedied the situation as a whole would not be decisively altered. The Marshall Plan might be administered without a thought for the interests of American business. The British might be as altruistic as they are alleged to be selfish. Trade restrictions among the Marshall Plan countries might be completely eliminated. There would still be no economically independent western Europe by the end of 1952.

The truth is that the Marshall Plan does not touch the real problem of western Europe. The Marshall Plan is based on the tacit assumption that western Europe was temporarily knocked out by the war and that what it needs is help in getting back on its feet again. This is a totally inadequate diagnosis. In fact, the war was merely the climax of a long-term trend. The *status quo ante* in western Europe is dead; no amount of outside assistance can bring it to life again. To quote Thomas Balogh, an eminent Oxford economist: "Western Europe's crisis is not a temporary or short-lived departure from an 'equilibrium position' to which it is easy to return. It is a historically unique, harsh break with all that has gone before, a fundamental crisis."

In broad outline the nature of this crisis is clear and simple. Western Europe was the original home of capitalism. During the eighteenth and nineteenth centuries it was economically by far the most advanced region in the world. It used its wealth and power to establish relations with the rest of the world which were enormously advantageous to western Europe. On the strength of these advantageous relations with the rest of the world, western Europe developed a very numerous population and provided it with a relatively high standard of living.

It is easy to see now, looking back, that the foundation of western Europe's extraordinary prosperity was temporary. The rest of the world was bound to catch up and to demand a redefinition of its relations with western Europe. When that happened western Europe could no longer go on living in the old way. It would have to face up to the problem of reconstructing and reorienting its economy to meet the requirements of a changed world.

The two world wars greatly accelerated this inevitable historical development. Already in the interwar period, the day of reckoning was clearly approaching. By the end of World War II it was obvious that it had at last arrived.

What were the practical alternatives?

First, outside aid which would permit western Europe to evade the real problem but would in no sense contribute to its solution.

Or, second, a thoroughgoing economic revolution which would cut through centuries-old vested interests, drastically redirect and reorganize the utilization of human and material resources, and open the way for a planned coordination of the western European economy with the economies of other regions which would be both willing and able to enter into firm long-term commitments of a mutually beneficial nature. The watchword of such a revolution would have to be planning and still more planning — vigorous, disciplined, comprehensive.

Only a political imbecile could believe that the traditional ruling classes of western Europe would or could carry through such a revolution. It would have to be done by the working class, which has few privileges to lose and is capable of toil and sacrifice for a communal goal. And in the very process of carrying out this great revolution, the workers of western Europe would inevitably be forced to scrap the old capitalist system of production for profit and to substitute a new socialist system of production for use.

In the actual circumstances which prevailed after World War II, such a revolution was a very real possibility. On the Continent the Resistance movements, under the leadership of Socialists and Communists, were everywhere spearheading the drive for radical economic reform. In England the Labor Party was swept into power on a wave of popular enthusiasm for its stated socialist aims. A firm Socialist-Communist front could have led the way forward despite all obstacles.

But the leaders of the United States, and especially those who have their offices in the skyscrapers of New York rather than in the government buildings of Washington, feared nothing so much as a real revolution in western Europe. They had one, and only one, weapon with which to fight it — economic subsidies which would give the old order a new lease on life and permit western Europe, for the time being at any rate, to evade rather than tackle the basic problem which confronted it. They used their weapon skillfully and ruthlessly; and they found valuable allies among the Social Democratic leaders of western Europe.

At first the subsidies took the form of a variety of loans and grants. Later they were systematized in the more effective form of the Marshall Plan with its centralized administrative apparatus, its network of bilateral treaties, and its agents in each of the countries affected.

Thus we see that while the Marshall Plan was sold to the American people as a *solution* to the crisis of western Europe, in reality it is just the opposite. It is the means by which American capitalism seeks to prevent western Europe from solving its own crisis in the only possible way it can solve the crisis, by the adoption of socialism.

It is only against this background that we can properly evaluate the relation of the Marshall Plan to peace and war. The relation is not a simple one and nothing is gained by pretending that it is.

If the ruling elements in the United States were prepared to continue the Marshall Plan indefinitely, if the support of the American people for such a policy could be secured, and if the economy of the United States could be stabilized by a continuing export surplus of this magnitude, then the Marshall Plan would have a tendency to reduce international tensions, at least for a considerable period. Western Europe would become the passive dumping ground for an economic system which is always in danger of choking on its own surplus product.

But none of these conditions is likely to be fulfilled. Subsidizing western Europe is not a directly profitable form of investment for American capitalists; the people of the United States are not sufficiently initiated into the mysteries of capitalist economics to understand the need for giving away five or six billion dollars a year forever; and in any case five or six billion dollars is not enough to keep American capitalism from choking.

Hence the Marshall Plan must be looked upon as a stopgap expedient which solves neither the problems of western Europe nor the problems of the United States. Being essentially temporary and inadequate by any standards, it cannot but play a disturbing role in international relations.

And yet it is hardly accurate to say that the Marshall Plan as such is a threat to peace.

The real threat to peace comes from the utter and complete inability of the rulers of the United States to devise a nonwarlike program for dealing with the overwhelming problems which are pressing in on them from all sides.

When the Marshall Plan runs out, the crisis of western Europe will be no nearer solution than it was two years ago — and it may be added that the obvious and continued success of socialist planning in eastern Europe will by that time have shown the western Europeans how they can solve their crisis if they but have the will and the resolve. American capitalism is already giving signs of sliding into the inevitable depression which all the world expects and which our rulers know will deal a body blow to their prestige and authority. Worst of all from their point of view, if something isn't done, even the American people may wake up from their propaganda-created nightmare of Soviet aggression and Communist plots to discover that the real world is one in which those nations and peoples who manage their affairs in their own interests go forward in spite of all obstacles, while those who put their trust in the gods of free enterprise find themselves hopelessly stuck in the mire of economic insecurity and political reaction.

These are the problems which stare the rulers of America in the face. They do not know how to overcome them. In truth there is no way to overcome them within the framework of the self-contradictory system to which they are wedded. In the long run the replacement of capitalism by a rational socialist order is as certain in the United States as elsewhere. But in the meantime, the greatest danger to world peace, and indeed to much that is best in human civilization itself, is that the rulers of America will seek to put off the day of reckoning by embarking on a career of unlimited militarism and imperialism.

They are already moving in this direction — whether consciously or not is beside the point. If they continue, war may not come soon; but it is hard to see how it can be avoided indefinitely. Militarism and imperialism have their own logic, and its final term is war.

Is it too late to call a halt? That will depend on how quickly the people everywhere, but especially the people of western Europe and America, can be brought to understand that the only possible guarantee of lasting peace is a new social order which puts the interests of producers and consumers above the interests of private capital.

5

Marxism in the East: Decomposition or Enrichment?

This is a review of Benjamin Schwartz, *Chinese Communism and the Rise of Mao* (Cambridge, Massachusetts, 1952). It appeared in *The Journal of Political Economy*, April 1952.

*C*HINESE *Communism and the Rise of Mao* is an interesting and thoughtful book on an extremely complicated and controversial subject. It is also something in the way of a curiosity these days — a study dealing with Communism which is carried out in a scientific spirit and without apparent ulterior purpose.

Mr. Schwartz's analysis is concerned entirely with what may be called the "inner history" of the Chinese Communist movement. He begins with its intellectual origins in the period immediately after the Russian Revolution — a very useful discussion, incidentally, since hardly any literature exists on the subject, at least in English — and brings us down to Mao Tse-tung's accession to undisputed leadership in the early thirties. The period of collaboration with the Kuomintang, the break with the Kuomintang in 1927, relations between the Chinese Communist Party and the Communist International, the repeated efforts which were made by the Party to win an urban proletarian base, the birth and gradual expansion of the Soviet regions, and the final triumph of Maoism — all these subjects are treated in considerable detail and with a candid appraisal of the sources used.

It would perhaps be presumptuous of a nonexpert to criticize Schwartz's reconstruction of the factual story of the development of Chinese Communism; but it is in order to report that the material available in this country, even to a student who commands Chinese, Japanese, and Russian (as Schwartz does), is extremely meager on many important points. The result is that Schwartz often has to resort to inference and conjecture, and here, of course, his conscious and unconscious biases play a crucial role. It is no paradox, I think, to say that another scholar with the same knowledge of the subject that Schwartz possesses and with a no less scientific attitude could paint a very different picture of the inner history of Chinese Communism. Under the circumstances, even the nonexpert will scarcely be able to avoid the frequent exercise of his own judgment on the evidence presented. It is to Schwartz's credit that he makes a conscientious effort to present the evidence in such a way as to make this possible.

Schwartz draws certain general conclusions from his study of Chinese Communism. Perhaps the most important is the following:

In general, it is our view that in spite of its seeming "successes," Marxism has in its movement eastward — into situations for which its original premises made little provision — undergone a slow but steady process of decomposition. This process had already gone some distance with Lenin, himself, and might have gone further if he had lived longer. . . . With Stalin, of course, this process has gone still further, and it has been one of the aims of this study to show how the process has been carried forward yet another step by the experience of the Chinese Communist Party. (P. 4.)

The "proof" that Marxism has "undergone a process of decomposition" in China is essentially that the Chinese Communist Party failed to establish roots in the urban proletariat and instead came to power on a revolutionary peasant base. This will no doubt satisfy non-Marxists who insist on seeing in Marxism nothing but a body of rigid dogmas, precluded *ex definitione* from learning anything new from the unfolding historical process. But those who understand that in essence Marxism is a method of analysis and a guide to action, not at all a body of dogmas, will be in little doubt that Schwartz has mistaken the enrichment of Marxism by the two great twentieth-century revolutions for its decomposition.

In conclusion, let me pay Schwartz what I think is a real compliment: his book is as valuable to those who disagree with him as to those who agree with him. There are few enough books of this kind being written today.

Part II

Imperialism

6

A Marxist View of Imperialism

This is the text of a paper delivered at a joint session of the American Historical Association and the Economic History Association, Hotel Mayflower, Washington, D. C., December 28, 1952. It was published in Monthly Review, *March 1953.*

LET me begin with one or two introductory remarks which may help to avoid misunderstanding.

In the first place, I call your attention to the fact that my title is "*A* Marxist View of Imperialism," not "*The* Marxist View of Imperialism." I do not presume to speak for others, and I regret that conditions in this country today are such as to make it extremely difficult for Marxists to engage in the kind of fruitful exchange of views that could lead either to agreement or at any rate to a clear definition of differences. Therefore, while I may hope that what I have to say will command the assent of other Marxists, I am in no position to claim that it does.

In the second place, the subject of imperialism is so large that in a short paper one must limit oneself severely if one is to accomplish any useful purpose at all. What I would like to do is to draw on the history of imperialism and of ideas about imperialism to show why and in what sense the United States is an imperialist country today. The problem has an obvious interest for its own sake, and it will serve as a convenient focus for a few remarks about imperialism in general.

I

According to Hallgarten, whose recently published study of imperialism before 1914 is a uniquely valuable work,[1] the term "imperialism" itself is of relatively recent origin, having first been employed by a group of British writers and administrators in the late 1870s. These men were advocates of the strengthening and expansion of the British colonial empire; "imperialism" was the name they gave to the policy they were urging on their countrymen. Originally, in other words, "imperialism" was roughly equivalent to "colonialism" — the establishment and extension of the political sovereignty of one nation over alien peoples and territories.

During the next three decades, the term came into increasingly common use and, as so often happens in the history of language, acquired a much broader meaning than it originally had. This was the period during which Britain's economic supremacy came under challenge, when the surface of the globe was pretty largely divided up among the advanced countries of Europe, and when the powers that were slow in starting and hence lagged behind in the race for colonies began to use new methods of economic and political expansion outside their own borders. Emphasis shifted from political colonialism to the economic penetration and domination of markets, sources of raw materials, and investment outlets. The newer writers on imperialism — whether they were for it, as in the case of Charles A. Conant in the United States, or against it, as in the case of John A. Hobson in Britain — saw economic forces and motives as primary and political forms as secondary. Moreover, Hobson — in his justly famous work entitled *Imperialism*, published in 1902 — went beyond the imperial relation as such to analyze the effects of imperialism on the societies concerned, stressing the exploitation of the backward peoples by the advanced

---

[1] G. W. F. Hallgarten, *Imperialismus vor 1914*, 2 vols. (Munich, 1951). This work is discussed in detail below, pp. 93-103.

nations and the development of what he called "parasitism" in the latter.

In some respects, Rudolf Hilferding, the most influential German Marxist writer on the subject of imperialism, went further than Hobson in broadening the concept. His magnum opus, *Das Finanzkapital*, with its conscious echoing of Marx's *Das Kapital*, was subtitled "A Study of the Latest Phase of Capitalist Development," and it treated imperialism as an inseparable part of the system itself. In Hilferding's view, imperialism became, as it were, an emanation of finance capital, the inevitable consequence of the world-wide struggle of the great industrial and financial monopolies for maximum profits.

Lenin took the final step on the road of broadening the concept when he gave the name "imperialism" to the system as a whole. In Lenin's own mind, there was nothing particularly original or new about this — it was merely the logical implication of a usage which had become common by the time World War I broke out. "During the last fifteen or twenty years," he wrote in the very first sentence of *Imperialism* (1917), "... the economic and also the political literature of the two hemispheres has more and more often adopted the term 'imperialism' in order to define the present era."

I have described this linguistic development, which reached its logical conclusion in the famous work of Lenin, as a broadening of the concept of imperialism. The term, from defining a particular political relation, gradually came to take in the entire politico-economic system of which that relation was merely one part. But there was another side to the development, too. Colonialism exists under conditions of modern capitalism, but it is by no means peculiar to such conditions: it has existed in a variety of historically known social systems. Hence if imperialism is identified with colonialism, it is not at all an historically specific concept. It is otherwise if imperialism is the name given to a certain historical era — or, more accurately, to the social system which dominates a certain historical era. It then becomes in the fullest sense an historically specific concept — one the validity and usefulness of which is strictly limited to an historical period which covers the lifetime of a definite social system.

Ever since the publication of Lenin's *Imperialism*, Marxists — and, I should add, many others of whom Hallgarten is one of the most recent and also one of the most distinguished examples — have used the term as Lenin did, to denote the specific international politico-economic system which took shape in the three or four decades before World War I. In what follows, I shall adhere to this usage.

II

Before we turn to the problem of American imperialism, we must acquire certain criteria of measurement and judgment. And for these we must, of course, go back to the years before World War I, to what Hallgarten appropriately calls "the classical period of imperialism."

Lacking the time to go into this problem from a methodological point of view, I can only state my own conviction that the existence or nonexistence of imperialism can be most satisfactorily tested by examining the pattern of economic relations between advanced and backward countries, and especially by observing the course of economic development in the latter.

The lessons of the classical period of imperialism in this connection are, I think, unmistakable. The advanced countries were interested in the backward countries for three main reasons. They wanted (1) sources of raw materials which could be profitably sold in world markets; (2) outlets for capital investment; and (3) markets for manufactured goods. These three requirements mutually conditioned and limited each other in such a way that capital flowing into the backward countries did not create replicas of the socioeconomic system existing in the lands of origin. Rather it turned the backward countries into economic appendages of the advanced countries, favoring the growth of those kinds of economic activity which complemented the advanced economies and blocking the growth of those kinds of activity which might compete with the advanced economies. The result, from the point of view of the backward countries, could not but be an unbalanced development which continually gave rise to new economic maladjustments and social tensions for which the system had no self-correcting mechanisms.

One of the distinguishing characteristics of this situation was the distribution by fields of employment of the foreign investments of the capital-exporting countries. Contrary to a widespread impression, which economists and economic historians have done much to foster, there was very little foreign investment in industry proper in the whole period before 1914; and what there was, was largely among the advanced countries rather than between the advanced countries and the backward countries. I refer you in this connection to Herbert Feis's classic study of pre-World War I foreign investment, *Europe, The World's Banker: 1870-1914*. The *significance* of the distribution of foreign investments largely escaped Feis, but the *facts* are carefully reported. Almost all foreign investment in backward countries went into government loans (largely for police, armies, and public works); transportation and communications (especially railroads, of course); mining; and the production of standardized agricultural raw materials.

Investment along these lines, taken together with the importation of cheap manufactured goods (especially consumers' goods) from abroad, naturally forced a special pattern of development on the backward countries. Pre-existing economies were disrupted, peasant cultivators uprooted, handicraft workers deprived of their means of livelihood. Native capital — what little there was of it — usually went into commerce or moneylending, since the obstacles to the growth of a native industry were for the most part insurmountable. On the one hand, therefore, you had modern technology and rapid growth in a few export industries affecting a relatively small proportion of the population; and on the other hand, stagnation and decay affecting the vast majority. Native agriculture was generally hit especially hard, whether because of the pre-emption of the best lands by foreigners, or because of the overcrowding of the available arable land as population grew and ruined handworkers moved to the countryside. In either case, the results were likely to be the same: subdivision of agricultural holdings, rack-renting to the profit of a parasitical landlord class, growth of a landless proletariat in the countryside, declining agricultural productivity, multiplication of the numbers of bloodsucking middlemen and usurers — in short, mounting agrarian crisis.

The economic impact of imperialism on the backward country can be summed up as follows: (1) exploitation by foreign capital of the country's natural resources, often by the most modern large-scale methods but directly affecting only a small percentage of the inhabitants; (2) creation of a transport network, but with a view to getting things out of the country, not to its people; (3) stagnation of industry and ruin of handicrafts; and (4) steady deterioration of agriculture.

III

This, then, was the general pattern of relations between advanced and backward countries which was already firmly established during the classical period of imperialism. It could be observed — of course with local variations — in India and China, together containing nearly half the world's population; in the entire continents of South America and Africa; and in innumerable smaller countries of Europe, Asia, North America, and on islands dotting the seven seas. It was so widespread, indeed, that Lenin, in 1917, could write with little exaggeration: "Capitalism has grown into a world system of colonial oppression and of the financial strangulation of the overwhelming majority of the people of the world by a handful of 'advanced' countries." (*Selected Works*, Vol. 5, p. 9.) For the advanced countries, or rather for their ruling classes, imperialism meant the exploitation at will of the natural and human resources of the backward countries; for the backward countries, it meant not only exploitation at the hands of the advanced countries but embarkation on a course of economic (and social) development which, if persisted in, could lead only to total disaster.

That there was little change in this pattern during the interwar period is, I think, self-evident. A good deal happened in those years: Russia dropped out of the comity of capitalist nations; Japan became a major imperialist power; the balance of economic and political power among the advanced countries shifted markedly. But through it all, the relations between the advanced capitalist countries and the backward countries remained much what they had been on the eve of World War I. Only the tensions grew—especially in the wake of the Great Depression — and the speed with which the backward countries hurried along the road to disaster increased.

World War II, however, unquestionably marked a turning point in the history of imperialism. As a direct result of the war, several of the backward countries of eastern Europe were brought into the orbit of the new social system which had emerged from the Russian Revolution of 1917. And a few years later, China, the most populous country in the world and in some ways one of the most backward, overthrew its old semifeudal, imperialist-dominated regime and joined hands with the Soviet Union and the countries of eastern Europe. By 1950, the period of unchallenged imperialist world domination had definitely come to an end: there were now two world systems, each containing economically advanced and economically backward countries and each vying for the support of peoples everywhere.

Nor was this the only change brought about by World War II. Simultaneously, there took place upheavals in the imperialist camp itself. Germany and Japan were at least temporarily knocked out of the ranks of the advanced countries with extensive imperialist connections; Britain and France were vastly weakened; India and Indonesia, largest and richest of the British and Dutch colonial possessions, won their political independence; and, finally, the United States emerged as the undisputed economic and political leader — if not boss — of all the advanced and most of the backward countries outside the Sino-Soviet orbit.

As a result of these momentous developments, world-wide interest in the relations between advanced and backward countries has been stimulated, a vast literature on economic development has grown up, and the United States has loudly proclaimed the adoption of new policies which have been hailed — and have been intended to be hailed — as foreshadowing nothing less than the end of the imperialist epoch.

IV

Has the pattern of relations between advanced and backward countries really changed in the capitalist camp? And what is the significance of present and prospective American policies in this respect? These are the questions which we must now attempt to answer.

That there have been no substantial changes *within* the old colonial empires is surely obvious. The function of the colonies is what it always has been — to provide raw materials for sale on the world market and to buy manufactured goods from the advanced countries. Investment in the colonies has for the most part followed the traditional pattern, with heavy emphasis on the development of standardized mineral and agricultural products. No structural reforms of a social or economic nature have been effected in the colonies, and there is no reason to anticipate that such will be forthcoming in the visible future.

Nor is the picture so very different when it comes to the relations between the advanced countries and the former colonies which have won their independence since the war. In fact, what has happened in the case of these countries proves how deeply rooted the imperialist pattern is, how impossible it is to abolish it short of a complete social revolution such as has taken place in China. India, for example, had what seemed like a magnificent opportunity in the late forties to extricate itself once and for all from the imperialist yoke and to strike out on a new course. The country had won its political independence; during the war it had repatriated much of Britain's huge capital investment in India and was still Britain's creditor on a substantial scale. The stage seemed to be set, in other words, for an ambitious development program which would raise India economically as well as politically out of the ranks of the colonial countries. But little was done, and the Indian economy continued to travel the downward road it had entered upon many decades before under British rule. The recently announced Five-Year Plan is essentially a desperate holding operation, not a development plan at all, and even so it cannot be carried out without considerable foreign assistance.[2] Meanwhile, the Indian government which, at the time of independence, had been willing to allow foreign investment only under the most careful safeguards, has been making increasingly attractive offers to foreign capitalists. The Indian ruling classes seem to have come to the conclusion that India's only hope lies in putting its neck once again into the imperialist yoke which it has hardly more than thrown off. But it must be admitted that there *is* a difference: the foreign capitalists, as everyone knows, will have to be Americans this time.

But what about Point Four and all that it implies, I can hear some of you saying. Is it justifiable to assume that American aid to backward countries, including investment

---

[2] Cf. H. W. Singer, "India's Five-Year Plan: A Modest Proposal," *Far Eastern Survey*, June 18, 1952.

of private American capital, must be of the same kind and have the same significance that foreign aid and foreign investment have always had in the past? "The old imperialism — exploitation for foreign profit — has no place in our plans," said President Truman in his inaugural speech announcing Point Four. But has the "old imperialism" in fact been abolished?

V

One thing certain is that, historically speaking, the United States has been as imperialist in its relations with backward countries as any of the other advanced countries. This fact has been somewhat obscured by a persistent strain of anticolonialism in American foreign policy, going back as far as the Monroe Doctrine, making a vigorous appearance in Hay's Open Door policy even while the United States was itself engaged in acquiring a colonial empire, and later manifesting itself in the voluntary granting of independence to Cuba and the Philippines. Anticolonialism, however, had little to do with economic relations — except in the sense that it was used as a weapon to pry open other countries' spheres of influence to American business. Where important relations existed between the United States and backward countries, the pattern in all essentials was indistinguishable from that which obtained within the great colonial empires themselves. To convince oneself of this, one need only read the Bell Report[3] analyzing the condition of the Philippines after a half century of close association with the United States — or, better still, visit one of the Latin American countries which have been the scene of heavy capital investments by United States corporations.

If there has been a change, it must have come very abruptly with the announcement of Point Four, and it certainly has not yet had time to make itself widely felt. But the question

---

[3] *Report to the President of the United States by the Economic Survey Mission to the Philippines,* Washington, October 9, 1950.

is whether there is *any* tangible evidence, aside from the pronouncements of official and semiofficial spokesmen, of such a change.

No such evidence can be found in the development of United States policy toward the older colonial empires. Far from trying to help the backward colonial countries to win their freedom, either political or economic, the United States has consistently aligned itself with the mother countries in their efforts to hold on to what they have. It is true that American capital has shown some signs of penetrating the colonies of other countries (for example, the Belgian Congo and Morocco), but of course that has nothing to do with anti-imperialism.

It would seem, therefore, that the whole burden of proving a change must be borne by the Point Four program. And I must confess that if one confines oneself to reading the literature extolling Point Four which has emanated in the last few years from a variety of New Deal, Fair Deal, and other liberal sources, it appears that the burden is easily borne. But if one analyzes the efforts which have so far been made to implement Point Four and examines the direction in which its sponsors have recently been pushing it, I suggest that one can hardly avoid coming to a very different, and in a sense paradoxical, conclusion, namely, *that Point Four is realistically to be regarded as a support for American imperialism and a stimulant to its further development.*

Point Four was first transformed from a statement of noble generalities into an outline of a concrete program by President Truman's message to Congress of June 24, 1949. In that message, Mr. Truman made several points unmistakably clear. First, the main purpose of "technical assistance" is to "create conditions in which capital investment can be fruitful." Second, while some capital may be invested in backward countries by public agencies such as the Export-Import Bank and the International Bank for Reconstruction and Development, nevertheless "private sources of funds must be encouraged to provide a major part of the capital required." Third, this encouragement will "in all probability" have to take the form of "novel devices," of which Mr. Truman proposed two kinds: (1) special treaties guaranteeing equal and nondiscriminatory treatment to American capital, and (2) government insurance to private investors against the special risks of foreign investment.

This may be a "bold new program," but its object is pretty clearly the encouragement and protection of American foreign investment, not the balanced development of backward countries.

Or are we to assume that from now on private investment will actually serve the purposes of balanced development in the backward countries? So far as the *direct* effect of private investment is concerned, I take it that not even the most enthusiastic supporters of Point Four are prepared to make such an assumption. They do not expect American capital to flow into the production of all the many goods and services which are required for balanced economic development. More than that: they do not want it to. They want American capital in the first instance to serve the needs of the United States, to go into the production of the raw and semifinished materials which are required in such vast quantities by the American economy. So much is evident from a perusal of *Partners in Progress* and *Resources for Freedom*, the two major reports which were prepared for the Truman administration — under the direction of Messrs. Rockefeller and Paley respectively — in an attempt to formulate policy toward backward countries and raw materials.

The Point Four theory, spelled out in some detail in the Paley Report, is that foreign capital by developing the raw material resources of the backward countries will provide them with the means to carry out a balanced development program on their own hook. In the words of the Paley Report:

Minerals development and expanded production for export offer great opportunities to the less developed countries. The yield to the source country in government revenues and foreign exchange earnings is usually a substantial percentage of the value of mineral output and can provide the financial basis for a domestic development program. (*Resources for Freedom*, Vol. I, p. 61.)

The weakness in this theory is painfully obvious. Why haven't backward countries which have long been provided with this "financial basis for a domestic development program" accomplished anything worth mentioning in the way of balanced development? Can it be that the corrupt and reactionary regimes which generally dominate these countries have other uses for the proceeds of their raw materials? And has the United States or any of the other imperialist countries ever done anything to help the backward countries get rid of regimes of this kind?

To ask these questions is, I think, equivalent to answering them.

The authors of the Paley Report seem to have sensed that something was missing from their theory, for they were driven to what I can only describe as the desperate expedient of arguing that Venezuela — of all countries — proves the possibility and feasibility of a backward country's carrying out its own development program with earnings from raw material exports. I wish I had the time to analyze in detail the special report on Venezuela published in Volume V of *Resources for Freedom*. It is a masterpiece of disingenuousness, to use no stronger term. But I shall have to content myself with a quotation from a recent eyewitness account, by a trained observer, of the blessings Venezuela has derived from its fabulous oil riches. Harvey O'Connor, author of many valuable works on American economic and social history, reported as follows after returning from a research trip to the oil-producing and oil-refining regions of the Caribbean:

Some ten percent of Venezuela is sitting in on the modern Belshazzar's feast, catered by Standard Oil and Shell; the other four million are on the outside looking in, with hunger in their bellies and disease in their bones. But some day, when the last oil is pumped out, the feast must end.

Then, in the words of Arturo Uzlar-Pietri [professor at the University of Caracas], the stricken land will need the disaster services of International Red Cross brigades doling out soup as its people expire surrounded by mountains of empty Frigidaires, silent Philcos, and gasless Cadillacs. . . .

What has happened to Venezuela is a gold-plated disaster moving on noiseless oiled bearings toward tragedy. Its ancient, static but self-sufficient economy has been tossed in the ashcan. Now it reaps billions of bolívars each year for its oil. With these bolívars it buys all the expensive trash in the world — baubles, Uzlar-Pietri calls them. When the oil runs out, he says, the nation will be like an old tailor's chest filled with useless spangles. Lacking subsidies, industry will collapse; agriculture will long since have perished.

Let me urge you to read the hosannas to Venezuela's marvelous development in the Paley Report and then compare them with O'Connor's somberly brilliant account of the actual state of that unhappy country, which appeared in the July 1951 issue of *Monthly Review*.

Let me now attempt to sum up in a few words what I have been trying to say. Imperialism is the international socioeconomic system which developed in the period of competing monopoly capitalisms. It produced a characteristic pattern of relations between a few advanced and many backward countries, and set the latter on the road to ultimate disaster. The United States which rapidly became the most powerful of all the monopoly-capitalist nations participated in this process from an early date. The relations now existing between the United States and backward countries are typically imperialist. Point Four, to the extent that it succeeds, will extend and intensify, not alter, these relations.

7

Three Works on Imperialism

This review article was published in the Spring 1953 issue of *The Journal of Economic History*. It deals with the following books: (1) Rosa Luxemburg, *The Accumulation of Capital*, translated by Agnes Schwarzschild, with an introduction by Joan Robinson (New Haven, 1951); (2) G. W. F. Hallgarten, *Imperialismus vor 1914*, 2 vols. (Munich, 1951); and (3) Fritz Sternberg, *Capitalism and Socialism on Trial* (New York, 1951).

IT CAN hardly be questioned that imperialism has been one of the decisive forces shaping the world of the twentieth century, or that the analysis of imperialism is one of the most important problems of the social sciences. The virtually simultaneous publication of three major works on imperialism is therefore an event which all social scientists should welcome. It may be hoped that it is also an event which will call forth renewed interest in the subject and stimulate fresh efforts to understand its innumerable complexities.

It is not necessary to say much about Rosa Luxemburg's famous work which was first published in German in 1912.[1] It is by now a classic which has won for itself a permanent place in the literature of both economic theory in the narrow sense and imperialism in the broadest sense.[2] An English

---

[1] The work is discussed at greater length below, pp. 291-294.
[2] I have discussed Rosa Luxemburg's work and its critics in detail in my *Theory of Capitalist Development* (especially pp. 202 ff.). I should perhaps note that my interpretation of her economic theory differs at several points from that supplied by Mrs. Robinson in her helpful and sympathetic introduction to the English translation.

translation is long overdue, and now that it has arrived we must welcome it with the greater enthusiasm because Dr. Schwarzschild has performed her translator's job with care and skill. My only regret is that the volume does not include Rosa Luxemburg's long answer to her critics which was written while she was in prison during the First World War and was published together with the original work in a 1921 German edition. The *Antikritik*, as it is usually called, contains a restatement of Rosa Luxemburg's basic theoretical position which, it seems to me, is indispensable to a proper interpretation of *The Accumulation of Capital* itself.

It is altogether appropriate that Rosa Luxemburg's book should appear at the same time as Sternberg's *Capitalism and Socialism on Trial*, for Sternberg was originally a disciple of Rosa Luxemburg and his early treatise on imperialism (*Der Imperialismus*, Berlin, 1926) was essentially a restatement and elaboration of her treatment of the subject. Since Sternberg devotes relatively little attention to theoretical underpinnings in the present work, it is valuable to have *The Accumulation of Capital* at hand to supply, as it were, some of the missing links. But before commenting further on *Capitalism and Socialism on Trial*, I want to direct the reader's attention to our third work, Hallgarten's *Imperialismus vor 1914*.[3]

I have no hesitation in saying that Hallgarten's is a great work. It throws a flood of light on the whole historical period which led up to the outbreak of World War I; and it expounds, and demonstrates the fruitfulness of, a method of

---

[3] For a book with the word "imperialism" in its title, Hallgarten's may seem to devote unduly little space to the colonial and semicolonial countries. This is explained, and in my judgment satisfactorily so, by the purpose of the work. "The present work," Hallgarten comments near the outset, "was undertaken with the intention of describing this hunt [for imperialist living space] and the mutual struggle of the hunters for the spoils. It is more concerned with the hunters and their struggles to the death with each other than with the game they killed...." (Pp. 32-33.)

studying international relations which can be equally effectively applied to other periods.

The book is not easily classified in terms of the conventional "fields" of social science. It is certainly not history in the usual sense, nor political science, nor sociology, nor yet economic history. It is, however, something of all these, and one of its greatest merits is that it combines them, not abstractly and in theory but in actual application. For the economic historian, the chief value of the work lies not only in the vast amount of new or specialized information it contributes, but also in the way it links development in the economic field to the political and diplomatic history of the period. Hallgarten shows how broad economic trends — the growth of trusts and monopolies, alterations between prosperity and depression, the accumulation of capital seeking investment outlets, the expansion of overseas trade, and so on — motivate classes, groups, and individuals to act in domestic and international politics. He does this with such a wealth of detail and with such massive documentation that the reader cannot help being convinced not only of the reality but also of the crucial importance of the relations which are being described and analyzed.

Hallgarten's method is to concentrate attention on the forces which can reasonably be regarded as decisive for the world situation as a whole in the period before World War I, that is to say, on the forces responsible for the international behavior of Britain, France, Germany, and Russia (hence his subtitle: "The Sociological Foundations of the Foreign Policies of the European Great Powers before the First World War"). The policies of the other powers — including even those that are generally accorded "great power" status — are treated as being of essentially secondary importance, which means not that they are neglected but that they are dealt with only in relation to the policies of the Big Four. Within this general frame of reference, Hallgarten has taken Germany as, so to speak, the point of vantage from which to view the scene as a whole. The choice was doubtless dictated in the first instance by practical considerations: Hallgarten was in Germany when he was working on and writing the book, and he was fortunate in having wide access to official and unofficial archive materials. But it is important for an understanding of the nature of the work to realize that it could just as well have been written with Britain as the vantage point. It would not have been the same book, of course; but it would have dealt with the same basic subject matter, only from a different angle. The book, in other words, is not primarily a study of German imperialism, despite the space allocated to Germany; it is a study of the entire international system of the pre-1914 world.

The underlying hypothesis which dominates the work is that every policy or course of action which has genuine political significance is the result of a complex or "aggregate" of interests. To understand a given situation it is therefore necessary to identify the decisive interests at stake and to trace the manner in which their representatives seek to protect or advance them. This may be a relatively easy task if the situation is simple and the interests are either avowed or obvious to the observer. Or it may be an enormously difficult task if the situation is complex and the interests are more or less elaborately disguised or hidden.

What, it may be asked, is the nature of these "interests" which play such a crucial role? Hallgarten repeatedly describes them as "sociological" interests, but the term is not very helpful. What he means would seem to be interests which are determined by the structure and development of society and which are shared by recognizable classes, strata, and subgroups. These interests are very largely economic but not exclusively so. For example, the interest of the German General Staff in preserving an elite army and an aristocratic officer corps — a by no means unimportant factor in pre-World War I German imperialism — could hardly be described as an economic interest, nor could the religious interest which bound the diverse elements of the Catholic Center Party together and enabled it to play a key role on the German political stage. True, these interests can be related to and in a real sense explained in terms of economic factors, including those operative at an earlier period of German history, but this is a very different thing from saying that they *are* economic interests. Finally, Hallgarten's schema allows plenty of room for the operation of individual interests, insisting only that they must make themselves felt within a framework of socially determined class and group interests. Thus a Joe Chamberlain, serving both the family fortune and the interests of the Birmingham arms industry, could play a significant role in the development of British imperialism; just as the Kaiser's partiality for a large navy could become a part of the "interest aggregate" that drove Germany along the fatal road of conflict with Britain.

This whole approach to the problem of interests, since it regards them as socially determined and considers individuals as essentially their representatives rather than their source, can be effectively applied only in conjunction with a working theory of society and social change. Without such a theory, the interests to which crucial importance is attached are left hanging in midair, their interrelation obscure, their direction of change over time arbitrary — a mere congeries of "pressure groups" and "special interests." Hallgarten seems to be fully aware of this problem. He begins with a chapter entitled "Capitalism and Imperialism Before 1914: A Theoretical Discussion," in the course of which he specifically recognizes that "the fate of those driving social elements — pressure groups, as they are called in America — depended upon the general course of social and economic development which dominated the whole era." (Vol. I, p. 33.) Hallgarten does not devote very much space to this underlying theoretical issue, but it is clear from what he does say, as well as from the way he handles his materials throughout, that his thinking in this regard was basically shaped by the dominant intellectual trends in the German socialist movement during the period of the Weimar Republic when the book was planned and written. His theory can perhaps best be described as Hilferdingian, and the book, despite the fact that it was not published until nearly two decades later, should properly be counted as one of the best examples of that period's extensive and creative literature in the field of the social sciences. This is, indeed, well symbolized by Hallgarten's dedication of the work to "the unforgettable Eckart Kehr," the young socialist historian whose tragic death at the age of thirty-one cut short a career already rich in achievement and full of promise for the future.[4]

This is not the place for a discussion of the theory of imperialism; I can only record my own judgment that Hilferdingian theory fits the facts of the pre-World War I period on the whole very adequately. In a sense, indeed, Hallgarten's book is its most convincing vindication: by actually using this theory on a grand scale, Hallgarten has, it seems to me, proved to the hilt its validity and usefulness. On the other hand, it should be noted that Hilferdingian theory is by no means of universal applicability. It works much less well for the interwar period, which may in part account for the fact that the best work of the pre-Hitler German socialists dealt with Wilhelminian Germany; and its direct usefulness in analyzing the present-day international scene, in which the two major powers have entirely different social systems, would be even more limited.

One of Hallgarten's central themes, of course, is the foreign policy of the Germany of Wilhelm II, a country with a

[4] Kehr's work, published in a number of papers in the theoretical organ of the Social Democratic Party, *Die Gesellschaft*, of which Hilferding was then editor, and in his one book-length study, *Schlachtflottenbau und Parteipolitik, 1894-1901* (Berlin, 1930), is of fundamental importance to an understanding of German imperialism. Hallgarten's method is similar to Kehr's, and both show a strong affinity to Hilferding's *Finanzkapital* (1910), especially to the last section ("Zur Wirtschaftspolitik des Finanzkapitals").

rapidly expanding and highly trustified capitalist economy seeking markets and raw materials in all directions at once. German foreign policy under these conditions came to be what Hallgarten calls the policy of *Sowohl als-Auch*, the policy of "not only but also" — not only continental imperialism but also world imperialism. With France already hopelessly antagonized by the loss of Alsace-Lorraine, this policy soon provoked the lasting enmity of Russia and made any serious rapprochement with Britain impossible. In the space of a few years Germany succeeded in driving Russia into the arms of France, and England into the arms of France and Russia, thus patching up what had been by all odds the severest imperialist conflicts of the nineteenth century and setting the stage for Germany's own downfall.

A remarkable performance without any doubt, and one which historians have been strongly inclined to regard as a remarkably stupid performance. Why, they ask, didn't Germany pursue a policy of "either-or" — *either* an understanding with Russia as a basis for overseas expansion *or* friendship with Britain as rear cover for an overland drive to the East? The advantages should have been obvious to an intelligent leadership; indeed they were obvious to many contemporary observers. That Germany persisted in its suicidal course of antagonizing everybody, they conclude, must have been owing to weak and ineffective leadership, with the Kaiser himself generally bearing a large part of the blame.

It is one of the great merits of Hallgarten's work that he demonstrates — conclusively, it seems to me — the superficiality and inadequacy of explanations of this kind. He does so not by denying the existence of the factors mentioned: after all, there is no doubt that the Kaiser was a headstrong dilettante in the field of international relations, nor is anyone likely to argue that his ministers, especially von Bülow and Bethmann-Hollweg, were strong and effective leaders. But Hallgarten shows that "causes" of this order are out of all proportion to the effects they are supposed to bring about, and he clinches his point by marshaling a massive and cumulative body of evidence to support an alternative pattern of causation which is wholly adequate to bear the burden put upon it.

To the foreign policy of *Sowohl als-Auch* there corresponded in domestic politics what has come to be known as Miquel's *Sammlungspolitik*, the policy of uniting the main factions of Germany's ruling classes on a program embodying the most important demands of each. The basic idea of this coalition policy, in Hallgarten's words, "consisted in the creation of a combined system of industrial and agrarian tariffs which was then made the financial basis for a navy expansion policy, all for the benefit of the Kaiser, the industrialists, and the big landlords, and naturally at the expense of the consumer." (Vol. I, p. 412.) As a reward for supporting this program, the Catholic Center Party received a larger share in the management of political affairs and concessions to its special socio-religious interests. Note that this arrangement was very profitable to all the participants, so much so that none of them was ever seriously tempted to abandon it. But also note that by its very nature it precluded the possibility of a rational foreign policy. Agrarian tariffs and naval building were insuperable obstacles to good relations with Russia and England respectively. "Inadequate attention to the requirements of German foreign policy was the innermost essence of this [coalition] economic policy. The crutches which supported industry and agriculture were created at the expense of the German people as a whole through spoiling their relations with the rest of the world." (Vol. I, p. 373.)

It might be thought that the way out of this dilemma lay in the direction of an internal struggle for supremacy between industrialists and landlords. But there were two decisive reasons why this apparent exit was in fact closed and barred. The first, which Hallgarten occasionally touches upon but the importance of which I think he underestimates, was the common fear of both groups that if they should quarrel among themselves they would simply be preparing the ground for a seizure of power by the working class. The second reason was that with the development of German interests in the Balkans, Turkey, and the Middle East, some of the very same elements that were already committed to an anti-English naval policy in the West plunged more and more deeply into an anti-Russian policy in the East. Hallgarten appropriately cites the example of the House of Krupp, "which while standing beside the Kaiser in support of his naval policy . . . helped, through establishing itself on the Bosporus and through its connection with the Bagdad railway, to poison relations with the only potential ally which could have given Germany a really sound base for its naval policy: the Russian Empire." (Vol. I, p. 394.) The truth is that Germany was by this time caught in a trap from which the only escape would have been a complete change of system, which only the socialists advocated and which they were still far too weak to achieve.

This does not mean, of course, that no attempt was made to escape from the trap. On the contrary, the two decades before the outbreak of war witnessed repeated efforts at rapprochement, now with Britain and now with Russia. But the overriding requirements of the ruling coalition always asserted themselves, and the upshot was in fact a steady deterioration of relations with both powers. Germany's mounting crisis was not a crisis of intelligence or leadership; it was the crisis of an entire socio-economic system. No one, I should think, who has seriously studied Hallgarten's work could ever again be in doubt about this fundamental point.

Criticism of Hallgarten's work is largely a job for specialists with a command of the relevant factual and literary material comparable to his. My impression is that they will find the book meticulously accurate in its scholarship, but that there will be many legitimate differences of opinion about the way Hallgarten has presented and interpreted the hundreds of incidents which he has fitted into his analysis of pre-1914 imperialism.[5] I should be very surprised, however, if any criticism of details could shake the general validity of the picture Hallgarten has painted. Here, I am convinced, is a work which is destined to become a social science classic, at once a source book for understanding "the foundations of the twentieth century" and a methodological model for others to learn from and emulate.

I am much less sure, unfortunately, that under existing conditions Hallgarten's work will receive the recognition it deserves. Its history to date is not reassuring. Completed immediately after Hitler's coming to power, the book could of course not be published in Nazi Germany. After long efforts to secure support for its publication elsewhere, Hallgarten finally concluded that the search was hopeless. He therefore published a severely abridged and popularized edition under the title *Vorkriegsimperialismus* (Paris, 1935) and deposited the original manuscript in the Musée de la Guerre Mondiale in Vincennes. During the mid-thirties several sections of the complete work were published in professional periodicals and attracted the attention of the Institute for Social Research in New York (successor to the famous Frankfurt Institut für Sozialforschung of the Weimar period). The Institute retrieved the manuscript from the museum in Vincennes and had five copies made which were bought in 1939 by the libraries of Harvard, Yale, Chi-

---

[5] The nonspecialist reader, incidentally, will want to study Hallgarten with a shelf of good reference works at hand. These should include at a minimum an encyclopedia, an atlas, and some standard historical treatises on the period 1871-1914. For all but the last twelve years of the period, the most useful works are Langer's *European Alliances and Alignments* and *The Diplomacy of Imperialism, 1890-1902*, to which Hallgarten pays generous tribute. Reading Langer in conjunction with Hallgarten does more than provide necessary factual background: it also shows how much more deeply one can penetrate into the "causes of things" by Hallgarten's methods than by those of the traditional diplomatic historian.

cago, Stanford, and the University of California (the Library of Congress and the New York Public Library acquired microfilm copies at about the same time). One of these copies formed the basis of a brief review by Langer in the *American Historical Review* in 1940.

All this, of course, was no substitute for publication, but it certainly should have been enough to introduce the work to specialists in modern European history and to create a demand that it be made available to the profession generally (which at that time, in view of the complete closing of the German market, would have meant a translation). Nothing of the kind seems to have happened, however, and it was not until 1949 when he was invited to Munich as a guest professor that Hallgarten could finally find a publisher, and even then, he informs us in the preface, publication was possible only at the cost of personal financial sacrifice.[6]

Unfortunately, publication in German will not go far toward making the work available to social scientists in this country. It is too difficult and long (over a thousand pages in all) even for most of those who have an adequate working knowledge of the language. But at any rate there is no longer any excuse for the continued failure of the specialists, and the foundations they advise, to recognize that Hallgarten's is a work of absolutely first-rate importance which should be translated into English and published at the earliest possible date.

Sternberg's *Capitalism and Socialism on Trial* begins with the rise of capitalism and ends with a look ahead into the second half of the twentieth century. In between, it covers an enormous range of subjects, with the focus of attention,

---

[6] Aside from useful notes, printed in italics and largely dealing with literature which appeared after 1933, the published version is substantially identical with the original manuscript. Hallgarten was wise to follow this course. The work gains in stature when viewed in the light of subsequent research more than it could have benefited by attempting to incorporate the detailed results of that research.

however, rarely straying far from the central theme of imperialism and its effects.

The best part of Sternberg's work, it seems to me, is the analysis of the impact of imperialism on the colonial countries which come within its orbit. (Part 1, Chapter 2; pp. 367 ff.; and *passim*.) In this respect, Sternberg provides a valuable supplement to Hallgarten who concentrates attention on the conflicts among the imperialist powers. Sternberg shows how and why the development of the colonial (and semicolonial) countries, comprising over half the world's total population, pursued a very different course from that of the metropolitan imperialist centers.[7] The mother countries were interested in the colonies as markets, sources of raw materials, and outlets for capital investment. For all three reasons, the colonial economies tended to develop a special pattern, with capital flowing into the production and transport of a few standardized commodities for sale on the world market, imports consisting of manufactured goods from abroad, and handicraft production being largely ruined. As a consequence of these economic changes, the old integrated societies tended to fall apart, while revolutionary movements looking to national independence — and beyond to social reconstruction — naturally emerged to threaten imperialist rule. The imperialist countries in self-defense allied themselves more and more closely with the parasitic ruling classes in the colonies. In this way the vicious circle was closed. Effective reform being permanently precluded by the structure of imperialist rule, the colonies were doomed to exploitation and stagnation which must sooner or later lead to an explosion.

Sternberg is much less effective in dealing with the development of the advanced imperialist countries themselves. He emphasizes — at times overemphasizes — the importance of imperialist expansion in their overall economic growth, and he attributes the crisis of European capitalism which

---

[7] On this subject, see also above, pp. 82-84.

set in with the outbreak of World War I to the cessation of external expansion. This cessation in turn is "explained" by the assertion that colonial imperialism had reached its "limits" by 1914. (See, for example, page 90.) But obviously this is no explanation at all. What were those limits, and why were they reached in 1914? Sternberg throws no light on these questions, which are clearly decisive for his whole analysis. For all he says, still less proves, one might just as well conclude that external expansion came to a halt, or reached its "limits," because European capitalism entered a period of crisis in 1914. Actually, I believe that Sternberg's thesis is nearer the truth, but the way he argues it will not convince anyone who is not already convinced — worse still, its obvious weaknesses will only tend to confirm in their views those who disbelieve in the causal connection he seeks to establish.

Sternberg is no more satisfactory when he deals with the Soviet Union and the countries which have become associated with it in the post-World War II period. According to Sternberg, the USSR is neither capitalist nor socialist. What is it then? No answer. He states repeatedly, and of every period of Soviet history, that the dictatorship is becoming narrower, more burdensome, and more terroristic. But no attempt is ever made to describe the social base of the Soviet regime, still less what is meant by its "narrowing"; and every competent history of the USSR with which I am acquainted shows that there have been ups and downs in the severity of Soviet rule. The inadequacy of Sternberg's analysis is only emphasized by his description of Soviet economic development, where the record is one of unbroken and in many ways unprecedented successes. One wants to know what kind of system it is that grows this way, whether economic success hasn't actually led to a *broadening* of the social base of the regime, and so on.

Sternberg is equally disappointing in his treatment of "Soviet imperialism" and the "Russian Empire" to which it is supposed to have given rise. In analyzing capitalist imperialism, both in this and in his earlier works, Sternberg leaves no doubt about what he considers to be the dominant economic forces which push countries toward external expansion and the conquest of empires. But when it comes to "Soviet imperialism" he specifically states that these economic forces are not operative. (See especially pages 529-530.) What, then, is it that is assumed to drive the USSR to acquire an empire? Here again, one will search in vain for an answer. Nor does he seem to be altogether clear on the nature of the empire which the Soviet Union is said to have acquired: sometimes China seems definitely to be a part of it, and Communist revolutionary activity in Asia is spoken of as though it were a manifestation of Soviet expansionism; but elsewhere the Chinese Revolution is treated as a specifically Chinese phenomenon and as "one of the greatest events in world history, and one fraught with tremendous possibilities for world developments in the second half of the twentieth century." (P. 532.)

All of these issues conceal very real problems, no doubt, but I suggest that Sternberg is either confused in his own thinking or has made no serious effort to state what the problems are and along what lines solutions are to be sought.

Finally, it is necessary to say that Sternberg's book is very badly in need of cutting and editing and, in parts, rewriting. As it stands it is inflated, repetitious, and often plain boring. Perhaps these weaknesses are in part due to bad translation — Sternberg wrote the manuscript in German — but the translator cannot be held responsible for frequent *non sequiturs,* absence of transition sentences and paragraphs, repetition of the same point on the same page, or even in the same paragraph, and so on. There is no apparent sense or logic in the way Sternberg quotes other authors and sources. Sometimes he quotes a whole paragraph to make a point which could have been put more briefly and just as convincingly in his own words; even more often an apt quotation or citation of authority which is *not* there would have greatly strengthened his argument. From a technical point of view, in short, *Capitalism and Socialism on Trial* is a thoroughly sloppy performance.

Part III

American Capitalism

8

Recent Developments in American Capitalism

This article was written expressly for the first issue of Monthly Review, *May 1949. Its purpose was not only to sum up the dominant features of American capitalism in the mid-twentieth century but also to make clear to readers some of the major premises of* Monthly Review *editorial policy.*

THE first obligation of socialists is to see the present in historical perspective, to understand those underlying economic and social trends which mold seemingly arbitrary contemporary events into a meaningful pattern.

During the period of the Great Depression and the New Deal, the American Left had a much clearer grasp of these underlying realities than it has today. Congressional committees and government agencies, beginning with the Pecora investigation of stock exchange practices and continuing through the Temporary National Economic Committee, poured out a steady stream of extremely valuable descriptive and analytical material. Economists, jolted out of their traditional complacency by the depression and the "heresies" of Keynes, began to see that capitalism is a system of contradictions and not of harmonies. The left-wing Keynesians, led by Alvin Hansen of Harvard, even went so far as to assert that the American economic system had entered a period of stagnation which could be relieved only by massive government action.

But now, a decade later, serious investigations are strictly out of fashion, and pessimistic views about the future of free enterprise are looked upon as little short of traitorous. Only occasionally does a government document give us a quick glance behind the scenes; the economists, whose memory was never good for much more than ten years, have gratefully forgotten about the gloomy forebodings of the thirties.

Under these circumstances the responsibility of socialists is greater than ever. They must apply themselves with redoubled energy to the task of penetrating the veil of official deception and academic evasion which prevents even conscientious students of social phenomena from grasping the basic structure and tendencies of American capitalism. It is the purpose of this article to assist in this task by placing in sharp relief the decisive developments of recent years.

By far the most important thing to understand about American capitalism is that its power to accumulate capital is much greater than its capacity to make sustained use of additional capital in private profit-making industry. Individual capitalists can do nothing about this; unless they take action as a class — through the state — the result is bound to be chronic depression and mass unemployment.

It is not possible to say precisely when American capitalism reached this stage of development. An economic crisis was undoubtedly approaching in 1914, and if there had been no war it might have inaugurated the period of chronic depression. But World War I intervened and provided the stimulus, directly and indirectly, to a decade and a half of abnormally prosperous conditions which were interrupted only briefly by the crisis of 1920-1921. By 1929 this stimulus had exhausted itself, and American capitalism rapidly sank into a depression of unprecedented scope and intensity.

The years 1933 through 1939 (roughly Roosevelt's first two terms) constituted the period of the New Deal, which was characterized by extensive social reforms and a relative lack of emphasis on imperialist and militaristic activities. Expenditures of the federal government for military purposes actually declined from $1.8 billion in 1932 to $1.6 billion in 1939. (Temporary National Economic Committee Monograph No. 20, p. 58.) The relative decline was much greater (from nearly 40 percent of total expenditures to less than 20 percent) because expenditures on public works and social services simultaneously increased from approximately $0.5 billion to $5 billion. (P. 61.) Despite this increase in government expenditures on public works and social services, the period was one of persistent and heavy unemployment. No one knows how many were unemployed in 1932-1933, but it was certainly more than fifteen million; and in only one year of the New Deal (1937) did unemployment fall appreciably below ten million.

It was only during the 1940s, when military expenditures increased rapidly, that unemployment disappeared and American capitalism achieved a volume of production approaching its full capacity. The wartime peak of federal government expenditures (very largely devoted, directly or indirectly, to military purposes) was $99 billion in 1945. Since the end of the war this figure has of course declined, but there has been no return to the *status quo ante*. According to the budget submitted by President Truman to Congress in January 1949, total expenditures in the fiscal year ending June 30, 1950, will amount to $42 billion, divided as follows:

National defense	14.3
International affairs	6.7
Veterans' benefits	5.5
Interest on public debt	5.5
All other	10.0

The first item on this list, national defense, is the military budget in the narrow sense; the second item, international affairs, comprises the Marshall Plan and other so-called "aid" programs which are primarily motivated by strategic and imperialist considerations; the third and fourth items, veterans' benefits and interest on the public debt, are almost exclusively attributable to the last two wars. Thus more than three quarters of the present unprecedented peacetime budget (before 1940, *total* peacetime expenditures never exceeded $10 billion) is devoted to paying for past wars or preparing for future wars.

There can be no doubt that but for these enormous outlays for direct and indirect military purposes we should have had an economic crash long since. This is now so widely admitted by business and government spokesmen that it is no longer necessary to cite evidence to prove it. But recent events have shown that even with present levels of military expenditure it is by no means certain that a serious depression can be avoided. The real figure for unemployment is now probably nearly five million — the official figure is about 3.2 million, but economists of the United Electrical Workers have demonstrated in a very able report that this is a substantial understatement — and a large part of the business press is anything but optimistic about the prospects for the months ahead. This situation clearly constitutes a standing invitation to the American ruling class to embark upon new militaristic and imperialist adventures.

We are led inescapably to the conclusion that at least for the last twenty years American capitalism has at no time been able to achieve high levels of production and employment except by means of enormous war-related expenditures by the federal government. This is more true today than ever before, even a war-related budget of more than $30 billion a year being insufficient to scotch the danger of an economic collapse.

At this point, however, we must pause to ask a question. It is certainly a fact that American capitalism has become increasingly geared to militarism and imperialism, but is it not conceivable that other forms of government expenditure (coupled, of course, with appropriate policies in such fields as taxation and price control) would be capable of achieving comparable or even more impressive economic results?

As a matter of pure logic, of course, such a possibility exists. A given number of billion dollars will affect the economic system in much the same way whether it is spent on armaments and soldiers' pay or whether it is spent on housing and social security: x billion \$ $=$ x billion \$, so much is clear. The liberal case for a "reformed" capitalism rests in the final analysis on this simple proposition. But what the liberals overlook is that the problem is not one of logic but of economic and political power. And under capitalism economic and political power are ultimately in the hands of the capitalist class — and the only forms of massive government spending which are acceptable to the capitalist class are those which have imperialist expansion and war preparations as their aim.

Why should this be so? Is it the result of ignorance or stupidity on the part of the capitalists? Or have they good reasons for their attitude?

The answer is clear: from the point of view of their own narrow interests they have very good reasons. To raise the purchasing power of the masses and to invest in socially useful projects on a large scale would involve a deliberate redistribution of income from the wealthier to the poorer sections of the population. Moreover, and this is at least as important, such a program would teach the workers the power of collective action, would raise their educational and cultural level, and eventually would convince them that society could get along very nicely without capitalists living off the fat of the land and interfering with the efficient functioning of the economy. In short, the capitalists would suffer a gradual loss of both economic and political power. This does not bother the liberals, but it does bother the capitalists.

By way of contrast, war-related expenditures are subject to none of these disadvantages. They cost the capitalists money, to be sure, but a good share comes back in the form of higher profits which are now defended as essential to military preparedness. The bigotry and chauvinism which accompany the militarization of society, moreover, play right into the hands of the capitalists. The institutions of the country are identified with the country itself, and the dissenter is stigmatized as a saboteur and a traitor.

For all these reasons, the capitalists resolutely reject the sweet reason of liberal reform and rely increasingly on imperialism and militarism to maintain the system from which they benefit.

Let us now turn to the question of monopoly and the concentration of economic power. The National Resources Planning Board, in its important study *The Structure of the American Economy*, published in 1939, established the fact that the relative importance of the biggest corporations had grown steadily up to 1933. In 1909 the 200 largest nonfinancial corporations held approximately one third of the assets of all nonfinancial corporations; the figure had risen to between 45 and 50 percent by 1929, and to between 55 and 60 percent by 1933. The same study likewise showed that a large proportion of these corporate giants were linked together in eight more or less tightly integrated "interest groups."[1] And the TNEC, in its Monograph No. 29 (1940), revealed, behind the fig leaf of the small stockholder, the naked fact that most of the largest corporations are substantially owned by a relatively few wealthy families.

What has been happening to the American economy in these very important respects during the last decade and a half?

Unfortunately, to assemble the relevant facts requires much laborious research and access to material which is not normally made public; the job, in short, can only be done by a liberally financed investigation which has the cooperation of a number of government agencies. Needless to say, neither money nor cooperation has been available for such obviously subversive activities in recent years. Hence it is impossible to make an accurate comparison between prewar and postwar conditions. Nevertheless, the Smaller War

[1] See below, pp. 158-188.

Plants Corporation and the Federal Trade Commission — each because it has a special ax of its own to grind — have disclosed enough information to leave us in no doubt about the direction of developments and in little doubt that the pace has been unprecedentedly rapid. Two composite quotations will give the gist of the story.

The first is from *Economic Concentration and World War II*, a report submitted in 1946 by the SWPC to a special Senate committee on the problems of small business. It relates to the period up to 1945.

The relative importance of big business, particularly the giant corporations, increased sharply during the war, while the position of small business declined. . . . In each of the war industries, with but one exception, firms with 10,000 or more employees grew in relative importance. In manufacturing as a whole, these few giants accounted for 13 percent of total employment in 1939, and for fully 31 percent of the total in 1944. . . . In the nonwar industries, which made few gains during the war, small business, generally speaking, held its own. Taking manufacturing as a whole, the giants expanded greatly, while all other firms, especially small business, suffered a substantial decline.

The second quotation is from an official press release summarizing the *Report of the Federal Trade Commission on the Merger Movement* (1948). The report relates primarily to the war and postwar years.

The sharp upward movement in mergers and acquisitions has been most pronounced during the last three years. In this respect the present trend has closely followed the pattern established after World War I. . . . Merger activity turned sharply upward with the end of World War II and has continued at a relatively high level through 1947. In the final quarter of 1947, more mergers and acquisitions were reported than in any fourth quarter — with the single exception of 1945 — since 1930. The recent merger movement has extended to virtually all phases of manufacturing and mining. . . . As in earlier periods, high corporate profits have fed the merger movement. . . . Not only do profits provide the financial wherewithal with which to effect mergers, but more than that, they exert a powerful pressure on business to expand, both internally by building new plant and equipment, and externally by absorbing existing firms. At the end of June 1947, the 78 largest manufacturing corporations had sufficient net working capital to buy up the assets of some 50,000 manufacturing corporations of less than $1 million in assets each, representing more than 90 percent of all manufacturing corporations.

This last quotation calls attention to a phenomenon of great and growing importance, the extent to which the huge corporate giants now finance their expansion internally (by plowing back profits instead of distributing them to stockholders) and have consequently become independent of the capital markets generally and of banker control in particular. Much evidence bearing on this subject was introduced into the hearings on corporate profits held last December by a subcommittee of the Joint [Senate and House] Committee on the Economic Report. In a report summarizing these hearings the subcommittee commented: "While the evidence was not always conclusive as to the causes, the fact was made amply clear that most expansion funds for business are now being, and are expected to be, provided through retained earnings." One consequence of this is that "Wall Street" is an increasingly misleading symbol of concentrated economic control in the United States. The investment banker, of whom J. P. Morgan was the prototype of an earlier day, is now a relatively minor figure in the American economy — so much so that his services can easily be spared and he can be sent to Washington as the ideal trustee of business interests in the government. So far as the big commercial banks are concerned, it is probably now more accurate to say that they are controlled by industry than vice versa. But until a serious investigation of the facts is undertaken, we shall have to be content with very general statements in this field.

This article has highlighted two basic features of present-day American society: (1) that without the support provided by enormous expenditures on imperialist and militaristic ventures, American capitalism would quickly sink into a morass of chronic depression and mass unemployment; and (2) that American capitalism is coming increasingly under the domination of a few giant corporations which in turn are owned and controlled by a handful of extremely rich capitalists. The editors of *Monthly Review* believe that a recognition of these facts is the beginning of realistic thinking about the world we live in.

9

The American Ruling Class

This two-part article was published in the May and June 1951 issues of *Monthly Review*.

I

ONE *Monthly Review* reader, a graduate student of sociology at one of our larger universities, writes to the editors that "in the December and January issues your editorials used the term 'ruling class' no less than eighteen times." He thinks that "by using this term so repetitiously you lay yourselves open to the serious accusation of surface-scratching analysis only." Don't we, he asks, owe MR readers "a probing analysis of a concept that is so complex and crucial"?

It would be easy to answer that the concept of the ruling class is well established in Marxian theory and that we are merely trying to apply the ideas and methods of Marxism to the analysis of the current American scene. But our correspondent would probably not be satisfied. He would hardly deny the relevance of Marxian theory, but he might say that, after all, Marx wrote a century ago, that he never made a special study of the American ruling class even of his own day, and that in any case the free and easy use of theoretical abstractions can be very dangerous. Wouldn't it be better to drop the appeal to authority and tell MR readers what we mean by the "ruling class" in terms that will permit them to judge for themselves whether our usage is justified?

The challenge seems an eminently fair one, and in this article I shall attempt to meet it.

First, however, let me enter a disclaimer. I couldn't give complete answers even if I wanted to. "The American ruling class" is a big subject. An exhaustive study of it would involve a full-dress analysis of the past and present of American society as a whole. That is a job not for an individual or even a small group of individuals; it is a job for all American social scientists working together and over a long period of time. But unfortunately American social scientists, with but few exceptions, are not interested in studying the ruling class; on the contrary, this is a "sensitive" subject which they avoid like the plague. The result is that relatively little valuable work has been done on the ruling class. Some day the American Left will no doubt make good this deficiency, but in the meanwhile there's no use pretending it doesn't exist. In the course of writing this article, I have become even more acutely conscious of it than I was at the outset.

This doesn't mean that American social scientists have done no work at all on the subject of class. The founders of American sociology — men like Lester Ward and William Graham Sumner — were very much interested in classes and their role in American society and wrote a surprisingly large amount on the subject. And in recent years, sociologists and social anthropologists have made a considerable number of field studies of American communities, studies in which problems of social stratification have played a prominent part.

These field studies (of which the Lynds' *Middletown* was one of the first and also one of the best examples) contain a great deal of useful information, but they all suffer from one fatal defect from our present point of view: they are confined to single communities and have almost nothing to say about social classes on a nation-wide scale. Contemporary sociologists and social anthropologists seem, almost as if by common agreement, to have decided that national social classes are not a proper subject of investigation.

The American Left, of course, does not share this view;

in fact, it has long been very much alive to the existence and importance of a national ruling class. And left-wing writers have contributed many studies which throw valuable light on the subject — such works as Harvey O'Connor's *Mellon's Millions* and *The Guggenheims*, Anna Rochester's *Rulers of America*, and Ferdinand Lundberg's *America's Sixty Families*. But these left-wing works have been for the most part factual studies of particular aspects or elements of the ruling class. Generalizations about the ruling class as a whole have tended to run in terms of an oversimplified theory of Wall Street control of the country. This theory has many merits, especially for mass propaganda purposes, but it can hardly be considered an adequate substitute for a scientific analysis of the structure of the American ruling class.

GENERAL CHARACTERISTICS OF SOCIAL CLASSES

As an initial step it will be valuable to review the general characteristics of social classes, or in other words to establish the main outlines of a usable theory of social class.

The first thing to be stressed is that social classes are real living social entities; they are not artificial creations of the social scientist. This can best be explained by an illustration. Suppose a social scientist is analyzing a given population. He can divide it into "classes" by dozens of different criteria: for example, by height, by weight, and by color of hair. Each system of classification will yield different results. One person in the six-foot class will be in the 200-pound class and in the brown-hair class; another will be in the 150-pound class and the blond-hair class. By choosing his criteria appropriately the social scientist can thus divide the population up in all sorts of different ways, and any given division is his own artificial creation which may not matter at all to the people themselves. It is not so with social classes. The members of the population are keenly aware of the existence of social classes, of their belonging to one, of their desires to belong (or to avoid belonging) to another. If the social scientist wants to investigate social classes he has to take these facts as his starting point, and any attempt to impose artificial criteria of class membership will result only in confusion and failure. In other words, social classes are obstinate facts and not mere logical categories.

Recognition of this is the beginning of any attempt to deal seriously with social classes. In the past, American social scientists have been all too ready to deny the reality of social classes, to assume that they exist only in the mind of the observer. Fortunately, however, this is becoming less and less frequent. One great merit of recent sociological field work is that it has shown conclusively that America is a class society and that the American people know it is a class society. In this connection, the best-known work is that of Lloyd Warner and his various associates. It is conveniently summarized in Warner, Meeker, and Eells, *Social Class in America* (1949), Chapter 1. (The reader should be warned, however, that this book does not live up to its title: it is about social classes in individual communities and has only a limited usefulness from the point of view of the problems analyzed in this article.)

The fundamental unit of class membership is the family and not the individual. The proof of this is simply that everyone is born into a certain class, the class to which his family belongs. The basic test of whether two families belong to the same class or not is the freedom with which they intermarry (either actually or potentially).

Families and their mutual relations are thus the stuff of a class system. But this does not exclude individuals from a crucially important role in the functioning of the system. Generally speaking, it is the activity (or lack of activity) of an individual which is responsible for the rise or fall of a family in the class pyramid. The familiar American success story illustrates the process: the lower-class lad who marries at his own social level, then achieves wealth and by so doing establishes his children in the upper reaches of the social hierarchy. But the process works both ways; there is also the man who loses his fortune and thereby plunges his family to the bottom of the social ladder. It should be noted that in nearly all cases the individual himself does not succeed in making a complete shift from one class to the other. The *nouveau riche* is never fully accepted in his new social environment; and the man who loses his position never fully accepts his new environment. It is only the families that in each case, and in the course of time, make the adjustment.

A social class, then, is made up of freely intermarrying families. But what is it that determines how many classes there are and where the dividing lines are drawn? Generally speaking, the answer is obvious (and is borne out by all empirical investigations): the property system plays this key role. The upper classes are the property-owning classes; the lower classes are the propertyless classes. This statement is purposely general in its formulation. The number of classes and their relations to each other differ in different systems. For example, there may be several upper classes based on different kinds as well as on different amounts of property. We shall have to examine the American case more specifically below.

But before we do this, we must note other things which hold pretty generally for all classes and class systems.

It would be a mistake to think of a class as perfectly homogeneous internally and sharply marked off from other classes. Actually, there is variety within the class; and one class sometimes shades off very gradually and almost imperceptibly into another. We must therefore think of a class as being made up of a core surrounded by fringes which are in varying degrees attached to the core. A fringe may be more or less stable and have a well-defined function in relation to the class as a whole, or it may be temporary and accidental. Moreover, we must not think of all the class members (in either the family or the individual sense) as playing the same role in the class. Some are active, some passive; some leaders, some followers; and so on. Here we touch upon all the complex questions of class organization, cohesion, effectiveness, and the like. And finally, we must not imagine that all members of a class think and behave exactly alike. There are differences here too, though clearly the values and behavior norms of the class set fairly definite limits to the extent of these differences. A person who deviates too far from what the class considers acceptable is, so to speak, expelled from the class and is thenceforth treated as a renegade or deserter (the common use of the expression "traitor to his class" is symptomatic — and significant — in this connection).

In all these respects, of course, there is wide variation between different classes and class systems. Some classes are relatively homogeneous, well defined, effectively organized, and to a high degree class-conscious. Others are loosely knit, amorphous, lacking in organization, and hardly at all class-conscious. Further, some classes in the course of their life histories pass through different stages, in the course of which all these variables undergo more or less thorough changes. These are all problems to be investigated in the particular case; there are no general answers valid for all times and places.

One more point has to be noted before we turn to the American case. There is no such thing as a completely closed class system. All systems of which we have historical record display interclass mobility, both upwards and downwards. In some systems, however, mobility is difficult and slow; in others it is easy and rapid. A social class can be compared to a hotel which always has guests, some of whom are permanent residents and some transients. In a relatively static system, the average sojourn is long; arrivals and departures are infrequent, and the proportion of permanent residents is high. In a dynamic system, guests come and go all the time; the hotel is always full but always with new people who have only recently arrived and, except in a few cases, will soon depart.

THE AMERICAN CLASS SYSTEM

The United States is a capitalist society, the purest capitalist society that ever existed. It has no feudal hangovers to complicate the class system. Independent producers (working with their own means of production but without hired labor) there are, but both economically and socially they constitute a relatively unimportant feature of the American system. What do we expect the class structure of such a pure capitalist society to be?

Clearly, the two decisive classes are defined by the very nature of capitalism: the owners of the means of production (the capitalist class), and the wage laborers who set the means of production in motion (the working class). There is no doubt about the existence or importance of these two classes in America. Taken together they can be said to constitute the foundation of the American class system.

The foundation of a building, however, is not the whole building; nor does the American economic system contain only capitalists and workers. For one thing, as we have already noted, there are independent producers (artisans and small farmers), and to these we should add small shopkeepers and providers of services (for example, the proprietors of local gas stations). These people make up the lower middle class, or *petite bourgeoisie,* in the original sense of the term. For another thing, there are a variety of types which stand somewhere between the capitalists and the workers and cannot easily be classified with either: government and business bureaucrats, professionals, teachers, journalists, advertising men, and so on. These are often, and not inappropriately, called the new middle classes — "new" because of their spectacular growth, both absolutely and relatively to other classes, in the last seventy-five years or so. Finally, there are what are usually called declassed elements — bums, gamblers, thugs, prostitutes, and the like — who are not recognized in the official statistics but who nevertheless play an important role in capitalist society, especially in its political life.

Viewing the matter from a primarily economic angle, then, we could say that the American class structure consists of capitalists, lower middle class in the classical sense, new middle classes, workers, and declassed elements. There is no doubt, however, that this is not a strictly accurate description of the actual living social classes which we observe about us. If we apply the criterion of intermarriageability as a test of social class membership, we shall often find that people who from an economic standpoint belong to the new middle classes are actually on the same social level as the larger capitalists; that smaller capitalists are socially indistinguishable from a large proportion of the new middle classes; and that the working class includes without very much social distinction those who perform certain generally comparable kinds of labor, whether it be with their own means of production or with means of production belonging to others.

These considerations lead us to the following conclusion: the social classes which we observe about us are not *identical* with the economic classes of capitalist society. They are rather *modifications* of the latter. This is, I believe, an important point. If we keep it firmly in mind we shall be able to appreciate the decisive role of the economic factor in the structure and behavior of social classes while at the same time avoiding an overmechanical (and hence false) economic determinism.

How shall we describe the actual social-class structure of America? This is partly a matter of fact and partly a matter of convention, and on neither score is there anything that could be called general agreement among students of American society. Warner and his associates, for example, say that in a typical American community there are exactly six classes, to which they give the names upper-upper, lower-upper, upper-middle, lower-middle, upper-lower, and lower-lower.

There are a number of objections to this scheme, however. It is based on studies of small cities; the dividing lines are largely arbitrary; and the labels suggest that the only important thing about classes is their position in relation to other classes. Warner and his associates admit that there are some communities which lack one or more of the six classes they believe they found in "Jonesville" and "Yankee City"; and one hesitates to speculate on how many classes they might plausibly claim to find, by using essentially the same methods, in a really big city. Their scheme, in other words, while representing a serious attempt to cope with the problem, is unsatisfactory. Its inadequacy is particularly obvious when we attempt to pass beyond the individual community and deal with social classes on a national scale.

What we need is a scheme which both highlights the fundamental economic conditioning of the social-class system and at the same time is flexible enough to encompass the anomalies and irregularities which actually characterize it.

The starting point must surely be the recognition that two social classes, at bottom shaped by the very nature of capitalism, determine the form and content of the system as a whole. I prefer to call these classes the ruling class and the working class. The core of the ruling class is made up of big capitalists (or, more generally, big property owners, though the distinction is not very important since most large aggregates of property have the form of capital in this country today). There are numerous fringes to the ruling class, including smaller property owners, government and business executives (in so far as they are not big owners in their own right), professionals, and so on: we shall have more to say on this subject later. The core of the working class is made up of wage laborers who have no productive property of their own. Here again there are fringes, including, especially, independent craftsmen and petty traders.

The fringes of the ruling class do not reach to the fringes of the working class. Between the two there is a wide social space which is occupied by what we can hardly avoid calling the middle class. We should not forget, however, that the middle class is much more heterogeneous than either the ruling class or the working class. It has no solid core, and it shades off irregularly (and differently in different localities) into the fringes of the class above it and the class below it. Indeed we might say that the middle class consists of a collection of fringes, and that its social cohesion is largely due to the existence in all of its elements of a desire to be in the ruling class above it and to avoid being in the working class below it.

This generalized description of the social-class structure seems to me to have many merits and no fatal defects. The terminology calls attention to the chief functions of the basic classes and indicates clearly enough the relative positions of the three classes in the social hierarchy. More important, the use of the fringe concept enables us to face frankly the *fact* that the dividing lines in American society are not sharply drawn, and that even the borderlands are irregular and unstable. This fact is often seized upon to "prove" that there are *no* classes in America. It cannot be banished or hidden by the use of an elaborate multiclass scheme like that of Warner and his associates, for the simple reason that such a scheme, however well it may seem to apply to some situations, breaks down when applied to others. What we must have is a scheme which takes full account of the fact in question without at the same time obscuring the fundamental outlines and character of the class system itself.

I shall next try to show that, at least as concerns the ruling class, the scheme proposed above does satisfy these requirements.

II

Every community study shows clearly the existence of an upper social crust which is based on wealth. The nucleus is always the "old families" which have transmitted and usually augmented their fortunes from one generation to the next. Around this nucleus are grouped the *nouveaux riches*, the solidly established lawyers and doctors, the more successful of the social climbers and sycophants, and people whose family connections are better than their bank accounts. Taken all together, these are the people who comprise what is called "society." Except in very large cities, the whole community is aware of their existence and knows that they constitute a more or less well-defined "upper class."

So much is obvious. Certain other things, however, are not so obvious. It is not obvious, for example, that these local "upper classes" are in fact merely sections of a national upper class, nor that this national upper class is in fact the national ruling class. What we shall have to concentrate on therefore are two points: first, the structure of the national ruling class; and second, how the ruling class rules.

THE STRUCTURE OF THE NATIONAL RULING CLASS

That the local upper crusts are merely sections of a national class (also of an international class, but that is beyond the scope of the present article) follows from the way they freely mix and intermarry. The facts in this regard are well known to any reasonably attentive observer of American life, and no attempt at documentation is called for here. I merely suggest that those sociologists who believe that only field work can yield reliable data could provide valuable light on the mixing of the local upper crusts by a careful field study of a typical summer or winter resort.

The national ruling class, however, is not merely a collection of interrelated local upper crusts, all on a par with each other. It is rather a hierarchy of upper crusts which has a fairly definite organizational structure, including lines of authority from leaders to followers. It is here that serious study of the ruling class is most obviously lacking, and also most urgently needed. I shall confine myself to a few hints and suggestions, some of which may turn out on closer investigation to be mistaken or at any rate out of proportion.

Generally speaking, the sections of the national ruling class are hierarchically organized with hundreds of towns at the bottom of the pyramid and a handful of very large cities at the top. Very small communities can be counted out: normally the wealth and standing of their leading citizens is no more than enough to gain them entry into the middle class when they go to the city. Even towns as large as five or ten thousand may have only a few representatives in good standing in the national ruling class. You can always tell such a representative. Typically, he is a man "of independent means"; he went to a good college; he has connections and spends considerable time in the state capital and/or the nearest big city; he takes his family for part of the year to a resort where it can enjoy the company of its social equals. And, most important of all, he is a person of unquestioned prestige and authority in his own community: he is, so to speak, a local lieutenant of the ruling class.

Cities, of course, have more — I should also judge proportionately more — national ruling-class members. And as a rule those who live in smaller cities look up to and seek guidance from and actually follow those who live in larger cities. Certain of these larger cities have in turn acquired the position of what we might call regional capitals (San Francisco, Chicago, Cleveland, Boston, and so on): the lines of authority in the given region run to and end in the capital. The relation which exists among these regional capitals is a very important subject which deserves careful study. There was a time in our national history when it would probably have been true to say that the sections of the ruling class in the regional capitals looked up to and sought guidance from and actually followed the New York section, and to a considerable extent this may still be the case. At any rate this is the kernel of truth in the Wall Street theory. My own guess, for what it is worth, is that economic and political changes in the last thirty years (especially changes in the structure and functions of the banking system and the expansion of the economic role of the state) have reduced the relative importance of New York to a marked degree, and that today it is more accurate to describe New York as *primus inter pares* rather than as the undisputed leader of all the rest.

The ruling-class hierarchy is not based solely on personal or family relations among the members of the ruling class. On the contrary, it is bulwarked and buttressed by a massive network of institutional relations. Of paramount importance in this connection are the corporate giants with divisions, branches, and subsidiaries reaching out to all corners of the country. The American Telephone and Telegraph Company, with headquarters in New York and regional subsidiaries covering forty-eight states, is in itself a powerful force welding the unity of the American ruling class; and it is merely the best-developed example of its kind. Formerly, a very large proportion of these business empires were centered in New York, and it was this more than anything else that gave that city a unique position. Today that proportion is much reduced, and cities like Pittsburgh, Cleveland, Detroit, Chicago, and San Francisco play a relatively more prominent part than they used to. In addition to corporations, an integrating role in the ruling class is performed by businessmen's organizations like the National Association of Manufacturers, the Chambers of Commerce, the Rotary and other so-called service clubs; by colleges and their alumni associations; by churches and women's clubs; by scores of fashionable winter and summer resorts (not all located in this country); and by a myriad other institutions too numerous even to attempt to list. (It will be noted that I have not mentioned the two great political parties in this connection. The reason is not that they don't to some extent play the part of an integrator of the ruling class: they do, and in a variety of ways. But their main function is quite different, namely, to provide the channels through which the ruling class manipulates and controls the lower classes. Compared to this function, their role *within* the ruling class is of quite secondary significance.)

Finally, we should note the key part played by the press in unifying and organizing the ruling class. To be sure, not all organs of the press figure here: the great majority, like the political parties, are instruments for controlling the lower classes. But the more solid kind of newspaper (of which the *New York Times* is, of course, the prototype), the so-called quality magazines, the business and technical journals, the high-priced newsletters and dopesheets — all of these are designed primarily for the ruling class and are tremendously important in guiding and shaping its thinking. This does not mean that they in some way make up or determine the *content* of ruling-class ideas — this content is basically determined by what I may call the class situation (about which more will be said presently) — but it does mean that they standardize and propagate the ideas in such a way that the entire ruling class lives on a nearly uniform intellectual diet.

All of the formal and informal, the personal and institutional, ties that bind the ruling class together have a twofold character: on the one hand they are transmission belts and channels of communication; and on the other hand they are themselves molders of ideas and values and behavior norms — let us say for short, of ruling-class ideology. And here we have to note another mechanism of the greatest importance, the mechanism by which the class passes its ideology on from one generation to the next. The key parts of this mechanism are the family and the educational system. Ruling-class families are jealous protectors and indoctrinators of ruling-class ideology; the public school system faithfully reflects it and even, contrary to popular beliefs, fosters class distinctions; and private preparatory schools and colleges finish the job of dividing the ruling-class young from their compatriots. (In this connection, we must not be confused by the fact that a considerable number of lower-class families succeed in getting their sons and daughters into the private preparatory schools and colleges. This is merely a method by which the ruling class recruits the most capable elements of the lower classes into its service and often into its ranks. It is probably the most important such method in the United States today, having replaced the older method by which the abler lower-class young people worked their way directly up in the business world.)

HOW THE RULING CLASS RULES

Let us now turn, very briefly, to the question of how or in what sense the ruling class can be said to rule. This is a question which can easily lead to much mystification, but I think it can also be dealt with in a perfectly simple, straightforward way.

The question has two aspects, economic and political. The ruling class rules the economy in the sense that its members either directly occupy the positions in the economy where the key decisions are made or, if they don't occupy these positions themselves, they hire and fire those who do. The ruling class rules the government (using the term as a shorthand expression for all levels of government) in the sense that its members either directly occupy the key positions (largely true in the higher judiciary and the more honorific legislative jobs, increasingly true in the higher administrative jobs), or they finance and thus indirectly control the political parties which are responsible for staffing and managing the routine business of government. In short, the ruling class rules through its members who (1) do the job themselves, (2) hire and fire those who do, or (3) pay for the upkeep of political machines to do the job for them. That this rule through the members of the class is in fact *class rule* does not require to be separately demonstrated: it follows from the nature and structure of the class as we have already analyzed them.

This analysis of the way the ruling class rules is, of course, sketchy and oversimplified. I think nevertheless that it will stand up provided we can meet one objection, namely, that if the ruling class really ruled it would not put up with New Deals and Fair Deals and trade unions and John L. Lewises and Sidney Hillmans and all sorts of other outrages — *you* may not think them outrages, but the important thing from our present point of view is that the upper class *does* think them outrages. I have found in lectures and conversations about the ruling class that this is by far the most important and frequent objection to this analysis.

A full answer, I think, would require a careful examination of the nature and limits of political power, something which obviously cannot be undertaken here. But the main point is clearly indicated in the following passage from Lincoln Steffens's *Autobiography*. The passage concludes a chapter entitled "Wall Street Again":

It is a very common error to think of sovereignty as absolute. Rasputin, a sovereign in Russia, made that mistake; many kings have made it and so lost their power to premiers and ministers who represented the "vested interests" of powerful classes, groups, and individuals. A dictator is never absolute. Nothing is absolute. A political boss concentrates in himself and personifies a very "wise" adjustment of the grafts upon which his throne is established. He must know these, reckon their power, and bring them all to the support of his power, which is, therefore, representative and limited. Mussolini, in our day, had to "deal with" the Church of Rome. A business boss has to yield to the powerful men who support him. The Southern Pacific Railroad had to "let the city grafters get theirs." The big bankers had to let the life insurance officers and employees get theirs. J. P. Morgan should have known what he soon found out, that he could not lick Diamond Jim Brady. Under a dictatorship nobody is free, not even the dictator; sovereign power is as representative as a democracy. It's all a matter of what is represented by His Majesty on the throne. In short, what I got out of my second period in Wall Street was this perception that everything I looked into in organized society was really a dictatorship, in this sense, that it was an organization of the privileged for the control of privileges, of the sources of privilege and of the thoughts and acts of the unprivileged; and that neither the privileged nor the unprivileged, neither the bosses nor the bossed, understood this or meant it.

There is, I think, more sound political science packed into that one paragraph than you will find in the whole of an average textbook. And it clearly contains the fundamental answer to the contention that the upper class doesn't rule because it has to put up with many things it doesn't like. Obviously the ruling class has to make concessions and compromises to keep the people, and especially the working class, in a condition of sufficient ignorance and contentment to accept the system as a whole. In other words, the ruling class operates within a definite framework, more or less restricted according to circumstances, which it can ignore only at the peril of losing its power altogether — and, along with its power, its wealth and privileges.

We must next consider the problem of "class position," which determines the basic content of ruling-class ideology. Here I can do no more than indicate what is meant by the expression. This, however, is not so serious a deficiency as at first sight it might appear to be; for once the nature of class position is understood it will be seen to be the very stuff of contemporary history, the constant preoccupation of anyone who attempts to interpret the world from a socialist standpoint.

Class position has two aspects: the relation of the class to its own national social system, and the relation of the national social system to the world at large. For purposes of analyzing the position of the American ruling class we can identify it with the body of American capitalists: in respect to basic ideology, the fringes of the ruling class have no independence whatever. The problem therefore can be reduced to the state of American capitalism on the one hand, and the place of American capitalism in the world on the other. American capitalism has now reached the stage in which it is dominated by a strong tendency to chronic depression; while world capitalism, of which America is by far the most important component, is faced by a young, vigorous, and rapidly expanding international socialist system. These are the conditions and trends which determine the basic content of ruling-class ideology.

One final problem remains, that of divisions and conflicts within the ruling class. We are now in a position to see this problem in its proper setting and proportions. Aside from more or less accidental rivalries and feuds, the divisions within the ruling class are of several kinds: regional (based on economic differences and buttressed by historical traditions and memories — the North-South division is the clearest example of this kind); industrial (for example, coal capitalists vs. oil capitalists); corporate (for example, General Motors vs. Ford); dynastic (for example Du Ponts vs. Mellons); political (Republicans vs. Democrats); and ideological (reactionaries vs. liberals). These divisions cut across and mutually condition one another, and the dividing lines are irregular and shifting. These factors introduce elements of indeterminacy and instability into the behavior of the ruling class and make of capitalist politics something more than a mere puppet show staged for the benefit (and obfuscation) of the man in the street. But we must not exaggerate the depth of the divisions inside the ruling class: capitalists can and do fight among themselves to further individual or group interests, and they differ over the best way of coping with the problems which arise from the class position; but overshadowing all these divisions is their common interest in preserving and strengthening a system which guarantees their wealth and privileges. In the event of a real threat to the system, there are no longer class differences — only class traitors, and they are few and far between.

In conclusion, let me say that I have tried to cover a great deal of ground in this essay on the American ruling class. I recognize that this procedure necessarily results in many gaps and omissions, but I hope that it also has compensating advantages. In particular, I hope that a bare outline of the whole subject may serve most effectively to bring into sharp relief the essential problems. I hope also that it will convince the reader not only that *Monthly Review* is justified in talking about the ruling class but that it would be impossible to discuss intelligently the current situation in this country and in the world at large without doing so.

10

Capitalism and Race Relations

This review article dealing with Oliver Cromwell Cox's *Caste, Class, and Race* (New York, 1948) appeared in *Monthly Review*, June 1950.

AMERICAN academic social science has a long and inglorious tradition of evading the burning social issues of the day. The powers-that-be hold the purse strings and on occasion crack the whip; the social scientists, bowing respectfully, either elaborate justifications of the existing social order or else escape into the relatively innocuous study of other times and other systems.

But there have always been a few who have insisted on dealing with the crucial issues of their times and on telling the truth as they see it, regardless of whose toes may be stepped on or whose sensibilities may be injured. They have prevented the complete stultification of academic social science and in the long run have exercised an influence on American life out of all proportion to their numbers.

Such a one is Oliver Cromwell Cox, a professor of sociology, formerly at Tuskegee Institute, now at Lincoln University in Missouri. Oliver Cox's book, *Caste, Class, and Race*, is unquestionably an outstanding product of American sociology. It measures up to the best standards of academic scholarship. And yet packed away in its long words and copious footnotes there is plenty of dynamite — and no pulled punches.

It has been my experience that very few people, even

among social scientists, have heard of Cox's work. This is perhaps not surprising. *Caste, Class, and Race* is the kind of book that publishers bury as quickly as they can; while the sociologists, unable to answer it, seem to have found it most expedient to ignore it. Nevertheless, its message is of vital importance, not only to scholars and students but even more to the whole American progressive movement.

The book is divided into three parts, corresponding to the three components of its title. Part I ("Caste") and Part II ("Class") are essentially preliminary: their function is to clear the ground and lay the foundation for the structure erected in Part III ("Race"). Hence, for the purposes of this brief summary, we can bypass Parts I and II and enter immediately into Cox's treatment of the problem of race. (I should like to add, incidentally, that this procedure has an added advantage from my point of view in that it enables me to avoid a critical analysis of certain of Cox's arguments, especially in Part II, with which I do not agree but which are related only indirectly, if at all, to the main theme of the book. For example, in my judgment Cox's formal theory of "social class" and "political class" is the weakest part of the whole work. But for the most part — and this holds particularly of Part III — his actual use of class concepts is consistent with a more satisfactory theory of class and class relations.)

Cox is interested in race and race relations as social, not anthropological, phenomena. He therefore quite properly defines his field of inquiry as "that behavior which develops among peoples who are aware of each other's actual or imputed physical differences." (P. 320.) The exact nature of these physical differences, or even whether they really exist at all, is thus not the issue. What the anthropologist can or cannot prove about races is important from some points of view, but it has no appreciable effect on the social attitudes and behavior patterns which it is the job of the sociologist to analyze and explain.

It is often maintained, even by social scientists, that people "naturally" react in a certain way to others who are, or are believed to be, physically different from themselves. But all the evidence is against this view. The historical record shows that peoples react differently to one another according to the particular situation in which they find themselves.

We are, of course, primarily interested in the kind of race relations which are found in the world in which we live. This means that we are primarily interested in race relations which are characterized by attitudes of antagonism, and by behavior which is exploitative and discriminatory. Again consulting the historical record, we learn that race relations of this description were unknown to the ancient and medieval worlds and first appeared only in early modern times. Moreover, the facts clearly point to the conclusion that

> racial exploitation and race prejudice developed among Europeans with the rise of capitalism and nationalism, and that because of the world-wide ramifications of capitalism, all racial antagonisms can be traced to the leading capitalist people, the white people of Europe and North America. (P. 322.)

In other words, the heart and core of modern race relations is "the phenomenon of the capitalist exploitation of peoples and its complementary social attitude." (P. 321.)

When capitalism began to expand in the sixteenth and seventeenth centuries, its greatest need was for readily exploitable labor power. In western Europe itself, this need was met by the dispossession and pauperization of peasants and handicraft workers — that process which is unforgettably described by Marx in the last part of the first volume of *Capital*. Here, since exploiters and exploited were alike white, there was no room for a racial rationalization of the inhuman treatment to which the exploited were subjected.

But overseas it was different. There the natives who were ruthlessly impressed into the service of capital were colored — red and black, brown and yellow. The whole situation invited, one might almost say demanded, a theory of white superiority and colored inferiority: "The capitalist exploitation of the colored workers . . . consigns them to employments and treatment that is humanly degrading. In order to justify this treatment the exploiters must argue that the workers are innately degraded and degenerate, consequently they naturally merit their condition." (P. 334.)

The exploiters, needless to say, have been ably aided and abetted by their priests and scribes. In accordance with the principle that the "ideas of each age have ever been the ideas of its ruling class," the theory of white superiority and colored inferiority took root and flourished throughout the capitalist world.

This analysis of the origin and development of modern race relations leads to a principle of great importance. Since the dominant pattern has been imposed by whites in their own interest, it has been more or less consistently opposed and resisted by peoples of color. Race relations are thus essentially relations of conflict, and the aims and strategy of the two sides are necessarily different. In every concrete situation of race relations, therefore, there are two distinct sets of problems: the controlling attitudes and behavior of whites toward colored, and the defensive attitudes and behavior of colored toward whites.

Having dealt with the crucial question of the genesis of modern race relations, Cox proceeds to analyze a number of specific "Situations of Race Relations" (Chapter 17), among which the most important are what he calls the "Ruling-Class Situation" (for example, the British in India) and the "Bipartite Situation," in which peoples of all classes live side by side (the American Southern states and South Africa are the outstanding examples). Cox shows very clearly how attitudes and behavior patterns differ from one case to another, thus once again proving that there is no such thing as "natural" race relations.

Chapter 18 ("Race Prejudice, Intolerance, and Nationalism") is essentially a digression which deals with anti-Semitism on the one hand and with the special race problems between whites and Asians on the American West Coast and in Hawaii. Neither discussion, of course, is exhaustive but both are highly stimulating. Here I shall only quote Cox's summary of what he considers to be the essential difference between race prejudice and anti-Semitism. Generally,

the dominant group or ruling class does not like the Jew at all, but it likes the Negro in his place. To put it in still another way, the condition of its liking the Jew is that he cease being a Jew and voluntarily become like the generality of society, while the condition of its liking the Negro is that he cease trying to become like the generality of society and remain contentedly a Negro. (Pp. 400-401.)

Race prejudice and anti-Semitism are thus distinct phenomena, though both are facets of ruling-class ideology.

The fundamental purpose of Cox's next six chapters (Chapters 19-24) is to evaluate the theories of race relations which are fashionable among American social scientists today. For this purpose, he has first to tie in the analysis of race with that of caste (given in detail in Part I). The reason for this is not that caste and race are identical phenomena, or even that they give rise to essentially similar problems, but rather that academic social scientists have made a regular fetish of the caste concept in dealing with race relations, and especially with the Negro problem in America.

Cox does a thoroughly workmanlike job in exposing the pseudo-scientific pretentiousness of the whole gamut of caste theories of race relations. The term "caste," of course, comes from India where for a period of years measured in the thousands there has been in effect an intricate system of mutually repellent and at the same time mutually cooperating castes. The origin of caste is shrouded in obscurity. A number of hypotheses have been advanced — Cox himself develops an ingenious theory on this subject — but the evidence is too scanty to provide conclusive support for any one of them. Whatever the origin of the caste system, however, there can be no doubt that it developed on the basis of the occupational division of labor characteristic of ancient Hindu society and that its chief social function has been to stabilize and rigidify the whole structure of that society. Castes have ever been extremely conservative institutions, what Marx once called "decisive impediments to Indian progress and Indian power." (Quoted by Palme Dutt in *India Today*, p. 263.) It is true, of course, that during the last two hundred years the caste system has been slowly crumbling under the impact of Western capitalism which forcibly breaks down the hereditary division of labor, the very foundation of the caste system. But even so, castes have proved remarkably resistant to change; and today they present enormous problems to an Indian bourgeoisie straining to turn its country into a modern capitalist nation. So far as we know, there has never been a comparable caste system anywhere else in the world.

Obviously, the race problem in America is of an entirely different sort from the caste problem in India. The latter grew up in the conditions of a prehistoric society, the former as a direct outgrowth of capitalist exploitation. Caste in India has been a stabilizing institution; race in America has always been a promoter of change, a source of profound threats to the *status quo*.

We must now ask what contribution the caste concept can make to the understanding of the race problem in America. The answer clearly is, none at all. On the contrary, to think of American race relations in terms of caste can only confuse the real issues and lead to false or misleading conclusions. And Cox shows, with a wealth of detail, that this has been precisely the effect.

Why, then, have so many eminent social scientists eagerly seized upon caste as the key to American race relations? Partly, no doubt, the explanation is to be found in the extreme poverty — one might almost say triviality — of their own theories. All too many sociologists operate on the principle that a lack of ideas can be made good by a lot of fancy words and concepts. The caste school of race relations is an excellent example of this. As Cox says,

the final achievement is a substitution of words only. One may test this fact by substituting in the writings of this school the words "Negroes" or "white people" wherever the words "Negro caste" or "white caste" appear and observe that the sense of the statement does not change. (P. 507.)

But the use of the caste concept serves another purpose, too. It smuggles into the discussion of American race relations all the ideas and connotations which are associated with the caste system in India: antiquity, social adjustment, stability, resistance to change, and so on. As a matter of fact, race relations in this country have none of these characteristics. They are the product of capitalism, a relatively modern phenomenon; they are symptoms of profound social disequilibrium; they are evolving rapidly; and they constitute a standing threat to the stability of the country's social structure. But these are explosive facts which the social scientists stay away from for fear of getting hurt. It is safer, and more "scientific," to escape into the make-believe world of caste. In Cox's remarkably restrained words:

By using the caste hypothesis, then, the school seeks to explain a "normal society" in the South. In short, it has made peace for the hybrid society that has not secured harmony for itself; and in so far as this is true, its work is fictitious. (P. 504.)

Cox devotes a whole chapter to Gunnar Myrdal's *An American Dilemma*, describing it as the "most exhaustive survey of race relations ever undertaken in the United States." This is one of the best chapters in the book. Myrdal borrowed the caste hypothesis from its American originators; and Cox shows, patiently and painstakingly, that his work suffers from all the essential defects of the caste school plus others which are more original and more insidious. What perhaps distinguishes Myrdal most sharply from the rest of the caste theorists is that he is at least aware of the challenging existence of Marxian theory, and much that he writes is designed to undermine its prestige and refute its conclusions. It is therefore in analyzing Myrdal's work that Cox makes the following profoundly true statement:

> Capitalist rationalizations of race relations have recently come face to face with a powerful theory of society and, in order to meet this, the orthodox theorists have become mystics. This evidently had to be so because it is exceedingly terrifying for these scientists to follow to its logical conclusion a realistic explanation of race relations; and yet they must either do this or stultify themselves. Here the social scientist is "on the spot"; he must avoid "the truth" because it is dangerous, regardless of how gracefully he eases up to it. (P. 528.)

I would add only that this holds not only in the field of race relations. It is increasingly true throughout the whole range of the social sciences. What Cox is really doing here is to describe the crisis of capitalist social science, a crisis which accompanies and reflects the general crisis of the capitalist system itself.

Let us now attempt to summarize Cox's theory of race relations in the United States today. Much of this theory is included in the final chapter entitled "The Race Problem in the United States," but parts of it (including many of the crucial supporting arguments) are scattered throughout Part III. My purpose is to put the various elements together as concisely as possible and at the same time in a logically consistent fashion.

The race problem in the United States, of course, is the problem of relations between Negroes and whites. Its origin was in the slave system of the old South, and this in turn "was simply a way of recruiting labor for the purpose of exploiting the great natural resources of America." (P. 332.) The Civil War abolished slavery but did not overthrow the social *system* of the South. It presented the Southern ruling class with the necessity of finding new methods of controlling its labor force and maintaining its own dominance. The way the Southern ruling class has solved this problem has been the decisive factor in shaping the development of race relations ever since. This is not to say that the whole issue is peculiar to the South; it also exists in the North, and the difference is "mainly in degree." (P. 545.) But the South is the decisive theater of race relations, and it is there that the problem can be most usefully studied.

The task of the Southern ruling class is to keep both Negroes and white workers ("poor whites") tractable and freely exploitable. For this purpose it has employed two main devices which are so closely interdependent that neither could survive without the other. On the one hand it has systematically incited and propagandized the whites against the Negroes. The resulting race prejudice is thus "an attitude deliberately built up among the masses by an exploiting class, using acceptable rationalizations derogatory to the Negro race." (P. 532.) On the other hand, the ruling class has erected all sorts of social and legal barriers between the races in order to segregate Negroes and to prevent the development *in practice* of Negro-white solidarity on a class basis. "All sympathetic contact between the white and black masses was scrupulously ruled out by a studied system of segregation." (P. 487.) Further,

explicit segregation is at the foundation of all the racial discrimination and exploitative practices of the whites. In fact, segregation is . . . absolutely necessary to maintain white ruling-class dominance. . . . What segregation really amounts to is a sort of perennial imprisonment of the colored people by the whites. Moreover, this imprisonment provides the proper milieu for the planned cultural retardation of the colored people. Here they may mill and fester in social degeneracy with relatively minimal opportunity for even the most ambitious of them to extricate themselves. (Pp. 381-382.)

Segregation thus not only bulwarks the policy of cultivating racial hatred but, by retarding the social development of Negroes, provides visible grounds for further anti-Negro rationalizations.

Among the various methods of segregation, none is more crucial than the prohibition of interracial marriages, or of interracial sexual relations in general. This is true, first, because sex is a highly charged subject around which strong feelings can be mobilized and directed into channels of race hatred; and second, because interracial breeding would tend to undermine the very foundation of the system. This is why

> the white woman holds a strategic position in the interracial adjustment of the South. To the extent that the ruling interest in the South can maintain eternal watchfulness over her, to that extent also the system may be perpetuated. The belief that Negroes are surreptitiously using white women to "mongrelize" the population produces a bitter sense of frustration, calling for practically unlimited violence against Negroes. It is principally on the latter score that the white ruling class has been able to corral the white masses for expressions of mob violence. Clearly a "mongrelized" South will ultimately mean not only a non-segregated South but also a non-aristocratic South, the perennial nightmare of the southern oligarchy. (P. 559.)

We thus see the real role of sex in race relations. It is not, as many writers have assumed, the heart of the matter: "Sex is not 'basic' in race relations, but it is basic in the system of rationalization which supports racial antagonism." (P. 528.) And again: " 'Pure blood' has value only when in preserving it a calculable social advantage can be maintained." (P. 389.)

The ultimate sanction of the system of white superiority is open and unrestrained violence. This is where lynching comes into the picture. This is why the Southern ruling class is adamantly opposed to any form of anti-lynching legislation.

> Lynching is crucial in the continuance of the racial system of the South. From this point of view lynching may be thought of

as a necessity. This is not to say, however, that lynching is "in the mores"; it is rather in the whip hand of the ruling class. It is the most powerful and convincing form of racial repression operating in the interest of the *status quo*. Lynchings serve the ruling class with the means of periodically reaffirming its collective sentiment of white dominance. (P. 555.)

Lynching ... is integral in the southern system. To remove the threat of it is to overthrow the ruling class in the South and to change the basis of southern economy. (P. 557.)

So far, we have analyzed the problem of race relations from the point of view of the purposes and strategy of the white ruling class. This is essential because the white ruling class is the architect and builder of the entire structure of American race relations. But it is far from being the whole story; we must also examine the problem of race relations from the point of view of the exploited Negro people, a point of view which is naturally very different from that of the white ruling class.

There are two fundamentally different ways in which Negroes might react to the situation into which they have been forced in this country. They might react nationalistically: that is to say, they might seek liberation as a group able to control its own affairs and to deal equally with other sovereign groups — in other words, as a nation. Or they might react by seeking to knock down the fences which imprison them and simply to merge into the larger society around them — the solution of the race problem which is usually known as assimilation.

For a variety of reasons, there is no strong tendency among American Negroes to react nationalistically to their situation. This, of course, has nothing to do with their being Negroes — "it is fairly certain that African Negroes in every continental colony will in time develop nationalism" (p. 403) — but is rather due to historical and cultural factors over which they have had little or no control. Their ancestors were uprooted when they were brought to this country as slaves;

they are "old" Americans; their culture is American; they have never accepted the anti-Negro shibboleth that "this is a white man's country." It is natural under the circumstances that their highest ambition should be to share in its resources and opportunities on equal terms with all the other inhabitants. As Cox puts it:

> The solidarity of American Negroes is neither nationalistic nor nativistic. The group strives for neither a forty-ninth state leading to an independent nation nor a back-to-Africa movement; its social drive is toward assimilation. (P. 545.)

The present solidarity of Negroes is thus essentially provisional and temporary: in so far as they succeed in achieving their goal of assimilation they will cease to be, or to think of themselves as, "Negro Americans" and will become just plain Americans. This view of Negro aspirations is not based on guesswork or the opinions of individuals. It is derived from the social practice of Negroes in their everyday living.

> The urge toward assimilation and away from group solidarity is so compelling among Negroes that few, if any, of the organizations maintained by whites which offer reasonably unrestricted participation to Negroes can be developed by Negroes for Negroes. As a rule, only those types of white enterprises which discriminate against Negroes can be developed among Negroes. If the white society were to be impartial to Negro participation, no business, no school, no church would thrive among Negroes. (P. 546.)

The final result of assimilation, of course, would be a society in which, as a result of generations of interracial breeding, the physical as well as the social basis of racial differences would disappear. This is the ultimate goal of American Negroes. And, we might add, *for that very reason* it will surely become, if it is not already, the goal of the entire American progressive movement.

In pursuit of assimilation, Negroes follow a policy of "whittling away at every point the social advantages of the whites.

By continual advances, no matter how small, the Negro hopes to achieve his status of complete equality as an American citizen." (P. 571.)

This policy is of utmost importance; it has brought substantial gains, and it can bring further gains. But it has its limitations. It may be compared to the policy followed by trade unions in attempting to eliminate the exploitation of workers by capitalists. This, too, is absolutely necessary and brings vital gains to the workers. But a policy of "whittling away" can never eliminate exploitation, which is rooted in the very structure of the capitalist system. And the same is true of racial discrimination: this, too, is rooted in the very structure of the capitalist system.

It follows that Negroes, like workers, are potential enemies of the system itself and sooner or later will be forced by the logic of their situation to adopt an anticapitalist position. It also follows that Negroes and workers are natural allies and that their goals — which, of course, overlap and to a large extent are even identical — will eventually be reached by a common struggle against the white ruling class which exploits them both in its own narrow interest.

Nor is there any mystery about the nature of the social system which will replace capitalism. Capitalism, indeed,

in our own day . . . has undoubtedly passed the noontide of its vigor and is giving place to another basic form of social organization. . . . The new economic system which will naturally replace the old is socialism. The relation of socialism to racial exploitation may be demonstrated by the fact that the greater the immediacy of the exploitative practice, the more fiercely is socialism opposed. . . . Indeed, the method of "solving the race issue" is identical with the method by which capitalism is being liquidated by proletarian action. (Pp. 578, 581.)

And again, in the words of Cox's concluding paragraph:

The problem of racial exploitation, then, will most probably be settled as part of the world proletarian struggle for democracy; every advance of the masses will be an actual or potential advance for the colored people. Whether the open threat of violence by the exploiting class will be shortly joined will depend upon the unpredictable play and balance of force in a world-wide struggle for power. (P. 583.)

11

The Heyday of the Investment Banker

This review of Louis M. Hacker's The Triumph of American Capitalism *(New York, 1940) appeared in* The New Republic, *October 21, 1940, under the title "A Marxist on American History." A more accurate title would have been "An Ex-Marxist on American History," for Hacker's subsequent career has shown that the abandonment of Marxism in the last chapter of this book, which is commented upon in the review, was final and complete.*

PRESENT-DAY professional historians are for the most part interested in the past for its own sake. For them the goal of historical research is, as nearly as possible, the re-creation of the past as it actually happened. The meaning of events is to be sought in people's utterances and emotions, and the most significant crystallizations of history are therefore those institutions and cultural patterns which express the thoughts and feelings of large numbers of people: religion, art, law, literature, and so on. No interpretative canon is required by this approach. Explanations are where you find them, and, more often than not, the actors on the historical stage are taken at their own word unless it can be clearly shown that they are liars.

The Marxist historian, however, has a very different outlook. He is interested in history not primarily for its own sake but because he believes that only through a study of the past is it possible to diagnose the present and plan for the future. Consequently he tries to cut through the outer crust of people's beliefs and emotions to the underlying forces of historical change which he finds in the economic structure of society and the class interests which it generates. Orthodox history is good if it satisfies its readers; Marxist history is right if it provides a valid guide to practical activity.

Hacker is a Marxist historian. It should, therefore, occasion no surprise that his version of American history as embodied in *The Triumph of American Capitalism* is something very different from the usual run of treatises on the subject. From the outset to (but not including) the last chapter, Hacker's interest is focused on a rigorous analysis of economic and class forces. His most important themes may be briefly stated. Twice in American history economic development has produced irreconcilable class antagonisms which could be resolved only by resort to arms. The first of these armed struggles was the Revolution, and it resulted in the freeing of American mercantile capitalism from the strangulation of the English colonial system. The second was the Civil War, and from it emerged a triumphant industrial capitalism standing over the prostrate form of Southern-planter capitalism. Hacker tries to show in detail why these bloody conflicts were inevitable and how the different classes in society reacted to the circumstances which were thrust upon them. On the whole the quality of the work is high. We have in this book the most ambitious attempt yet made to apply historical materialism to the interpretation of American history. Both as an example of method and for the light which it sheds, *The Triumph of American Capitalism* is a notable achievement.

There are in my opinion, however, certain deficiencies in Hacker's analysis, and by far the most important of these concerns his treatment of Northern capitalism in the second half of the nineteenth century. Full consideration of this question would require a great deal more space than is here available; I shall have to confine myself to a few rather general remarks.

THE HEYDAY OF THE INVESTMENT BANKER

Hacker thinks of Northern capitalism as being predominantly mercantile in character until the Civil War. The war gave the representatives of industrial capitalism, which had hitherto been retarded by the political power of the South, a chance to seize control and put through a political program in their own interests. Thenceforth until the end of the century the industrial capitalists held sway only to be replaced in the seats of power by the rising finance capitalists in the decade before the World War. The basic trouble with this picture, I think, is that it does not take adequate account of the railroad.

Northern capitalism was dominated by the railroad during almost the entire second half of the nineteenth century. Even the crisis of 1857, which Hacker tries to show was largely an affair of mercantile capital, was almost certainly a product of overinvestment in railroads. In every decade from 1850 to 1890, investment in railroads exceeded that in *all manufacturing industries put together* (including hand and neighborhood industries), and in the fifties, sixties, and seventies, it was more than twice as great. Now railroad construction and operation are certainly not functions of mercantile capitalism. The economic historian who called the railroad "the industrial revolution incarnate" was nearer the mark. But, in reality, it must be recognized that the railroad is in a class by itself, and that practically from the outset it is the preserve of finance capital. It is no accident that the giant corporation and the whole elaborate machinery of investment banking evolved in the railroad era. (By 1880 the Pennsylvania Railroad had 13,000 stockholders and total assets of more than $400,000,000!) Nor that Wall Street was a household byword long before Carnegie or Rockefeller made his first million. (Remember that Commodore Vanderbilt died in 1877 leaving a railroad fortune of $105,000,000 — an incredible sum for the time.) Moreover, railroads foster from their inception the kind of relationship between capital and the state which is so marked a characteristic of finance capitalism.

Aside from the significance of finance capital in the railroad field even before the Civil War, there is little real evidence to indicate that the war marked a decisive turning point in the quantitative progress of industrial capitalism, though, of course, the crushing of Southern power was a factor of enormous importance in permitting its uninterrupted growth. To be sure, the pace of industrial development quickened in the last quarter of the nineteenth century, but it was not until after the depression of the nineties that manufacturing experienced a truly sensational boom which made it for the first time the outstanding economic activity of the country. From 1890 to 1910 investment in manufactures (excluding hand and neighborhood) was double that of our whole previous history (including hand and neighborhood). And the greater part of *this* industrial activity, as Hacker realizes, was carried on under the auspices of finance capital, which had long been preparing itself for the task in the railroad field.

My conclusion from considerations of this sort is that Hacker's conception of the Civil War as the "Victory of American Industrial Capitalism" requires considerable modification. *All* types of Northern capital benefited from the war. Mercantile capital had an enormous stake in the South and stood to lose heavily from successful secession; industrialists fattened on war orders and finally achieved the protection for which they had long been clamoring. It was, however, finance capital, and particularly the railroad interests, which came off best of all. The Pacific railroad charters, with their princely grants from the public domain, are the most obvious evidence of this. But it is only a little less clear (though Hacker misses the point entirely) that the methods of financing the war, the establishment of the national banking system, and later on the adoption of the single gold standard and the resumption of specie payments, were all measures which were devised primarily in the interests of finance capital. Sound money has always been the program of the financial community; industrial entrepreneurs usually benefit from inflation so long as it is not carried to extremes.

In short, Wall Street very early achieved a dominant economic position as a result of the Civil War and the unique importance of the railroad in American development. This position in economic affairs it has never relinquished.[1] When manufacturing grew to full stature, it was under the wing of Wall Street. And when utilities in their turn occupied the center of the stage, even though they were largely local in character, Wall Street found a way of taking them to its heart. On the other side of the picture, national politics, substantially ever since the Civil War, has been a long and none too successful struggle to curb the enormous power of finance capital.

This brings me to what I regard as by far the weakest part of Hacker's book, namely, the conclusion. Here, in place of a prognosis based on rigorous analysis of economic and class forces, such as characterizes earlier parts of the book, we find an incongruous note of wishful idealism. Everything is going to be all right, he assures us, because of the strength of the "American tradition" of freedom and equality. In other words, Hacker, for reasons best known to himself, has abandoned Marxism just at the point where it begins to serve as a potential guide to action. He would have done better to stop at the end of the nineteenth century, leaving his readers to draw their own conclusions about the future.

Finally, a word about the first two chapters which comprise the introduction. These, it seems to me, give every indication of having been hastily thrown together. The writing is sloppy, the thinking rambling and confused. In a new edition Hacker would do well to drop them out entirely.

---

[1] But see below, pp. 189-196.

12

Interest Groups in the American Economy

This study was undertaken at the invitation of the National Resources Committee, a characteristically New Deal agency which would be unthinkable in the Washington of today, and was published as Appendix 13 to Part 1 of the NRC's well-known report, *The Structure of the American Economy* (Washington, 1939).

By dividing America's dominant financial-corporate giants among eight clearly definable "interest groups," this study set a precedent which has since been widely followed. It is all the more incumbent on me, therefore, to call attention to the fact that the situation here described and analyzed was that which obtained in the United States not later than 1935, and to a considerable extent earlier than 1935. The research was done in the summer of 1937, two years before publication; and while every effort was made to secure statistical data relating to 1935, much of the material drawn upon inevitably concerned conditions which preceded, and indeed to a considerable extent led to, the New Deal.

Needless to say, great changes in the structure and control of the American economy have taken place during the years of the New Deal, World War II, and the Cold War. Some of these are described in the next article, "The Decline of the Investment Banker." A study of interest groups in the early 1950s would almost certainly yield results differing in many respects from those embodied in this paper. No such study, as far as I know, has been made in recent years, though there is an obvious need for one. I hope that the republication of this earlier attempt to deal with what was and remains one of the crucial aspects of our whole social system will stimulate the interest of younger social scientists and provide them with both a starting point and some useful methodological pointers.

It IS the purpose of this study to throw light on the degree to which the large corporations are linked among themselves through common control, community of interest groups, or more or less loose alliances.

It is of the very nature of the relationships which form the subject matter of this study that they are overwhelmingly qualitative in character. No statistical technique has been or is likely to be devised for reducing them to a quantitative scale. Furthermore, informed observers will inevitably differ in their judgments about the weight to be attached to the various bits of evidence out of which a general picture must be pieced together. For this reason it is necessary to be as careful as possible in indicating the method of analysis which has been followed. Clearly no claim to unbiased accuracy can be set forth in a study of this sort; that fact alone puts the author under an obligation to present his material in a way to make critical appraisal possible and easy.

The kind of relationships which we are studying clearly have to do with the way in which corporations are managed and this in turn depends upon how and by whom they are controlled. How they are controlled may or may not be determined by their ownership. Consequently *control* is the central issue around which the study must turn.

Now it is a fairly simple task to classify corporations by the techniques employed in controlling them. The classification used by Berle and Means,[1] while not exhaustive, is an excellent working scheme. They distinguish five major types, each one pretty much self-explanatory: (1) control through almost complete ownership, (2) majority control, (3) control through a legal device without majority owner-

---

[1] *The Modern Corporation and Private Property* (New York, 1933), Chapter V.

ship, (4) minority control, and (5) management control. It is one thing, however, to be able to place a corporation in one or other of these categories and quite another to be able to identify and name the controlling individual or group. To a certain extent, to be sure, the two problems overlap. It is quite likely that if enough is known to place a corporation in one of the first four categories, enough will also be known to identify, at least in a general way, the controlling interest. This is not necessarily true, however, and in the case of the fifth category it is likely not to be true. Since Berle and Means estimated that somewhere around one half of the 200 largest nonfinancial corporations in 1929 were management-controlled, the importance of this reservation will be at once apparent.

Once a corporation has been classified by type of control, however, it is usually possible to go further and make a more or less accurate judgment about who controls it. The most important aid is undoubtedly a knowledge of the history[2] of the corporation and of the individuals who comprise its management (officers and directors).[3]

Once the identity of controlling interests has been established it is possible to begin grouping companies together. This is, however, the most difficult task of all. Some corporations clearly belong together. For example, if one individual or well-defined group of individuals owns a majority of the voting securities of two or more concerns, then it will scarcely be denied that these companies should be placed together

---

[2] The history of every corporation has certain critical phases: organization and promotion, expansion, and possibly bankruptcy and reorganization. The role which certain individuals or groups play during these periods commonly determines their importance in more normal times. It is for this reason that it is so important to have a knowledge of historical facts.

[3] In this connection, undoubtedly, the most valuable source of information is the magazine *Fortune*, which combines a high regard for accuracy with a special interest in personalities. On the other hand, there is very little to be found in the professional writings of economists and economic historians except in a few cases where the subject matter is specifically biographical.

in what we may call a single interest group. We can safely say the same about any number of corporations which are completely under the control of the same interests, whatever the form of that control may be. But the concept of an interest group should surely comprise more than merely such corporations as are altogether under the same control. For example, if two brothers or close friends each own a business, and if at many points the policies of the two businesses are made in common, it would seem desirable to group the one with the other as belonging to the same interest group. Or if an investment banker promotes and takes a continuing and significant interest in several different concerns, it would appear that good grounds exist for putting these concerns into a single interest group. Most likely in the latter case the investment banker will be part of the management in each, sharing the control with others. We could generalize, then, and say that companies ought to be grouped together if, in the absence of counterbalancing factors, they have a significant element of control in common.

Does this mean that any two companies whose directorates interlock should be classed together in one interest group? The answer to this question is, emphatically, No. Anyone starting out on this principle would have little difficulty in putting all but a few of the 200 largest nonfinancial corporations into a single interest group. This fact is not without significance, but the classification achieved by this method would cover up the kind of grouping it is desired to disclose. For present purposes, material on interlocking directorates is unquestionably important, but it must be used with care and discrimination.[4] Some general rules can be laid down,

---

[4] *Cf.* the statement made in a recent government investigation of railroads: "In investigations of control it has generally been the custom to lean rather heavily on interlocking directorates as a line of evidence. The present study prompts the view that such evidence can easily be overworked unless it is very exhaustively examined." *Regulation of Stock Ownership in Railroads*, 71st Cong., 3d Sess., H.R. No. 2789, Part 1, p. lxxvi. This report will hereafter be referred to as *Splawn Report: Railroads.*

but in no case are they a complete substitute for knowledge of the relationships on which interlocking directorates are based. Interlocks may be classed as primary and secondary. A primary interlock exists between companies X and Y if a director of X, *whose main business interest is with X*, sits on the board of Y. If this same person also sits on the board of Z, then a primary interlock also exists between X and Z. These two relations, however, necessarily involve an interlock between Y and Z, and this we call a secondary interlock. It goes without saying that more weight should be given to primary than to secondary interlocks and that the latter should be interpreted only with caution.

More important in evaluating the significance of interlocking directorates is a knowledge of the general policies of the companies and individuals involved. Some firms and individuals regard the position of directorship as one of responsibility which involves their own reputations. They are not likely to assume such a responsibility unless they are in harmony with the general policy of the management of the company concerned and in a position to make their influence felt. This is clearly the case with the firm of J. P. Morgan & Co., for example. As a rule, a Morgan partner sits on the boards of only two or three large companies, frequently in related lines of activity. He is supposed to keep himself thoroughly informed and to take an active part in the affairs of these companies. When one considers the tremendous prestige which attaches to the Morgan name, it is easy to understand that the directorship of a Morgan partner is a fact of first importance in determining the orientation of a corporation. On the other hand, some individuals are perfectly willing to act as directors in a purely ornamental capacity, a function which in England is peculiarly reserved for members of the nobility. Directors with no active business interests and no apparent asset except a name with prestige value should always be regarded in this light unless there is specific evidence to the contrary.

It is obvious that multiple interlocks should be given more weight than single interlocks. In this connection, it is noteworthy that about half of the large companies in which J. P. Morgan & Co. is represented have two or more Morgan partners on their boards.

There are industrial and financial alliances which manifest themselves in other ways than through complete or partial common control. Most important are alliances based on banking and underwriting relations which do not result in formal interlocks. The connection between financier and manufacturer is generally not a casual one but a continuing one which gives rise to an active interest on the side of each party in the affairs of the other. Nevertheless, relations may remain entirely informal. For example, it was the general policy of Kuhn, Loeb & Co., under the leadership of Jacob Schiff, to eschew formal representation on the boards of its clients. Yet their responsibility for success was no less keenly felt.

Once a commitment had been made [Schiff's biographer comments], the important task was to guide the borrower's financial projects in such a way as to promote their success. This essential service was not one which was legally due anyone concerned; yet it had to be rendered for the ultimate welfare of all. One way in which bankers can watch the interests of investors who look to them for guidance is to be represented in the management or board of directors of the concern for which they have issued loans. So far as Schiff was concerned he preferred, as a rule, that his firm should not be so represented. He felt that by personal conference and advice he could do as much as through formal representation.[5]

When relations are of the kind preferred by Schiff, they can only be recognized and evaluated by knowledge of the history of the companies involved.

Some alliances are of a kind which does not permit of gen-

---

[5] C. S. Adler, *Jacob H. Schiff: His Life and Letters* (2 vols., 1928), Vol. I, p. 27.

eralization. Such, for example, is the close connection which has long existed between J. P. Morgan & Co. and the First National Bank of New York. It began as a personal relationship between the elder J. P. Morgan and the elder George F. Baker, but long since took on an institutional character. Outwardly this alliance manifests itself in close cooperation between representatives of the two concerns in the affairs of various third companies. Appointment to a partnership in J. P. Morgan & Co. is regarded as the most desirable form of promotion by junior officers of First National. Before the Banking Act of 1933, two Morgan partners were on the directorate of First National's securities affiliate, the First Security Co., since dissolved. It would be misleading to call the Morgan-First National alliance unique, but it is certain that it would be difficult to fit into any general category. The list of such connections which defy generalization would be a long one; probably many exist which have altogether escaped the attention of the present writer. The best that can be done is to note them down and incorporate them in the general picture as they are discovered and checked.

From what has been said the reader will gather that the method followed in this study is thoroughly empirical and involves at every stage an exercise of practical judgment. An interest group is not a clear-cut concept which can be given concrete content according to mechanical rules. Accordingly the writer makes no claim to either completeness or finality. What follows should be regarded as tentative and subject to revision at many points if and when more adequate evidence is brought to bear on the problem. Only one general rule has been observed throughout and that is to disregard connections which are not based on pretty direct relations between two parties concerned.

There are, of course, no a priori limits to the scope which might be determined upon for this study. Ideally it should perhaps cover all significant interest groups judged by their relation to the economy as a whole. But such an ambitious project would take years to carry through, and the results would be difficult to present in a concise and readily intelligible form. Consequently, more or less arbitrary limits had to be imposed, firstly, on the segment of the economy considered, and, secondly, on the number of groups analyzed.

As to the first limit, the starting point was the list of the 200 largest nonfinancial corporations as of the end of 1935. The list had to be used before it had assumed final form, so there may be minor discrepancies between figures used in this section and those appearing in the final version of the list. The 200 largest nonfinancial corporations, for the purposes of this paper, then, include 107 industrials, 54 public utilities, and 39 railroads. It is inconvenient to handle the railroads as separate companies since many of them are grouped together through majority stockholdings into large systems. In accordance with the procedure of the Splawn Report on railroads, the bulk of the mileage has been grouped together into 13 major systems.[6] This, of course, involves the inclusion of a number of smaller roads which belong to one or other of the major systems. The net result is that discussion is limited to 13 major systems and 8 other roads with assets of $100 million or over.[7]

---

[6] *Splawn Report: Railroads,* Part 1, p. lii. The report names 14 major systems, but suggests (p. li) that "the assignment of the Illinois Central to the Union Pacific system would perhaps be justified by reason of the fact that the latter owns by far the largest block of Illinois Central stock, representing 28.94 percent of the total." This assignment has been made here, and, consequently, the number of systems is reduced to 13.

[7] There has been very little change in the composition of the major systems since the Splawn Report. Nevertheless, in order to make the data as recent as possible, the grouping has been carried out in accordance with a chart compiled and published by Robert A. Burrows (Pittsburgh) entitled *Inter-Relation and Capitalization of the Principal American Railroads, As of January 1, 1933.* This chart is believed to be accurate and to embody all developments up to the time of its publication. In compiling asset figures for the systems, the assets of roads in which two systems have an equal interest have been divided between the two.

In addition to nonfinancial companies, it is necessary to consider at least banking companies in order to get a satisfactory view of the scope of important interest groups. This has been accomplished by including in the companies to be analyzed the 50 largest commercial banks as of the end of 1935.[8]

The total assets of the companies considered are set out in the following table.

Total assets at the end of 1935

	Millions of dollars
107 industrials	24,943
54 utilities	25,428
13 major railroad systems and 8 other roads with assets in excess of 100 million dollars	24,258
50 banks	23,722

It is possible to give a fairly accurate idea of the proportion of the total *corporate* assets of each class owned by the companies included in this table. At the end of 1933 the 104 largest corporations classified as "Manufacturing," "Mining and Quarrying," "Trade," and "Other," possessed 33.8 percent of the total corporate assets in these categories. The list is not quite the same as that for 1935, but the difference is of a small order of magnitude. These classifications correspond to what have been summed up here under the heading "Industrials."

The 1933 figures indicate that the 96 largest corporations engaged in "Transportation and Other Public Utilities" owned 87.4 percent of all corporate assets in these fields. No precise breakdown between railroads and public utilities is available, but it is likely that the figure for rails should be somewhat higher and for utilities somewhat lower than 87.4 percent in their respective fields. In the case of rails, data compiled from the *Splawn Report: Railroads* show that the 13 major systems and 8 other roads included in the above table

[8] "Largest" by total resources as reported in Moody's *Banks* for 1936.

owned at the end of 1929 about 95 percent of total railroad mileage. Assets figures would doubtless be roughly in proportion. Taking 95 percent as the correct figure for rails would mean, of course, that 75 percent would be about right for utilities.

In the case of banks it is possible to give a figure which is very nearly accurate. The 50 largest banks held, on December 31, 1936, deposits which amounted to 47.9 percent of the average deposits of all commercial banks for 1936.[9] Assets figures would certainly not differ materially.

Summing up, then, it may be estimated that the corporations included in this study own about 34 percent of the assets of all industrial corporations, 48 percent of the assets of all commercial banks, 75 percent of the assets of all public utilities, and 95 percent of the assets of all rails. It would probably not be denied that this sector of the economy is the seat of economic power out of proportion to its relative size.

The other limitation mentioned above, namely, the number of interest groups, has been more or less naturally dictated by the material itself.

From a careful company-by-company study there gradually emerged eight more or less clearly defined groups which so far overshadowed all the others that it seemed only logical to confine further attention to these eight.

It is manifestly impossible to rank these groups either by size or by influence. The interests of no two are equally divided among the different spheres of economic activity considered, nor are they at all strictly comparable from the point of view of the strength of the ties which bind them together. This point is important to emphasize. If it is kept in mind there is little danger of interpreting figures, despite their misleading appearance of precision, as more than general indicators of orders of magnitude.

---

[9] Data on the 50 largest are taken from the *American Banker*, January 19, 1937, p. 11; and for all commercial banks from the *Annual Report of the Federal Deposit Insurance Corporation for the Year Ending December 31, 1936*, p. 125.

The groups which will be considered may be designated for convenience as follows: (1) Morgan-First National, (2) Rockefeller, (3) Kuhn, Loeb, (4) Mellon, (5) Chicago, (6) Du Pont, (7) Cleveland, and (8) Boston. The reasons for these particular labels should become clear in the course of the further discussion.

1. MORGAN-FIRST NATIONAL.[10] This group is for the most part based upon partial control by one or the other, or more commonly both, of the financial institutions after which the group is named. This partial control in turn is based upon long-standing financial relations and the very great prestige attaching to the Morgan and First National firms. Neither of these banking houses, however, operates through ownership to any significant extent. Some of the relationships which entitle corporations to membership in this group are more complex than ordinary partial control and require separate explanation.

The industrials included are 13 in number, listed with the number of Morgan-First National representatives in their management.[11]

Pullman, Inc. (6)
General Electric Co. (4)
U.S. Steel Corporation (3)
Kennecott Copper Corporation (3)
Phelps Dodge Corporation (2)
American Radiator & Standard Sanitary Corporation (2)

---

[10] The Banking Act of 1933 enforced the divorce of deposit banking from underwriting. J. P. Morgan & Co. elected to continue in business as a deposit bank, and a new firm, Morgan, Stanley & Co., Inc., was formed by a number of the partners of J. P. Morgan & Co. and Drexel & Co. (the Philadelphia branch of J. P. Morgan & Co.), to take over the investment banking business. Though J. P. Morgan & Co. and Morgan, Stanley & Co., Inc., are, of course, legally entirely separate entities, they have nevertheless been treated as one for purposes of this analysis.

[11] This refers, as throughout this study whenever possible, to the end of 1935.

Continental Oil Co. (2)
Montgomery Ward & Co., Inc. (1)
National Biscuit Co. (1)
Philadelphia & Reading Coal and Iron Corporation (1)
Baldwin Locomotive Works (1)
Glen Alden Coal Co.
St. Regis Paper Co.

The last two named are special cases. Glen Alden owns and operates the coal properties which once belonged to the Delaware, Lackawanna & Western Railroad.[12] The ownership of the two are probably substantially identical, and we know that the D. L. & W. belongs to the extent of about 22 percent to the Bakers, the Vanderbilts, and the New York Central.[13] Two representatives of the First National are directors of Glen Alden's subsidiary, Delaware, Lackawanna & Western Coal Co., which handles sales. St. Regis can be more advantageously discussed under utilities.

There is good reason to believe that all the companies which are listed as having Morgan-First National representation on their managements have more than merely formal relations with the two financial institutions. To review all the evidence would carry us much too far afield into the sphere of economic history. The list errs if at all, in the writer's opinion, on the side of understatement. These 13 industrials have combined assets of 3,920 million dollars.

The utilities included in the group are as follows:

American Telephone & Telegraph Co.
International Telephone & Telegraph Co.
Consolidated Gas Co. of New York.[14]
United Corporation group
    Commonwealth & Southern Corporation

---
[12] Moody's *Industrials*, 1935, p. 1276. The railroads were obliged under the antitrust laws to divest themselves of coal properties.
[13] *Splawn Report: Railroads*, Part 1, pp. 134-135.
[14] Now Consolidated Edison Co. of New York.

United Gas Improvement Co.
Public Service Corporation of New Jersey
Niagara Hudson Power Corporation
Columbia Gas & Electric Corporation

Electric Bond & Share group[15]
American Power & Light Co.
American Gas & Electric Co.
National Power & Light Co.
Electric Power & Light Corporation

American Telephone & Telegraph has three directors in common with First National, but its informal relations with J. P. Morgan & Co. are probably even more important.[16] Two Morgan partners are on the directorate of International Telephone & Telegraph.

The next group of companies, with which Consolidated Gas may well be considered, heads up into a super-holding company called the United Corporation. United was formed in 1929 by J. P. Morgan & Co. and Bonbright & Co., acting in closest harmony.[17] Its avowed purpose was to foster "closer relations among the great public utility systems in the east."[18] The first set of directors of United comprised five partners of a leading New York law firm, and soon after its formation "these directors resigned to make way for Messrs. Whitney and Gates of J. P. Morgan & Co. and Messrs. Thorne and Loomis of Bonbright & Co., Inc."[19] There is not the slightest doubt that these two companies were in sole

---

[15] American & Foreign Power has been omitted from this study because all of its properties are held abroad.

[16] The development of these relations has been traced in detail by the Federal Communications Commission in its investigation of the Bell system. See Federal Communications Commission, *Special Investigation Docket No. 1*, "American Telephone and Telegraph Company: Corporate and Financial History," 3 vols., Reports Nos. 22, 23, and 24.

[17] For the story of the formation and development of United Corporation see "High Finance in the 'Twenties: The United Corporation," *Columbia Law Review*, May 1936, June 1936.

[18] *Columbia Law Review*, June 1936, p. 936.

[19] *Ibid.*, May 1936, p. 787.

control of later operations. The steps subsequently taken and the interrelations among companies in the United Corporation group are much too complicated to detail. In spite of the fact that stockholdings in Consolidated Gas are insignificant, nevertheless this company is very closely tied in with the rest of the group, particularly through the fact that one man, Floyd Carlisle, is chairman of the boards of Consolidated Gas, Niagara Hudson, and St. Regis Paper Co. This, plus substantial stockholdings, also explains the inclusion of St. Regis Paper in the group.[20]

The inclusion of the Electric Bond & Share system rests on less secure foundations than in the case of the United Corporation system. Nevertheless it is believed that the supporting evidence is amply convincing. Electric Bond & Share Co. was originally formed by General Electric Co. as a subsidiary to take over securities acquired by the latter in exchange for generating machinery and equipment.[21] Though General Electric divested itself of legal control in 1925, there was no change in management and there is no reason to suppose that the two concerns do not continue to cooperate as before. General Electric, it will be recalled, is one of the industrial corporations closest to the Morgan and First National banking houses. Furthermore Electric Bond & Share has had in the past, and may still have, relatively small minority holdings in stocks of United Corporation, American Superpower, Commonwealth & Southern, Public Service of New Jersey, and Niagara Hudson.[22] "From the point of view of legal control," according to Bonbright and Means, "these stock in-

[20] For interrelations within the United Corporation and Electric Bond & Share group, see *Inter-Relation and Capitalization of the Principal Public Utility, Holding, Operating and Investment Companies, As of January 1, 1936*, compiled and published by R. A. Burrows (Pittsburgh).

[21] *Relation of Holding Companies to Operating Companies in Power and Gas Affecting Control*, 73d Cong., 2d Sess., H.R. No. 827, Part 3, pp. 437 ff. This report will henceforth be referred to as *Splawn Report: Utilities*.

[22] J. C. Bonbright and G. C. Means, *The Holding Company*, 1932, p. 133.

terests of the Electric Bond & Share Co. in the United Corporation System are probably negligible. They become significant, however, by virtue of the fact that Electric Bond & Share Co. has long been closely affiliated with the banking house of Bonbright & Co., Inc.,[23] and they point strongly to the conclusion that the policies of the Electric Bond & Share Co. and of the interests controlling the United Corporation will be harmonious rather than antagonistic."[24] Nothing has happened since to change this judgment.

The 12 utility companies included in the Morgan-First National group have combined assets of 12,191 million dollars.[25]

The assignment of railroad systems to the Morgan-First National group has been done sparingly. Only five major systems and one other road are included in the list, though an excellent case could be made out for according similar treatment to two more major systems and at least two other smaller roads. Those included are as follows:

New York Central system[26]
Alleghany system[27]
Northern system[28]
Atchison system[29]

---

[23] Up to 1935, Sidney A. Mitchell, president of Bonbright & Co., was a director of Electric Bond & Share and three of its major subsidiaries.

[24] Bonbright and Means, *loc. cit.*

[25] The assets of United Corporation, American Superpower, Electric Bond & Share, and American & Foreign Power are not included in this total.

[26] Includes New York Central; Delaware, Lackawanna & Western; and a one-half interest in Rutland.

[27] Includes Chesapeake & Ohio; Missouri Pacific; Erie; New York, Chicago & St. Louis; Pere Marquette; Chicago & Eastern Illinois; Wheeling & Lake Erie; and a one-half interest in Denver & Rio Grande Western.

[28] Includes Great Northern; Northern Pacific; Chicago, Burlington & Quincy; Spokane, Portland & Seattle; and Gulf, Mobile & Northern.

[29] Includes only Atchison, Topeka & Santa Fe.

Southern system[30]
Western Pacific[31]

Morgan and/or First National representatives partake in the managements of all the major systems listed, except Alleghany, and Western Pacific. Financial relations have been in every case close and of long duration.[32]

Alleghany is a special case. This giant railroad system was built up, through the lavish use of holding companies, by the late Van Sweringen brothers of Cleveland. Almost from the inception of their career in the railroad field, the Van Sweringens relied heavily on both J. P. Morgan & Co. and the First National for advice and financial support. It is reasonably certain that without that assistance the Van Sweringens never would have built a railroad empire, nor would they have been able to remain in control once it was built.[33]

Since the last of the Van Sweringen brothers died in November 1936, a struggle for control of the profitable parts of the empire has developed between Robert R. Young and the Guaranty Trust Co., which is closely allied to the Morgan house. It is still too early to predict the outcome of this contest, but there is a possibility that the bankers will lose out. Since this study, however, does not attempt to go beyond the end of 1935, it is clearly correct to classify the Al-

---

[30] Includes Southern, and a one-half interest in Chicago, Indianapolis & Louisville.

[31] Includes Western Pacific, and a one-half interest in Denver & Rio Grande Western.

[32] See, for example, Lewis Corey, *The House of Morgan*, 1930, especially Parts IV, V, and VII; Stuart Daggett, *Railroad Reorganization*, 1908, *passim*.

[33] For the story of the Van Sweringens' career see the following: *Stock Exchange Practices*, Hearings Before the Committee on Banking and Currency, U. S. Senate, 73d Cong., 1st Sess., on S. Res. 84 (72d Cong.) . . . and S. Res. 56 (73d Cong.), Part 2; *Investigation of Railroads, Holding Companies and Affiliated Companies*, Hearings Before a Subcommittee of the Committee on Interstate Commerce, U. S. Senate, 74th Cong., 2d Sess., pursuant to S. Res. 71, Parts 1, 2, 3, 4, 7, 10; also *Splawn Report: Railroads*, Part 2.

leghany system in the Morgan-First National interest group. The combined assets of the listed railroads amount to 9,678 million dollars.

In the banking field only three banks beside J. P. Morgan & Co. and the First National have been admitted to the list, though this decision was not taken until several further promising candidates had been rejected. The banks are as follows:

Guaranty Trust Co.
Bankers Trust Co.
New York Trust Co.

In the case of the first, three Morgan partners are directors, and in the case of the others, two each. The combined assets of the five banks amount to 4,421 million dollars.

To sum up: the Morgan-First National group includes 13 industrial corporations, 12 utility corporations, 5 major railroad systems and one other road, and 5 banks. Total asset figures are as follows:

	Millions of dollars
Industrials	3,920
Utilities	12,191
Rails	9,678
Banks	4,421
Total	30,210

2. ROCKEFELLER. The Rockefeller group has been limited to companies about which there can be very little argument. It extends only into industrials and banks and comprises all told only seven corporations.

In the industrial field, the Rockefeller interests hold what amounts to a controlling minority position in six large oil companies, successor firms to the old Standard Oil Co., which was dissolved by court decree in 1911. These companies, together with the percentage of voting power held by John D. Rockefeller and/or Rockefeller-endowed institutions, are as follows:[34]

Standard Oil Co. of New Jersey	16.5
Socony Vacuum Oil Co., Inc.	20.8
Standard Oil Co. of Indiana	13.8
Standard Oil Co. of California	16.6
Atlantic Refining Co.	7.1
Ohio Oil Co.	24.0

These six companies have more than half the total assets of the oil industry. Rockefeller control is mostly exercised in a negative fashion, but is none the less real on that account. This was illustrated dramatically in 1929 when the management of Standard of Indiana, under the leadership of Robert W. Stewart, challenged the Rockefeller dominance and was decisively routed in a battle of proxies.[35] It will be noticed that the Rockefeller interest is smaller in Standard of Indiana than in any of the other companies except Atlantic Refining.

The total assets of the Rockefeller oil companies amount to 4,262 million dollars.

One bank, the Chase National, has been assigned to the Rockefeller group. John D. Rockefeller is probably the bank's largest stockholder, and Winthrop Aldrich, its chairman, is a long-time Rockefeller legal and business representative.[36] Chase National is the country's largest bank, with assets of 2,351 million dollars.

3. KUHN, LOEB. The main activity of the investment banking house of Kuhn, Loeb & Co. has, at least until quite re-

---

[34] As reported in *Report on Pipe Lines*, 72d Cong., 2d Sess., H.R. No. 2192, Part 1, p. xxxvi.

[35] The incident and its implications have been discussed at length by Berle and Means, *The Modern Corporation and Private Property*, pp. 82-84.

[36] "Chase National Bank," *Fortune*, January 1936. No study of stock ownership in banks, such as the House Committee on Interstate and Foreign Commerce has carried out for rails, utilities, and communications, has ever been made. It would be very desirable that this should be done.

cently, always centered in the field of railroads. In financing, reorganizing, rehabilitating, and advising railroads, Kuhn, Loeb has since the 1890s been the peer of J. P. Morgan & Co. As previously noted, it has never been the policy of Kuhn, Loeb to maintain more than a few of its contacts by means of directorships, but the reality of the community of interest between the firm and its clients is certainly not open to question on that account.[37] Only those contacts which have been very close and of long duration have been admitted as evidence of membership in the Kuhn, Loeb interest group. Besides railroads, of which five major systems and two other roads are included, only one utility and one bank are on the list. These are as follows:

Major railroad systems
    Pennsylvania[38]
    Union Pacific[39]
    Southern Pacific[40]
    Chicago, Milwaukee, St. Paul & Pacific[41]
    Chicago & Northwestern[42]
Other roads with assets over 100 million dollars
    Missouri-Kansas-Texas[43]
    Delaware & Hudson[44]

---

[37] The peculiarly intimate connection which exists between a railroad and its banker is very clearly set forth and vigorously defended in a statement prepared by Kuhn, Loeb & Co. for the Interstate Commerce Commission in 1922, and reprinted under the title "The Marketing of American Railroad Securities" in *Sale of Foreign Bonds or Securities in the United States,* Hearings Before the Committee on Finance, U. S. Senate, 72d Cong., 1st Sess., Part 2, pp. 305-322.

[38] Includes Pennsylvania; Norfolk & Western; Lehigh Valley; New York, New Haven & Hartford; Detroit, Toledo & Ironton; Boston & Maine; and a half interest in Rutland. For relations with Kuhn, Loeb, cf. Adler, *Jacob H. Schiff,* Vol. I, especially pp. 71-82.

[39] Includes Union Pacific and Illinois Central. *Ibid.,* pp. 88-123, 131-144.

[40] *Ibid.,* pp. 117-121.
[41] *Ibid.,* pp. 150-151.
[42] *Ibid.,* pp. 50-51.
[43] *Ibid.,* p. 131.
[44] *Ibid.,* pp. 148-150.

Utilities
    Western Union Telegraph Co.[45]
Banks
    Bank of the Manhattan Co.[46]

It is quite likely that Kuhn, Loeb exercises less in the way of active control than J. P. Morgan & Co., and for that reason the group at present under consideration should be considered as less closely knit and more in the nature of a loose alliance.

Asset figures for the Kuhn, Loeb group are as follows:

	Millions of dollars
Industrials	—
Utilities	342
Rails	9,963
Banks	548
Total	10,853

4. MELLON. The Mellon group is probably the best integrated and most compact of all the interest groups considered. It is based on a solid core of industrials and banks which are closely held by members of the Mellon family and a small number of close associates. Aside from companies of this description, two other types have been included, namely: (1) those on the management of which three or more members of the Mellon group are active and probably dominant, and (2) those allied to the closely held Mellon companies by significant primary interlocks, and in the affairs of which no other group is represented. On this basis the Mellon list is as follows:

Industrials
    Closely Held
        Gulf Oil Corporation

---
[45] *Ibid.*, pp. 171-172.
[46] Cf. "Mr. Kuhn and Mr. Loeb," *Fortune*, March 1930. This article also has additional information on relations with railroads.

Koppers Co.[47]
Aluminum Co. of America
Pittsburgh Coal Co.

Probably Mellon-dominated
Westinghouse Electric & Manufacturing Co.

Allied
Jones & Laughlin Steel Corporation
American Rolling Mill Co.
Crucible Steel Co. of America
Pittsburgh Plate Glass Co.

Rails
Virginian Railway Co.[48]

Utilities
United Light & Power Co.[48]
Brooklyn Union Gas Co.[48]

Banks (closely held)
Mellon National Bank
Union Trust Co.

Total assets of the Mellon group are as follows:

	Millions of dollars
Industrials	1,648
Utilities	859
Rails	153
Banks	672
Total	3,332

5. CHICAGO. The Chicago group has been defined solely on the basis of interlocking directorates. Of 11 companies designated as belonging to this group, all with headquarters in

[47] In computing Mellon asset figures, the assets of Koppers have been divided as accurately as possible between industrials and utilities.

[48] The Mellon interests have, through Koppers and directly, by far the largest stockholdings in these companies. On Virginian, see the report in the *New York Times*, August 10, 1937, of Hearings Before the Senate Committee on Railroad Finance; and, on the other two, the Security and Exchange Commission's *Official Summary of Holdings of Officers, Directors and Principal Stockholders*, as of December 31, 1935.

Chicago, one interlocks with the other ten, one with nine, one with eight, two with seven, three with six, one with five, and one with four. In every case at least one of the interlocks is double and several are triple. It is scarcely to be questioned that such a welter of interlocks signifies a substantial community of interest between the firms involved. The following are the 11 companies:

Industrials
    International Harvester Co.
    Armour & Co.
    Marshall Field & Co.
    Wilson & Co.
Utilities
    Commonwealth Edison Co.
    Public Service Corporation of Northern Illinois
    Peoples Gas, Light & Coke Co.
Banks
    Continental Illinois National Bank & Trust Co.
    First National Bank of Chicago
    Northern Trust Co.
    Harris Trust & Savings Bank

The assets of the Chicago group are as follows:

	Millions of dollars
Industrials	858
Utilities	813
Rails	—
Banks	2,595
Total	4,266

6. DU PONT. The Du Pont group comprises only four companies, three industrial and one bank, but they are all in the top rank with respect to size. Like the Rockefellers, the Du Ponts exercise control through substantial minority stockholdings. Theirs is a compact, closely knit group. The key company is E. I. du Pont de Nemours, which the Du Ponts

control through a family holding company, the Christiana Securities Co. The latter owns about 25 percent of the voting stock of E. I. du Pont de Nemours.[49] E. I. du Pont de Nemours in turn owns approximately the same proportionate interest in General Motors Corporation.[50] Du Ponts and Du Pont representatives dominate the management of both companies. The third industrial in this group is United States Rubber Co., in which another Du Pont family holding company, called Rubber Securities Co., owns about 20 percent voting power.[51] F. B. Davis, Jr., a Du Pont executive, was installed as president soon after the Du Ponts bought into United States Rubber. The Du Pont bank is the National Bank of Detroit, on the board of which sit five General Motors officials.

Assets of the Du Pont group are as follows:

	Millions of dollars
Industrials	2,232
Utilities	—
Rails	—
Banks	396
Total	2,628

7. CLEVELAND. The Cleveland group centers around the Mather interests in Cleveland. The corporations involved are as follows:

Industrials
    Cleveland-Cliffs Iron Co.
    Republic Steel Corporation
    Youngstown Sheet & Tube Co.
    Inland Steel Co.
    Wheeling Steel Corporation

---

[49] Prospectus of the E. I. du Pont de Nemours Co., dated June 30, 1937.

[50] *Ibid.*

[51] Securities and Exchange Commission, *Official Summary of Holdings of Officers, Directors and Principal Stockholders*, as of December 31, 1935.

Goodyear Tire & Rubber Co.
Interlake Iron Corporation
Banks
Cleveland Trust Co.

The interrelation of these companies, so far as stock ownership is concerned, is as follows. The Mather interests control the Cleveland-Cliffs Iron Co. by means of 100 percent of the voting common stock held through the Cliffs Corporation plus a substantial share of the voting preferred stock held directly. The Cleveland-Cliffs Co. has minority voting interests in the four steel companies. Relations are by no means confined to stock ownership, but so complicated is the whole picture that it defies brief and simple exposition. We shall have to be content with stating a few additional facts. The key company in the iron and steel group, Cleveland-Cliffs Iron Co., owns, next to U. S. Steel, the largest supply of unworked iron ore in the country.[52] The alliance between Cleveland-Cliffs and four of the so-called steel independents, Republic, Youngstown Sheet & Tube, Inland, and Wheeling, is consequently seen to have a solid and durable economic foundation. These companies do not have any elements of management in common, because a large number of interlocks were successfully attacked under the antitrust laws in 1935 and had to be abandoned.[53] There is no reason, however, to suppose that this altered their relations to one another except in a purely formal way. The Cleveland Trust Co. interlocks with Cleveland-Cliffs and Republic Steel in addition to the following smaller Mather interest concerns: Interlake Iron (twice), Interlake Steamship, and the Sam-

---

[52] "Iron and Steel," *Fortune*, May 1931.
[53] *Equity No. 5153, District Court of the United States, Northern District of Ohio; United States v. William G. Mather et al;* petition filed February 7, 1935. For the final disposition of the case, whereby the defendants voluntarily agreed to give up their interlocking directorships, see press release of the Department of Justice, February 11, 1936.

uel Mather Estate, Inc. Goodyear Tire & Rubber belongs to the Cleveland group by virtue of its having two directors in common with Cleveland Trust and two others with Cleveland-Cliffs.[54]

Total asset figures for the Cleveland group are as follows:

	Millions of dollars
Industrials	1,066
Utilities	—
Rails	—
Banks	338
Total	1,404

8. BOSTON. The Boston group heads up into the First National Bank of Boston and the Old Colony Trust Co.[55] First National-Old Colony banking interests interlock to a very great extent with the other companies which have been assigned to this group, and they with each other. Most of the relations have roots reaching back thirty or more years, and there is little doubt of the reality of the community of interest which is symbolized in these interlocking directorates. The companies included follow:

Industrials
 United Shoe Machinery Corporation
 U. S. Smelting, Refining & Mining Co.
 United Fruit Corporation[56]

---

[54] Cyrus S. Eaton, of Cleveland, who joined with the Mathers in forming the Cliffs Corporation just before the depression set in, was at one time in control of Goodyear. He lost control during the depression and for a time a number of banks, of which Cleveland Trust was one, were large stockholders. The story is told in detail by H. and R. Wolf in their book *Rubber*, 1936, Book V, Chapter III.

[55] These two banks merged their interests in 1929. Old Colony is now in effect the trust department of First National. See any of Moody's bank manuals for 1930 or after for details.

[56] Some question might be raised about the inclusion of United Fruit since there is no doubt that active control is in the hands of its managing director, Samuel Zemurray, of New Orleans. See "United Fruit," *Fortune*, March 1933. The fact that Zemurray retains the old directorate unchanged, however, would seem to indicate that he has reached a friendly understanding with the Boston group.

American Woolen Co.
Utilities
Stone & Webster, Inc.
Edison Electric Illuminating Co. of Boston
Banks
First National Bank (including Old Colony Trust)

Total asset figures are:

	Millions of dollars
Industrials	425
Utilities	554
Rails	—
Banks	740
Total	1,719

Eight interest groups have been sketchily outlined in so far as they cover a sector of the economy which includes corporations with total assets of very nearly 100 billion dollars, fairly evenly distributed between industrials, rails, utilities, and banks.

What percentages of these totals fall into the various groups and into all the groups together? This question is answered in the following table:

PERCENTAGES OF ASSETS CONSIDERED WHICH FALL INTO THE VARIOUS INTEREST GROUPS*

	Morgan-First National	Rockefeller	Kuhn, Loeb	Mellon	Du Pont	Chicago	Cleveland	Boston	Total
Industrials	15.7	17.1	—	6.6	8.9	3.4	4.3	1.7	57.7
Rails	39.9	—	41.1	.6	—	—	—	—	81.6
Banks	18.6	9.9	2.3	2.8	1.7	10.9	1.4	3.1	50.7
Utilities	47.9	—	1.3	3.4	—	3.2	—	2.2	58.0

* This is the percentage of total assets in the interest groups to the total assets in each of the four listed fields held by the 250 large corporations.

The reader should be cautioned against reading into this table implications which are not there. It does not relate to the whole economy but only to that segment which is roughly coterminous with the area controlled by the 200 largest nonfinancial corporations and the 50 largest banks. It is possible to argue that the influence of this segment is far greater than any statistical measure would indicate, but, of course, such an argument must rest on grounds different from any presented in this study. Secondly, it is not intended to imply that these aggregations of capital ever act as a unit under the rule of individual or oligarchic dictatorships. The social and economic content of the relationships which bind them together is far more subtle and varied than this. This study should be regarded as doing no more than posing the problem of the larger significance of the facts which it seeks to portray.

The method of procedure followed up to this point tends to give the impression that each of the groups considered is more or less isolated and unrelated to the others except, of course, by way of normal commercial transactions. This is very far from the actual state of things. Some idea of the way they overlap and interconnect is conveyed by the following list, very incomplete though it is, of contacts.

1. BETWEEN MORGAN-FIRST NATIONAL AND MELLON. Six representatives of Morgan-First National and three of Mellon are on the board of Pullman, Inc. This relationship resulted from the merger in 1930 of Pullman and Standard Steel Car, previously one of the closely held Mellon industrials. Texas Gulf Sulphur Co., which with the Freeport Sulphur Co. has a practical monopoly of the country's sulphur output, has two Morgan partners on its board, while Mellon's Gulf Oil Corporation owns one third of its capital stock.

2. BETWEEN MORGAN-FIRST NATIONAL AND CHICAGO. Three prominent members of the Chicago group are on the directorates of Pullman, Inc., and Montgomery Ward & Co., Inc.,

both of which have been assigned to the Morgan-First National group.

3. BETWEEN MORGAN-FIRST NATIONAL AND DU PONT. Three high representatives of Morgan-First National are directors of General Motors, controlled through minority ownership by the Du Ponts. Additionally, the Morgan firms are chief bankers and underwriters for the Du Pont interests.

4. BETWEEN MORGAN-FIRST NATIONAL AND BOSTON. At least three men who rate as members of the Boston group are directors of General Electric, and five are directors of American Telephone & Telegraph. These two corporations are among those which have had longest and closest relations with both Morgan and the First National of New York.

5. BETWEEN MORGAN-FIRST NATIONAL AND CLEVELAND. The Cleveland group is represented on the directorates of Alleghany Corporation and several of its subsidiaries. Alleghany has been assigned to the Morgan-First National group. Furthermore, three men are directors of both Alleghany and Goodyear Tire & Rubber.

6. BETWEEN KUHN, LOEB AND CLEVELAND. The records of the Securities and Exchange Commission indicate that, at least since the beginning of 1935, Kuhn, Loeb has been the leading underwriter for the four steel companies in the Cleveland group, namely, Republic, Youngstown Sheet & Tube, Inland, and Wheeling.[57]

7. BETWEEN KUHN, LOEB AND DU PONT. One of the few large companies in which Kuhn, Loeb partners hold directorships is United States Rubber, and in this case two Kuhn, Loeb partners are directors. United States Rubber is controlled by minority ownership by the Du Ponts.

8. BETWEEN DU PONT AND ROCKEFELLER. The Du Ponts' General Motors and Rockefeller's Standard Oil of New Jersey own on a half-and-half basis the Ethyl Gasoline Corporation. The latter exercises a virtual police power over the terms

---

[57] Also for two of the other large steel independents, Bethlehem and National.

and conditions of sale of 85 percent of the gasoline with high-octane rating sold in the country.[58] This amounts to about 70 percent of all gasoline sold.

9. BETWEEN ROCKEFELLER AND BOSTON. One of the difficult problems which had to be decided in making up the various interest groups was whether the giant International Paper & Power Co. should be assigned to Boston or Rockefeller. Boston is particularly closely associated with its power subsidiary, New England Power Association, which holds well over half the total assets of International Paper & Power. For example, F. D. Comerford is at one and the same time a director of the First National Bank of Boston, chairman of New England Power Association, and president of Edison Electric Illuminating Co. of Boston. The latter has five directors in common with the First National and/or the Old Colony. On the other hand, Chase National Bank now holds 16.6 percent of the voting power in International Paper & Power,[59] a holding exceeded only by that of the Phipps family. Furthermore, Chase and International Paper & Power have two directors in common.

The dilemma created by this situation was solved by assigning International Paper & Power to neither the Boston nor the Rockefeller groups.[60] That it provides a strong link between them, however, is evident.

10. BETWEEN BOSTON AND MELLON. Gas in Boston is pro-

---

[58] The facts came to light in an antitrust suit initiated by the Department of Justice early in 1937; *Equity No. E. 84-321, District Court of the United States, Southern District of New York; United States v. Ethyl Gasoline Corporation, Earle C. Webb, and John Coard Taylor;* petition filed February 19, 1937.

[59] As of May 1937. SEC File 33-22.

[60] Alternatively, the assets of International Paper & Power might be considered as evenly divided between Chase and Boston, thus raising the asset figures for Boston utilities from $554 to $942 millions. In assigning the other 50 percent of assets, it seems desirable to add them to Chase rather than directly to the Rockefeller total. This raises the Rockefeller bank total to $2,739 millions but adds nothing to utilities.

vided by Koppers's subsidiary Eastern Gas & Fuel Associates. Halfdan Lee, president of Eastern Gas & Fuel, is a director of First National Bank of Boston. Three prominent members of the Boston group are on the board of trustees of Eastern Gas & Fuel.

11. BETWEEN MELLON AND KUHN, LOEB. Westinghouse Electric & Manufacturing, certainly under Mellon influence and probably under Mellon control, has had long and close relations with Kuhn, Loeb. The late Jerome Hanauer, former Kuhn, Loeb partner, was a director of Westinghouse until his death.

Before leaving the subject of the interrelation of the various groups, it is well to note the role played in particular by the American Telephone & Telegraph Co. The American Telephone & Telegraph Co. covers the greater part of the country with its score or more associated companies. Each of these subsidiaries has a complete corporate structure with a board of directors and banking relations at least partially unconnected with those of the parent company. It has been a deliberate policy of the Bell system to foster relations with the important industrial and financial groups in all the large centers where it does business.[61] The result is that every one of the groups which have been analyzed interlocks in greater or lesser degree with one or more of the Bell system companies, and probably most of the large banks have financial relations with the local Bell company. It is of course difficult to gauge the importance of connections of this sort, but the extent to which they have been developed leads to the belief that they are by no means insignificant. It is probably true that relations like those just described are of more importance and interest in so far as they form a bond between the major groups and apparently independent corporations both large and small. It is obvious, however, that

---

[61] A similar policy is adopted by other large companies which have subsidiaries scattered over the country. The American Telephone & Telegraph is simply the best-developed case.

the discussion of the implications of the Bell system and kindred organizations cannot be a part of this study.[62]

The material here presented raises questions to which no answer can here be attempted. What is the significance of the existence of more or less closely integrated interest groups for the pricing process? What are its implications for the relation between economic and political activity? How and to what extent do the views of leaders in the economic sphere make themselves felt in the life of the community?

These questions, and many more, are raised with an urgency proportionate to the degree of concentration of economic leadership in the hands of a few. The present study will perhaps have helped to demonstrate that they have now attained the status of central issues.

---

[62] Ample raw material for a thorough analysis of this problem exists in the study of the Federal Communications Commission cited in note 16 above. See particularly the volumes entitled *Outside Contacts of the Bell System* and *Banking Relations of the Bell System*.

13

The Decline of the Investment Banker

This paper summarizes one of the important structural changes in the American economy which was wrought by a decade of depression and social reform. Subsequent events have shown that the change was a permanent one. The Cold War period brought a large-scale revival of business investment, and the investment banking fraternity has enjoyed very good times indeed in contrast to the dark days of the 1930s. But there has been no comparable recovery of the power and authority of the investment banker. On the whole, the conclusions of this article remain essentially sound. It was originally published in *The Antioch Review*, Spring 1941.

THE growth of Big Business in the last quarter of the nineteenth century brought to the fore a new figure in American life, the investment banker. With the domineering elder J. P. Morgan as prototype, the American investment banker became internationally famous, revered or reviled, feared or hated, as the very symbol of concentrated economic power. To the press, to Congressional committees, to the public at large, it was the investment banker who was the overlord of the new economic order of trusts and banks and imperial adventure and international intrigue.

The picture was, as all such pictures must be, somewhat overdrawn; but it was not without a solid foundation in the bedrock of economic fact. The investment banker, combining the roles of promoter, financier, and bond salesman, had been largely instrumental in building up, reorganizing, and consolidating the nation's vast railroad network in the 1880s and 1890s. Entering the industrial field after the long depression of the nineties, he was the outstanding figure in the great wave of promotions and combinations which culminated in the crisis of 1907; he took the lead in financing the victors in the World War of 1914-1918; during the prosperity of the twenties he again turned his hand to promoting mergers and combinations, with still unconcentrated fields like public utilities, automobiles, food processing, and retail distribution as his main sphere of activity, but without in the least neglecting the older fields of railroads and heavy industry. By 1929 he exercised sway over what were absolutely, if not relatively, larger aggregations of capital than ever before.

The picture of the investment banker firmly seated on the throne of economic empire has become so deeply implanted in all our minds that it is difficult to realize that in the short space of a single decade he has suffered a dramatic eclipse, and that such power as he still retains is largely rooted in a past that is gone forever. Yet such is unquestionably the case, and a proper analysis of our present-day economy demands that we face the fact and seek to understand its implications.

So far as the declining importance of investment banking is concerned, the main facts are plain and well known to the financial community. New large-scale promotions and mergers, which have always been the chief source of profit and power to the investment banker, have been virtually nonexistent since 1930. For this and other reasons, the traffic in new securities, and therewith the potential field for investment banking activity, has been drastically curtailed. Moreover, the overwhelming proportion of new securities, running up to 75 percent in some years, has been issued for refunding purposes; that is to say, the new securities have merely replaced old securities which have matured or been called. Refunding operations are, for the most part, of a routine nature; they neither require special skill from the investment banker nor offer him a strategic opportunity to extend his power over the issuing corporations. Finally, and perhaps most significantly, an ever larger part of even this reduced business in new securities has been altogether circumventing the traditional investment banking channels through the device of what is known as "private placement." Securities are privately placed when they are sold directly by the issuing corporation to a group of institutional investors, which usually means in practice to a group of life insurance companies, without the aid or participation of the investment banker. An item on the financial page of the *New York Times* of November 28 tells the story in this respect with concise eloquence: "Formal announcements will be made today of no less than four separate private placements of new securities involving $145,720,000. To say that these private sales, particularly the $140,000,000 American Telephone and Telegraph deal, is a stunning blow to the underwriting community is putting it mildly." When we recall that A. T. & T. was taken over in its infancy and nursed to its present enormous size under the guiding and controlling hand of J. P. Morgan & Co., once the greatest investment banker of them all, we get an illuminating insight into the hard times on which the trade has currently fallen.

The decline in business, which has just been sketched, has of course been reflected in the composition of the investment banking community. Many of the largest and most active houses, which were set up as subsidiaries by the great commercial banks during the twenties, simply folded up when the Banking Act of 1933 decreed a divorce of investment from deposit banking. Several firms, long active in the field, have found it expedient to merge their interests in order to cut out unnecessary duplication of facilities. Most significantly of all, J. P. Morgan & Co itself, when presented by the Banking Act of 1933 with the alternatives of giving up its deposit or its investment banking business, chose to abandon the latter. A new firm, Morgan, Stanley & Co., Inc., was established to carry on the investment banking business, but J. P. Morgan & Co. itself, along with all but one of its leading partners, saw the handwriting on the wall and elected to desert the field in which it had won international fame and power in favor of one which had long been regarded as merely a side line. Today, if one looks through the roster of investment bankers, one finds mostly unknowns or has-beens but very few who play a leading role in the business world.

What are the underlying reasons for the decline of the investment banker? Businessmen, with their customary propensity to seek for causes on the surface of things, have been inclined to lay the blame on the Securities Act of 1933 and on the Securities and Exchange Commission's administration of that legislation. These factors doubtless have played a part, but even in their absence it is inconceivable that the trend of events could have been significantly different. Looking beneath the surface, we can discern four causal influences at work which, operating in close coordination, may be regarded as controlling:

(1) A sharp decline in the pace of economic expansion and an unwonted paucity of important new industries have been responsible for a drastic contraction of the traditional field of investment banking activity.

(2) Such expansion as has taken place, and such new industries as have been developed, have been from the outset under the control of already existent large corporations disposing of vast internal financial resources and hence under no need to resort extensively to the capital market.

(3) The rapid growth of institutional investment, particularly of life insurance, straight through the depression years has completely transformed the buyers' side of the market for new securities. Studies by the Temporary National Economic Committee have shown that the greatest part of even those securities which are still distributed by investment

bankers soon gravitate into the portfolios of institutional investors. Under these circumstances, it is clear that the growth of the simple and direct method of private placement is inevitable.

(4) The federal government, particularly through the Reconstruction Finance Corporation but also through other agencies set up under the New Deal, is performing more and more of the financial functions which once required the services of the investment banker. This is most dramatically illustrated by the financing of plant expansion under the defense program in which the government is playing the leading role and the investment banker a very minor part, at least up to the present.

A careful consideration of the implications of these basic tendencies in our economic life will make it plain that the decline of investment banking must be attributed in large measure to a simple atrophy of functions. The potential field for investment banking has shrunk, and the business which is left is being carried on to an increasing extent by new methods and by new agencies better suited to the task.

One further question must be raised, though to answer it satisfactorily within the compass of a short article would manifestly be impossible. Who has fallen heir to the leadership and power which once resided in the investment banker?

In one sense, it is clearly too soon to be able to answer this question with anything approaching finality. J. P. Morgan & Co. still exercises an enormous power which was *acquired* in investment banking, though the firm itself no longer operates in the field. It is probably even true to say that J. P. Morgan & Co. is still the focal point of the greatest economic power in American society; and this situation will doubtless persist until the older generation of businessmen, who now occupy most of the positions of authority, passes from the scene. Relationships which have been established over a long period of time do not simply disappear when the factors which were responsible for them are suddenly removed. Nevertheless, it is not impossible to discern some of the outlines of the situation which is shaping up for the future.

In the first place, it is clear that the expansion of the economic functions of government will place an increasingly large share of economic power and responsibility in the hands of those who control the state. In other words, we are moving in the direction of state capitalism, which may be defined as a society which is entirely capitalist in its class structure but in which there is a high degree of political centralization of economic power. Needlesss to say, certain other countries, notably Germany, Italy, and Japan, have already gone further along this road than we have. Also needless to say, there could be no more serious error than mistaking this for a trend toward socialism, though it does undeniably prepare the way for socialism in certain important respects.

Secondly, within the business community itself two tendencies are apparent. On the one hand, there has been a consolidation and extension of the scope of industrial empires based on family ownership and control of key corporations and banks. Family control is frequently buttressed by such relatively new devices as trust funds and endowed institutions for educational, scientific, or charitable purposes. In this connection the recent revelation by the Temporary National Economic Committee that thirteen families own $2,700,000,000 worth of stock in the country's 200 largest nonfinancial corporations is significant, though it is a long way from telling the whole story. It is in a sense ironical that the family, which once was the basic unit for all economic activity and the guarantee of some degree of economic equality and security, has lost most of its pristine economic functions and acquired one new one, namely, that of fostering and consolidating the inequality of economic power. This whole subject needs much more study than has yet been devoted to it. The second tendency within the business community is less clear, but it appears that there is developing a more or less stabilized, and hence closed and self-perpetuating, group of corporate executives (including bank and insurance company executives) which is to an increasing degree engrossing the key positions in those corporations which are owned not by particular family groups, but rather by the capitalist class at large. This incidentally seems to be what is meant by the "democratization of ownership" which we have heard so much about in the last twenty years or so.

So far as the location of private economic power is concerned it is clear that both of the tendencies noted point in the direction of a merger of financial and industrial interests. The dominance of financial over industrial capital, which for a while was widely interpreted as a more or less permanent state of affairs, is thus seen to have been a temporary stage of capitalist development, a stage which was characterized above all else by the *process* of forming trusts, combinations, and huge corporations. It was this process itself which thrust the financier forward, and now that it has been substantially completed the latter ceases to play a *special* role in the economic life of the country. In general terms the decline of investment banking is merely the outward manifestation of an inevitable adjustment.

A more difficult problem concerns the relation of the trend to state capitalism on the one hand and the tendencies in progress within the business community on the other. It has been generally held, and particularly among businessmen, that we have to do here with a fundamental conflict. This idea, however, is certainly an illusion which has its origins in the rather special circumstances surrounding the New Deal. The severity of the depression of 1929-1933 shook the structure of the American economy to its very foundations; a policy of reform and concessions, involving greatly increased government activity in the economic sphere, became the only possible way of saving the system itself. The carrying through of this policy, necessarily under progressive and at times even radical slogans, created a split in the capitalist class. In perspective, however, it is now possible to see clearly that this split was of a temporary character. The advance to a new period of greatly intensified imperialist conflict and threat to the capitalist system on a world scale quickly closed the breach. "Reform" has given way to "defense"; the policy of concessions has been scrapped; and the representatives of Big Business have been called in to take charge of the government's economic functions. Private economic power and public economic power are now rapidly being concentrated in the same group. It is probably safe to assume that this state of affairs will continue to obtain for some time to come. It may even be that it will prove to be as durable as the capitalist system itself.

14

Critics and Crusaders

This review of Charles Madison's Critics and Crusaders: A Century of American Protest *(New York, 1947) appeared in* The American Economic Review, *December 1947.*

AT A TIME of anti-radical hysteria like the present, this book comes as a welcome reminder of America's proud tradition of nonconformity and protest. Mr. Madison, an editor by profession and apparently an historian by predilection, writes with enthusiasm and at times with eloquence about a representative collection of American radicals all of whom, despite great diversity, obviously excite his admiration and sympathy.

The book is divided into six parts: The Abolitionists, The Utopians, The Anarchists, The Dissident Economists, The Militant Liberals, and The Socialists. Each part is divided into four chapters, one devoted to the background and one each to three individuals. As can be readily seen, this scheme is formal and rigid; it permits hardly any consideration of the developing pattern of American radicalism as a whole, and it inevitably conveys the impression that the various groups and individuals treated by Madison are all of approximately equal importance. On the other hand, it has the advantage that any one part — or for that matter any one chapter — can profitably be read separately; the work is, in fact, a collection of two dozen largely independent essays. This fact will no doubt make it more generally useful for teaching purposes. At the same time, however, a reviewer has the right to complain that it makes a coherent review of the book as a whole virtually impossible.

The quality of the various essays is by no means even. There are a number which have little more to them than an article in the magazine section of a Sunday newspaper; still others are written in the rococo style of a freshman theme. The chapter on Albert Brisbane falls in the former category, that on Margaret Fuller in the latter. On the other hand, Madison has painted several memorable portraits which combine sympathetic insight with careful analysis. The best of these, I think, is Altgeld; though Steffens and Debs are not far behind. One is inclined to assume that Madison's real interests lie in the social movements of relatively recent times and that much of the earlier material was included because the plan of the book called for it. This impression is strengthened by the various "Background" essays which tend to be somewhat perfunctory in the earlier parts but which become both considerably longer and very much more substantial in the last two parts. "The Socialist Background" is, I think, as good as anything that has been written on the subject, which unfortunately is not very much. One can easily find minor errors in it, and Madison's interpretations will not always command full assent; but it is comprehensive, accurate in its main outlines, and eminently fair to all parties and individuals concerned.

There are at least two cases in which Madison's classification of his subjects seems open to question. On his own showing, it is hard to see why Margaret Fuller should be put in with the Utopians, though perhaps there are good reasons which he does not adduce. On the other hand, early American history is so rich in Utopians that it should have been easy to find at least a half dozen about whom no question could be raised. More serious, I think, is the classification of Lincoln Steffens as a "militant liberal." On the basis of my own reading of the *Autobiography*, I would say that Steffens was neither militant nor a liberal. He was much too inquisitive, experimental, and tolerant to be militant; and he utterly lacked what I should call the *differentia specifica* of the liberal, namely, the belief that a free market in ideas will ultimately produce the good society. What liberal would say, as Steffens did: "The reformation of politics and business by propaganda and political action was impossible. Nothing but revolution could change the system." (P. 406.) Though he apparently never belonged to a Socialist or Communist organization, there can be little doubt that, at least in the years after World War I, Steffens was much more of a socialist than a liberal.

Readers of *The American Economic Review* will perhaps be most interested in the part dealing with the "Dissident Economists": Henry George, Brooks Adams, and Veblen. On the whole, however, these are not among the best essays of the book. Madison has been somewhat too ready to accept the judgment of Henry George's disciples: George's criticism of existing social conditions was unquestionably brilliant and incisive, but he was a long way from being one of "the pre-eminent social thinkers of our time." The summary of the life and work of Brooks Adams is useful, and it makes one realize that the economic theories of this (relatively) early critic of American imperialism have received much less attention than they deserve. Now that the United States has embarked on a course that bids fair to put all previous imperialisms in the shade, it is possible that American economists will examine the whole problem more attentively than they have been accustomed to do in the past. If so, they will find Madison's introduction to Brooks Adams a valuable stimulant to further study. Madison's treatment of Veblen, on the other hand, is less useful if only because Veblen's work is widely known and he has already been the subject of several careful and illuminating studies. This is not to imply that the last word on Veblen has been said, only that the picture which Madison paints of Veblen is already a fairly familiar one.

As noted above, the essay on Altgeld is perhaps the best in the book. Madison obviously feels close to the great Illinois democrat, and he is able to write about him with warmth and understanding. But what struck me most forcibly in reading this essay was the many remarkable similarities in philosophy and political approach between Altgeld's conception of democracy and Franklin D. Roosevelt's New Deal. One could wish that Madison had seen fit to omit Randolph Bourne from the category of "Militant Liberals" — especially since he has a doubtful claim to be there — and to include Franklin D. Roosevelt instead. And I would suggest at the same time that Lincoln Steffens might better be moved in with the socialists to make way for La Follette senior. Altgeld, La Follette, and Roosevelt are three genuine militant liberals, and it would be highly interesting to have them treated together by so sympathetic an observer as Madison.

This is the kind of book which ranges over a rather wide field and is hence likely to meet with the sharp criticism of specialists who have a vested interest in this or that corner of the field. In fact, at least one carping review by a professional American historian has already appeared in print, and others may be confidently expected. In my opinion, however, it is really irrelevant that the book contains a certain number of errors and occasionally indulges in generalizations which offend the conscience of the scholar. The book is written for the intelligent layman — and most economists whom I know can hardly claim to be more in the premises — and it is meant to bring to the fore in a readable and generally correct way certain ingredients of the American tradition which are all too easily lost sight of. I think it succeeds in this aim, and I hope it will be as widely read as I am sure it deserves to be. I especially recommend it as salutary reading to those who are afraid to say what they think because of loyalty orders and Un-American Activities Committees; they may well gain courage by reflecting on how the eighteen Americans brought to life again by Madison would have acted under similar circumstances.

15

Socialist Humanitarianism

This is a review of *Writings and Speeches of Eugene V. Debs,* with an introduction by Arthur M. Schlesinger, Jr. (New York, 1948). It appeared in *The Journal of Political Economy,* December 1948.

THIS is a useful selection from the works of Eugene V. Debs, America's most famous socialist figure.

The book opens with a proclamation to the American Railway Union, issued when the Supreme Court upheld a jail sentence against Debs for having defied an injunction during the great railroad strike of 1894. It closes with selections from *Walls and Bars,* a book written by Debs after he had served three years in a federal penitentiary for opposing participation by the United States in World War I. The intervening pieces — more than seventy in number — are all concerned in one way or another with Debs's unremitting struggle for the industrial and political organization of the American working class.

In the years since his death in 1926, Debs has become something of a legend; and nowadays it is fashionable for writers of all shades of political opinion to eulogize him as a great and noble humanitarian. There is a strong tendency to forget, or to hide, the fact that, just because he was a great and noble humanitarian, he was also an uncompromising revolutionist. There is hardly an article or speech in this entire collection which does not reveal the inseparable connection which existed in Debs's mind between love of humanity and hatred of capitalism. In reading what he actually wrote and said, one cannot avoid the conclusion that if Debs were alive today most of those who now praise him would be reviling him as the most un-American of un-Americans. And one also cannot avoid the conclusion that he would scorn their praise and welcome their abuse.

The articles and speeches in this volume are arranged chronologically and cover a wide range of specific subjects. They reveal Debs as more orator than writer, more agitator (in the best meaning of the term) than theorist. He was a good Marxist in the sense that millions of class-conscious workers throughout the world are good Marxists, but his conception of capitalism was too simple to permit him to come to grips with many of the peculiar problems of American society. Debs is more important as a part of American history than as a commentator on American history.

To say this, however, is in no way to detract from the significance of Debs's works, for he represents an aspect of our national development which the accredited historians are too prone to neglect. It is indeed refreshing in these days of fear and hysteria to read the articles and speeches of an American who said exactly what he thought no matter how unpopular his views, never retreated an inch under pressure, and preferred jail to any compromise on questions of principle. To Debs, John Brown was "history's greatest hero" who "set an example of moral courage and of single-hearted devotion to an ideal for all men and for all ages." (P. 280.) The example was one which Debs himself lived up to with complete success. One likes to think that America has a genius for producing John Browns and Gene Debses. Let us hope that there will be many more in the years ahead.

The introduction by A. M. Schlesinger, Jr., is a slight affair which adds nothing to what is generally known about Debs and is chiefly remarkable for its attempt to portray Debs as holding firmly to what Schlesinger calls "democratic traditions of change through debate and consent." Quite apart from the obvious fact that American democratic traditions are as revolutionary as those of any country, the implication of Schlesinger's evaluation is grossly unfair to Debs. Like all great socialist leaders, he was of course opposed to the use of force and violence; indeed, it was this opposition which more than anything else motivated his deep hatred of capitalism. For Debs believed — and repeatedly stated his belief — that capitalists would stop at nothing to preserve their privileges in a society which could not exist without the continual use of force and violence. It followed that workers would be justified in using any method which would enable them to overthrow this system and substitute a classless society. (See especially the article on "Sound Socialist Tactics," pages 350-357, where this argument is developed in the most explicit terms.) In practice, Debs was convinced that the use of violence by workers would hurt rather than help their cause; but he made specific allowance for "acute situations" and "grave emergencies" in which this might not be so. Furthermore, he refused time and again to condemn the use of violence — however misguided it might be — by workers in their struggle against their oppressors. (In this connection, see particularly the eloquent article on "The McNamara Case and the Labor Movement," pages 343-350.) When Schlesinger dismisses all this with a breezy reference to "the violence of his Socialist rhetoric," he merely demonstrates his incapacity to understand either Debs or the roots of the modern socialist movement.

It is a serious weakness of this volume that there is no explanation by the (unnamed) editor as to how the included material was selected. For all the reader knows, the book may contain nearly all the published articles and speeches of Debs; or it may contain only a small fraction of them. What was excluded and why? In particular, why is there so little from the postwar period? Without knowing the answers to these questions, one can hardly draw conclusions about many aspects of Debs's thought on the basis of the materials in this volume.

16

An Economic Program for America

This essay was written for Welfare State, *the 1950 edition of the National University Extension Association's annual Debate Handbook. It was reprinted in 1951 as part of a Monthly Review Pamphlet entitled "Socialism Is the Only Answer."*

I AM going to plead a case which is unpopular in our country and probably will remain so for some time to come. Socialism is a bogy with which you frighten little children, and no one who wants to get ahead in the world can be suspected of having the least sympathy with it. But this is no excuse for ignorance, and I ask the reader's attention not because I expect to convince him but because I think he owes it to himself to learn the reasons and the arguments which could persuade at least one person to embrace the horrid doctrine. In addition, I think a look at history may convince him that socialism has more of a future, even in the United States, than its opponents would be willing to admit. Is it not true that the heterodoxies of today have ever been the orthodoxies of tomorrow?

I

The American economic system is called capitalism. It is a system in which most of the means of production — the factories and farms, the mines and forests, the railroads and ships — are owned by a relatively few capitalists and operated for their profit. Most of the rest of us work for wages — if and when the capitalists will hire us.

Now the power and prestige of a capitalist are, generally speaking, in proportion to his wealth, and it follows that his main object in life is and must be to get richer than he is. He therefore operates his business in such a way as to make the greatest possible profit, and he takes a good part of that profit and adds it to his capital. The process goes on and on; there is no end to it. With all the capitalists doing the same thing, the natural result is that all their businesses, which is another way of saying the total social means of production, tend to expand at the same time and without limit.

But it is obvious that society's capacity to produce cannot be expanded indefinitely and without reference to the size of the final market for consumer goods. Sooner or later the result is bound to be "overproduction" — piling up of unsold goods in the hands of retailers and wholesalers, collapse of prices, shrinkage or disappearance of profits, and finally a stagnation of production coupled with heavy unemployment. After a while, stocks will be sold off, durable consumer goods (like automobiles and refrigerators) will wear out, and factories will begin to need new machinery to keep up even a low level of production. Then things pick up again, and the merry chase for more profits and more capital is resumed.

That's the way the system works. It's a system of booms and busts — not by accident or because of some superficial defect, but by its very nature. Moreover, the more advanced a capitalist country is, that is to say, the more highly developed its productive resources and the richer its capitalists, the weaker will be the booms and the more devastating the busts.

The United States is the most advanced capitalist country in the world. Its major problem is how to keep bust, or in other words low production and high unemployment, from being the normal state of the national economy.

During the 1930s it *was* the normal state of the national economy. Despite strenuous efforts on the part of the federal government (efforts which included extraordinary expenditures for doles, work relief, and public works), the period was one of continuing and massive unemployment. No one knows how many were unemployed at the bottom of the depression in 1932-1933, but the figure was certainly more than fifteen million; and in only one year (1937) did unemployment fall below ten million.

World War II saved American capitalism. It put everyone to work and doubled productive capacity and brought undreamed-of wealth to the big corporations and capitalists.

Many people, including some very able economists, predicted that soon after the war was over there would be another bust and the old problem of the thirties would be back with us again. It has not worked out that way, however. The reason is not that the capitalist system has changed its nature but that cold war has taken the place of the hot war as the dominant factor in the American economy. Cold war is not as expensive as hot war, and it does not keep the productive machine going at the same breakneck speed. But the $20 billion a year which are currently being spent on arms and on foreign aid programs have so far been enough to hold off the bust and to keep unemployment from going much above the five-million mark.

The result is that the whole capitalist class now has a vested interest in keeping the Cold War going — and in warming it up and making it more expensive if necessary. And the capitalists have the means to keep it going, too. They control the press, the radio and television, the movies, schools and colleges; their representatives sit in the halls of Congress and in the key positions in the State and Defense Departments. They systematically spread stories of impending Russian aggression, of Communist spies, and of subversive plots to overthrow the United States government. They whip up mass hysteria which provides the proper atmosphere of intolerance, bigotry, and bellicosity in which the Cold War, with all its blessings to American capitalism, can be fought to the limit.

This is not the place to discuss American foreign policy or to examine the reality behind the "Russian menace"; but one thing is sure, and that is that if we are ever to bring the Cold War to an end, if we are ever to establish a world in which we can live in peace and security, we must reform the American economy so that prosperity is no longer completely dependent on war or war preparations.

That is the Number 1 problem of an economic program for America.

There are many other problems, some closely related to the Number 1 problem, some overlapping it, some relatively independent. It is obviously impossible, in a brief essay, to discuss them all. I shall therefore limit attention to the few that seem to me to be most important and that everyone must surely agree are of major national concern.

(2) How to achieve a fairer and saner distribution of income.

(3) How to provide for the welfare and security of the aged, the sick, and all others who, for whatever reason, are unable to provide for their own livelihood.

(4) How to eliminate the overbearing power of private monopoly to exploit the worker, the consumer, and the farmer.

(5) How to conserve and husband our natural resources.

(6) How to eliminate the enormous waste entailed in our present system of production and distribution (for example, the employment of brains, manpower, and resources in the wholly wasteful business of competitive advertising and salesmanship) and to realize the full potentialities of modern science and technology for the benefit not only of the American people but also of other countries which are economically and technically less advanced.

I am convinced that not a single one of these problems can be satisfactorily solved within the framework of a capitalist economy. On the other hand, their solution flows easily and naturally from the adoption of one master reform: the socialization of the means of production (except those which are actually used by their owners) with its inevitable corollary, the introduction of overall economic planning.

II

A socialized and planned economy — in other words, the economic system which is known as socialism — functions according to principles and laws which are very different from those which govern a capitalist system. The individual productive and trading units are not operated with a view to the maximization of profit; their aim is to fulfill the tasks which are prescribed for them in the national economic plan. Under capitalism an industrialist is successful in proportion to the amount of money he makes for himself or for the stockholders he represents; under socialism he is successful to the degree that the plant which has been entrusted to his management carries out the tasks which society assigns to it through the medium of the plan.

This is a crucial difference. It means that the basic tendency of capitalism which we already noticed, that is to say, the tendency for society's aggregate means of production to expand without limit and without reference to the size of the final market for consumer goods, does not and cannot manifest itself under socialism. Under both systems, society's productive forces are (or at any rate can be) known with a reasonable degree of accuracy. The difference is that under capitalism the allocation of these resources — and especially the division between those that are to produce more means of production and those that are to produce consumer goods — is the outcome of millions of decisions of capitalists acting in their own interest and independently of each other; while under socialism the allocation of resources is planned in advance, to satisfy consciously felt social needs.

This is not to say that a socialist economy would never make any mistakes: that would be foolish. But it is to say that a socialist economy would always and as a matter of course strive to adjust the expansion of the means of production to the requirements of the people's rising consumption needs (including, of course, such collective needs as highways, education, and national defense). Mistakes would always take place within the framework of a planned and balanced economy and could always be rectified without the danger of precipitating a general depression. And as experience and skill in making and executing national economic plans grew, mistakes would naturally become less and less important.

What this means is that socialism *by its very nature* solves the central dilemma of a capitalist economy. There is simply no problem of boom and bust, of unemployment, of stagnant production under socialism. There is no need for a special program to eliminate the business cycle or to combat depressions. These economic disasters are specific products of capitalism, and only a capitalist system has to worry over what to do about them. It follows, of course, that prosperity under socialism could *never* be dependent on war or war preparations. In a planned economy, such activities would directly and obviously appear as what they are, the unfortunate and impoverishing diversion of resources from purposes of construction to purposes of destruction.

III

At this point, however, a fundamental question arises. The American people, it may be argued, are not ready for socialism. Must we not therefore devote our energies to solving the problem within the framework of capitalism? And have not the theorists of what has been called the "New Economics" — that is to say, the school founded by the late English economist, John Maynard Keynes — shown us how the problem can in fact be solved within the framework of capitalism?

In order to answer this question, we must indicate very

briefly the nature of the solution recommended by the Keynesians. Without entering into their underlying theories, we can perhaps best convey the nature of their reasoning by quoting a question which Stuart Chase says was asked of him during the war by a GI tank driver on his way to France: "Well, if the country can keep prosperous making tanks for men like us to die in, why can't it keep prosperous making houses for people to live in?"[1] The Keynesians answer that the country can do just that — with the understanding that in this context the term "houses" includes all sorts of constructive projects in the fields of education, welfare, resource conservation, public utilities, and even industry. Thus the Keynesians would say that if the economy is now being maintained in a satisfactory state of prosperity by roughly $20 billion of Cold War spending, it would likewise be kept in that state by $20 billion of what might be called Welfare State spending. Hence if America is now dependent on Cold War for its prosperity this is only because of a lack of understanding. Capitalism can be made to work well enough, according to this view, if the people and their representatives will only abandon old-fashioned economic orthodoxy and allow the government — through its borrowing and taxing policies on the one hand and its lending and spending policies on the other — to become the balance wheel of the economy in peacetime as well as in wartime.

The answer to the Keynesians does not lie in the realm of abstract economic theory. *If* an American capitalist government could spend $20 billion — and if necessary $30 billion or $40 billion — for peaceful, constructive purposes, then the Keynesians would doubtless be right. But the point is precisely that the ruling capitalist class, the very class whose enormous wealth and power is assured by the structure of capitalism itself, will never approve or permit spending on this scale (or anything even approaching this scale) for peaceful, constructive ends. Nor is this a matter of ig-

---

[1] "If Peace Breaks Out," *The Nation*, June 11, 1949, p. 656.

norance or stupidity. It is a plain matter of class interest, which, to the capitalist class (as to all ruling classes in history), appears to be the national interest and indeed the interest of civilization itself.

Take housing, for example. Why not a gigantic program to rebuild and rehouse America? Heaven knows, we need it badly enough! But everyone who has passed the age of ten knows the answer: the real estate interests. They will put up with a small amount of government housing, preferably in the field of slum clearance; but when it comes to anything big they say No, and they get the solid backing of all the propertied interests of the country.

Or take social security. Why not a real social security program? Here again, there is no lack of need.[2] But a real social security program would involve a considerable degree of income redistribution from rich to poor. And besides, capitalists do not *want* too much security — for others. It is bad for morale, dulls the incentive to work, leads to exaggerated expectations and pretensions. Capitalists believe — and not without reason — that their system requires enormous re-

---

[2] Since interested propaganda has sought to create the impression that we already have in this country a welfare state which takes care of the needs of its citizens, it may be salutary to quote a passage on this subject from President Truman's "Economic Report to Congress," dated January 6, 1950: "The present programs of social security are grossly inadequate. Because of the limited coverage of the present laws, and the exhaustion of benefits by many workers, one-third of the unemployed are now receiving no unemployment insurance benefits, and in some areas the proportion approaches two-thirds. Many communities provide no public funds for the relief of jobless workers and their families. There are also several million disabled workers, many with families to support, who are not eligible for public insurance benefits. In some places, they do not even receive public relief. Only 650,000 of the millions of bereaved or broken families with very low income are receiving survivors' insurance. Only 30 percent of the aged population are eligible for social insurance benefits, which are so meager that few can retire voluntarily. Needed medical care is denied to millions of our citizens because they have no access to systematic and adequate methods of meeting the cost." A fine welfare state!

wards at the top and poverty and insecurity at the bottom to keep it going. A real social security program contradicts both these requirements and will therefore always be opposed to the limit by the capitalist class.

Or take government investment in industry or public utilities or transportation. There is no end of useful projects which government could undertake at any given time — *if* it were free to compete with private enterprise. But of course government is not free to compete with private enterprise; in fact it is here that the resistance of the capitalists to the extension of government activities is at its maximum. They regard all branches of the economy that can be made to yield a profit as their own private preserve at the entrance to which they have posted a huge NO TRESPASSING sign. If anything seems certain it is that as long as we have capitalism we shall have very little government investment in the production of useful *and salable* goods and services.

And so it goes. To every form of peaceful, constructive government spending the capitalists have an objection: it redistributes income, or it increases the power and independence of the working class, or it competes with private enterprise. A New Deal government, enjoying overwhelming popular support, may be able to make some headway against these objections; but as long as the capitalists have the levers of economic power in their hands, they will be able to block, or if necessary sabotage, any program which would make the government the balance wheel in an expanding peace economy.

It is very different in the case of spending for military purposes. The flow of orders for armaments benefits the biggest capitalist monopolies; there is no competition with private enterprise; and the whole atmosphere of the Cold War — the witch hunts, the jingoism, the worship of force — creates the conditions in which the ruling class finds it easiest to control the ideas and the activities of the underlying population.

And so we must tell the "realists" who urge the necessity of working within the framework of capitalism that they are being hopelessly unrealistic. It is not possible to maintain a system that guarantees wealth and power to capitalists and at the same time to make it work in ways to which they are irrevocably opposed. If the American people are not ready for socialism — and it can hardly be denied that they are not — then the real realist will recognize that the most urgent task of our time is to get them ready.

IV

So much for our Number 1 problem. Let us now turn very briefly to the other problems on our list. We shall find in each case (a) that they are insoluble under capitalism, and (b) that there are no inherent obstacles to their rational solution under socialism.

INCOME DISTRIBUTION. The real reason for the grossly unequal and unfair distribution of income in America today is private ownership of the means of production. About two thirds of our national income is paid out in the form of wages and salaries and about one third in the form of profit, interest, and rent. Most of this latter one third goes to a relatively very small proportion of the population, and it is this fact that gives the distribution of income as a whole its characteristic shape.[3]

The experience of Great Britain strongly suggests that

---

[3] Statisticians have devised an index of inequality which would stand at zero in case of perfect equality (that is, if everyone's income were the same) and at 1 in case of perfect inequality (that is, if one individual had all the income and everyone else had nothing). Thus the lower the index the greater the equality, and the higher the index the greater the inequality. Calculations based on 1945 federal income tax returns show that wages and salaries (with an index of .38) are much more equally distributed than business and partnership income (.68) on the one hand and than interest and dividend income (.82) on the other. Selma F. Goldsmith, "Statistical Information on the Distribution of Income by Size in the United States," *Papers and Proceedings of the 62nd Annual Meeting of the American Economic Association*, 1949, p. 327.

this situation cannot be fundamentally changed within the framework of a capitalist economy.[4] It seems to be pretty generally agreed that the Labor government in Britain has gone about as far as it is possible to go in the direction of taxing the rich while still maintaining a private-enterprise economy. But even so, as the following table shows, the fundamental distribution of income between labor and property has not changed very drastically since 1938 and does not differ greatly from the ratio of two thirds to one third which obtains in the United States.

PERCENTAGE DISTRIBUTION OF INCOME IN THE
UNITED KINGDOM, 1938 AND 1948*

	Before Taxes		After Direct Taxes		After All Taxes	
	1938	1948	1938	1948	1938	1948
Labor	61	60	64	65	63	63
Property	38	38	34	32	35	34
Armed Forces	1	2	2	3	2	3
Total	100	100	100	100	100	100

* Computed from figures given in the official White Paper on *National Income and Expenditure of the United Kingdom, 1946-1948* (Cmd. 7649).

Socialism, of course, solves this problem automatically by doing away with private property in the means of production

[4] Contrary to a widely held belief, Britain today is still a capitalist country. At the present time about six sevenths of all employment in the United Kingdom, excluding only the normal functions of government, is in private firms, and only about one seventh in socialized firms. See my *Socialism* (New York, 1949), pp. 45-47. It is true that the Labor government has actively and extensively intervened in the British economy in the last five years, but it has done so in response to immediate problems and emergencies, not in accordance with an overall plan. We must always remember that — as an anonymous British writer has put it — "making life difficult for capitalism is not the same thing, by any means, as transforming it into socialism." "British Labor and Socialism," *Monthly Review*, September 1949, p. 143.

and placing at the disposal of society as a whole the income (as we have seen, roughly one third of the total) which now goes to the relatively small class of capitalists.

SOCIAL SECURITY. Not much needs to be added on this subject to what has already been said above. As long as capitalists have the power they will use it to oppose the building up of a really adequate social security system. This does not mean, however, that nothing can be accomplished under capitalism. Unsatisfactory as our present social security system is, it is nevertheless much better than what we had twenty years ago; and the experience of other capitalist countries — chief among them the Scandinavian countries, New Zealand, Australia, and Britain — proves that much more can be done in this line than the major American political parties have yet been willing even to consider. Hence all liberals and radicals will as a matter of course consistently press for improvements in our social security system. But this does not in any way change our conclusion that progress will ultimately require the effective elimination of the capitalists' power to oppose and obstruct.

MONOPOLY. Almost everyone agrees that the monopoly problem arises from two closely interrelated causes: large-scale production, and the combination of many productive units under unified corporate managements. Big production units and even bigger management units have long since become the characteristic feature of the industries which dominate American economic life. Almost everyone — except, no doubt, the big businessmen themselves — also agrees that something should be done about the monopoly problem, that the degree of concentration which now exists is both economically and politically dangerous.[5]

---

[5] This view has been repeatedly stressed before the latest Congressional monopoly investigation, which is still in progress at the time of writing. Four volumes of hearings have so far been published under the general title, *Study of Monopoly Power*. The investigation got under way in the summer of 1949; it is being conducted by a subcommittee of the House Judiciary Committee under the chairmanship of Representative Emmanuel Celler of New York.

One common proposal is that the antitrust laws should be more vigorously enforced. But this is precisely what has been happening in recent years. Herbert A. Bergson, chief of the Antitrust Division of the Department of Justice, told the Celler Committee that

> more cases have been instituted in the last 10 years than in the entire 50 years before that. Our record of wins against losses in the courts has been most impressive. Nor do the court cases tell the whole story. Approximately 25 percent of our cases result in consent judgments, in which relief against illegal practices is obtained without the necessity of going to trial. Finally . . . the mere existence of the antitrust laws, coupled with the knowledge that violations will be punished, has a tremendous influence in keeping our economy democratic and competitive.[6]

And yet despite all this activity and these many victories, witness after witness testified to the growth of monopoly in the last ten years. The inference is plain, that the antitrust laws are powerless to deal with the situation. And it follows that to advocate relying on them is merely another way of opposing any effective action on the monopoly problem.

A second approach to the monopoly problem would establish regulatory commissions, on the model of the Interstate Commerce Commission and the various state public utility commissions, to control the activities of the large concentrated industries. There are, however, many and compelling objections to this proposal. Commission regulation has proved itself to be unwieldy and inefficient; it spawns red tape and bureaucracy in the worst sense of the terms; and the commissions always end by becoming the friend and backer of the private industries they are supposed to regulate rather than the protector of the public interest.[7] Regulatory com-

---

[6] *Study of Monopoly Power*, Part 1, p. 381.

[7] Note the following statement of former Governor Ellis Arnall of Georgia to the Celler Committee: ". . . since those regulatory bodies dealt only really with the people they regulated, through the course of years, since politics cost money at the state level where they run for

missions are no more effective than antitrust laws as a method of dealing with the monopoly problem, and they are likely to do a great deal more harm.

Finally, it is often urged that the solution of the monopoly problem is to be found in a new approach which would enforce competition through putting a limit on the size of firms. Those who advocate this method, however, are obliged to admit that the proposed maximum size would have to be different in different industries. Hence it would be necessary to establish a commission to determine the permissible limit in each industry; and after the commission had made its findings each case would have to go through the courts. This would be merely an extension of traditional antitrust procedure. It could be expected to lead to endless litigation, weighty pronouncements by the Supreme Court, perhaps a few highly publicized splitting-up actions — and for the rest a more secure tenure for monopoly because some of the pressure "to do something about it" would have been removed. But even if this method would work, it would be highly objectionable. Big Business, on the whole, is efficiently and expertly conducted. To attempt to solve the monopoly problem by pulverizing Big Business would be like throwing out the baby with the bath.

The trouble with Big Business under capitalism is not that it is big but that it is private and socially irresponsible. The remedy for that is obvious: make it public and socially responsible.

NATURAL RESOURCES. There is writ large in the annals of American history the lesson that private enterprise is wasteful and destructive of natural resources, that government regulation is at best negatively effective, and that social

---

reelection and at the federal level where pressures are not unknown, very soon we find ourselves with an amazing situation whereby many of these regulatory bodies . . . exist not to protect the public, but to stand as a bulwark against the public to protect the people they regulate." *Ibid.*, Part 1, p. 208.

ownership and planning are not only effective but yield positive results out of all proportion to the costs involved. The case of timber will serve to illustrate the comparison. The ruthless cutting-over of our forests by private capitalists had to be stopped by government action; but only where far-reaching government ownership and planning have been instituted — most notably in the case of the TVA — has it been possible to evolve a rational forestry policy as part of a comprehensive program of conserving and developing our natural resources.

Another industry, coal mining, underscores the point. Coal is a sick industry, losing its markets to competing fuels, throwing out of work more and more miners who find it practically impossible to move into other occupations, and beset by periodic labor disputes which each time threaten the economic life of the country. This is a problem which private enterprise and government regulation alike are powerless to cope with. It requires for its solution much more radical action: nothing less than the scrapping of private enterprise — not only in coal but also in oil and natural gas and all the other fuels which provide the lifeblood of modern industrial society — and the substitution of social enterprise operating in accordance with a long-run plan of conservation and development.

THE WASTEFULNESS OF CAPITALISM. The real wastefulness of capitalism certainly does not lie in the organization of its big corporations, as many well-meaning reformers seem to believe; nor, in the final analysis, even in its undoubted prodigality with our heritage of natural resources. It lies rather in the structure and functioning of the system as a whole — in the making of exquisite luxuries for a few while millions are condemned to misery and poverty; in misdirecting brains and energy and resources into the insanities of competitive salesmanship; in the foregone production and the blighted lives of depression; in the destruction and slaughter of wars to divide and redivide the world; and now in the monstrous waste of a Cold War to preserve the *status quo* at home and abroad.

In its day, capitalism was a progressive system. It created the productive forces which have completely revolutionized the world we live in. Its big corporations are in many ways models of rational and efficient organization. But capitalism does not know how to utilize constructively what it has created. If we are to enjoy the benefits of modern science and technology, if we are really to help others and not merely exploit them under the pretense of helping them, we must get rid of this blind, socially wasteful, destructive system, and we must put in its place a system which permits rational intelligence and common sense to play a role not only in the lives of individuals but also in the life of society as a whole.

Part IV

German Capitalism

17

The German Problem

In form, this article, which appeared in *Monthly Review*, June 1949, may seem dated. It was written as a commentary on the situation which existed immediately after the lifting of the Berlin blockade. The substance of the article, however, has a more enduring interest, both as regards Germany and as regards the policies of the Great Powers toward Germany. For Germany is once again coming to the fore as the central problem of a European peace settlement, and I think it is no exaggeration to say that all the main points I stressed on a similar occasion four years ago are equally relevant today.

AS I WRITE these lines, the Berlin blockade has been lifted and the foreign ministers of the Big Four are about to resume discussion of the German problem after an interval of nearly a year and a half. It is clear that these events initiate a new phase of postwar international relations, one in which the Soviet Union, undoubtedly genuinely alarmed by the recent rapid drift toward war, is prepared to make concessions in order to reduce tensions and avert the threatening catastrophe of World War III.

This development is, of course, to be welcomed. Everyone who retains an elementary sense of responsibility knows that the preservation of peace is of paramount importance and that the idea that international or social problems can be solved by war is an evil fallacy. We need and must have what the diplomats call a *détente* between East and West, and under present conditions it can come only through genuine concessions by both sides. The lifting of the blockade and the calling of the foreign ministers' conference are essential first steps.

What is "the German problem"? It is not a new problem, nor is it a very old problem. Before the last third of the nineteenth century there were a number of German problems; *the* German problem as we know it today emerged only after the unification of the Reich under Prussian leadership in the 1860s and 1870s. What are the main elements of the German problem in this latter-day sense of the term?

Basically, the German problem can be summed up in a brief phrase: viciously aggressive imperialism. All capitalist countries without exception are inherently expansionist and hence potentially aggressive, but special historical conditions have combined to make Germany into an extreme case. (In this respect, incidentally, Japan resembles Germany very closely.) Let us quickly review the most important of these special conditions.

First, national disunity prevented Germany from playing a pioneer role in the development of industrial capitalism. This relative economic backwardness had very important political consequences. As the events of 1848 proved, the German middle class was too weak to overthrow feudalism and establish a bourgeois democracy. National unity was finally established not by the bourgeoisie, as had been the case in other Western countries, but by the Prussian Junkers under the astute political leadership of Bismarck. At that time there existed a liberal-democratic opposition of considerable strength, but the rapid economic development and huge profits which followed the achievement of national unity soon convinced the German capitalists that the Junker world in which they lived was the best of all possible worlds. Liberalism has never since been a serious force in German political life, and the ruling alliance of Junkers and capitalists has combined the most reactionary and militaristic features of feudalism with the economic strength and expansionism of a highly dynamic capitalism. This is the root of the German problem.

The fact that capitalism developed in Germany at a relatively late stage had further important consequences. As Veblen so often pointed out, it meant that German industry could, so to speak, start from scratch with an already highly developed technology. This was the underlying factor in the extremely rapid growth of monopoly in Germany. In addition, Germany as a latecomer found the most desirable colonial areas, which yield such a rich harvest of raw materials and surplus value, already pre-empted by the older imperialist powers. Monopoly greatly intensified the expansionism inherent in German capitalism, while the lack of suitable "colonial space" transformed this drive into a kind of aggressivism which has long been a standing threat to all Germany's neighbors.

Finally, the character and role of the German working-class movement have been significantly shaped by the conditions surrounding the development of German capitalism, though in this respect the experience of Germany has been more or less similar to that of the other Western imperialist countries. For roughly half a century, from the 1840s to the 1890s, the German working class, forced to fight an independent battle for elementary economic and political rights, led the whole world, both theoretically and organizationally, in building the international socialist movement. Karl Marx and Friedrich Engels, the founders of scientific socialism, were Germans; and the German Social Democratic Party was the first example in the world of a great mass party of workers. For a long time the rulers of Germany attempted to suppress the socialist movement; but failure, coming simultaneously with the great upswing of capitalism in the 1880s and 1890s, brought about a change in strategy. During the quarter century preceding World War I, an attempt was made, by means of economic and political concessions, to reconcile the workers to the existing system and to identify the interests of the trade union and party leadership with the interests of German imperialism. This new strategy was on the whole successful, and when the old order seemed to be in a state of complete collapse, following World War I, it was the Social Democratic leadership which came to the rescue and which alone commanded the mass support necessary to head off a genuine socialist revolution.

The German problem, then, may be described as hopped-up imperialism, minus effective liberal opposition, plus support from working-class leadership at times of critical danger. It has been, without question, the most serious problem of the first half of the twentieth century — a major factor in one world war and virtually the sole cause of another. If it is not solved by a fundamental alteration in the structure of German society — and this is the only way it can be solved — it will live on to plague the second half of the twentieth century and very possibly to produce another and still more terrible world war.

I have said, and I repeat, that the German problem can be solved only by a fundamental alteration in the structure of German society. There is no mystery about the nature of the required changes; they have been spelled out time and again by generations of socialists both inside and outside of Germany. The roots of aggressive imperialism are the great privately owned, profit-hungry trusts and cartels which have long controlled German economic life and which under the Nazi regime acquired a dominating position in nearly every branch of the state apparatus. These roots must be torn up and utterly destroyed. Private ownership of trusts and cartels must be abolished, and the means of production over which they dispose must become public property to be utilized in accordance with a comprehensive plan which has as its goals: first, the building of a decent and secure life for the masses of the German people, and second, for some years to come, the provision of a measure of reparation and restitution to the victims of former German aggression. In short, the German economy must be socialized and German productive power must be utilized to bring life to the common people of Europe, not profits to a few exploiters and ultimately ruin and death to their victims.

Measured by these standards, the occupation policies of the Western powers — which are at bottom the policies of the United States government — have been a failure. There has been no socialization of industry, no land reform worthy of the name. Even a milk-and-water antitrust program, which was proclaimed at the outset of the occupation with much fanfare, has remained a dead letter. Private business has been largely freed of controls. Wages have been kept at low levels — according to *Barron's* of May 9, the average weekly manufacturing wage in Germany last summer was $16, compared to $26 in Britain and $54 in the United States. Profits have zoomed upward, and, by the early months of 1949, production in the three western zones combined had climbed to four fifths of the 1938 level. The policy, vigorously pushed at the outset, of denazifying the personnel of government and business has ironically turned into a policy of removing the Nazi stigma from former stalwarts of the Hitler regime. Says John Herz, former State Department official now teaching at Howard University, in an article entitled "The Fiasco of Denazification in Germany":

A detailed analysis of available facts and figures reveals . . . that denazification [in the western zones], which began with a bang, has since died with a whimper, that it opened the way toward renewed control of German public, social, economic and cultural life by forces which only partially and temporarily had been deprived of the influence they had exerted under the Nazi regime. (*Political Science Quarterly*, December 1948, p. 569.)

The overall picture in the western zones is thus crystal clear. It can be summed up very simply in one phrase: return, so far as conditions permit, to the *status quo ante*. And the implications are no less clear: revival, sooner or later, of aggressive German imperialism.

The record in the Soviet zone of occupation has been better. (In order to avoid misunderstanding, we emphasize that we are judging by standards which relate to the degree of fundamental change in the German social structure, not by the level of industrial production or the extent to which German politicians are free to resume business at the old stand.) Unfortunately, comprehensive and detailed information is not available, but enough is known to give a clear view of the outlines of Soviet policy. Big business has been socialized (turned over to the provincial governments pending establishment of a zonal or national government). Large agricultural estates have been divided up, and in this way the traditional East Elbian Junker aristocracy has been deprived of its economic base. Workers' organizations have been given a more important role in administration at all levels. Planning for community ends has, to a considerable extent, been substituted for profit-making as the guiding principle of production and distribution. And — considering Germany's past, a point of no small importance — a new educational system has been introduced which opens the ladder of advancement to children of working-class and peasant families.

Of course, the Soviet zone is no paradise. The Russians have removed a considerable amount of capital equipment, and they continue to tap current production on reparations account. Eastern Germany, cut off from its natural ties with the rest of the country, would limp economically even under much more favorable conditions than have existed in Europe since the war. There is doubtless plenty of opposition from Germans who have been trained for generations to regard themselves as superior beings and to look upon the old way as the best way. Nevertheless, when all is said, it remains true that the Soviet occupation has resulted in basic economic and social changes which really strike at the roots of aggressive imperialism.

There can be no doubt whatever that the only kind of

settlement which would really solve the German problem would be unification of the country coupled with the generalization and completion of the kind of structural reforms which have already been instituted in the Soviet zone. There is no reason to suppose that the Russians would not welcome such a settlement, and the British Labor government certainly ought to if it takes its socialist declarations seriously. But, unfortunately, the policies of the three Western powers are rigidly controlled by the State Department, and there is little chance of a reversal of the American policy of restoring the old order in Germany.

Under these circumstances we may well wonder whether there is any hope at all of a settlement, or even whether a settlement would be worth the price which clearly would have to be paid for it. Can the Soviet Union afford, even for the sake of an agreement with the United States and a consequent relaxation of international tensions, to meet terms which could only be designed to assure to all of Germany the blessings of the kind of regime now enjoyed by the western zones? Would not the strengthening of German imperialism inherent in such an agreement be a greater threat to Soviet security than a continuation, and even a possible intensification, of the Cold War?

Many socialists will be inclined to say at once that the price of an agreement is too high, that the Russians should stand firm. The Russians may come to the same conclusion. In that case there will be no agreement at this meeting of the foreign ministers, just as there has been none at previous meetings. But no one should be surprised, and no one should blame the Russians, if they figure it the other way and acquiesce in the unification of Germany even on substantially American terms and with only relatively minor concessions to protect as far as possible the reforms that have been carried out in the eastern zone.

If the Russians should accept such a settlement — and it is by no mean impossible — we ought to be clear about the motives and calculations behind such a decision. The purpose would not be to further the socialist movement in Germany; in fact the very acceptance of such a settlement would signify that for the foreseeable future the Russians had given up hope of seeing the German problem solved in the only way it can be solved, that is to say, by the uprooting of German imperialism. The Russian purpose would rather be to make German imperialism more independent, to loosen and if possible break the ties which now bind Western Germany to the United States, and ultimately, by playing off Germany against the United States and the other countries in the American-dominated (Atlantic Pact) bloc, to disrupt the united front of capitalist nations which now threatens the very existence of the Soviet Union.

It is not hard to understand that this is a realistic program which would have a reasonable chance of success. Exports from Western Germany are already threatening the British recovery program, and their pressure is even beginning to be felt in markets which American exporters had come to regard as their own private preserve. These key conflicts would certainly be greatly intensified if Germany were united and free of occupation forces.

When German manufacturers are free to sell as they please, unhampered by U.S. and British pressure to keep selling prices in line with world levels, Germany will emerge again as a truly formidable competitor in international trade. Britain is getting the brunt of that competition today, and British engineering, automobile, and scientific instrument industries have begun to call Germany's competition "unfair" and German labor too cheap. British and American exporters have had the field all to themselves since the war's end, but rivalry will now be keener for narrowing foreign markets. (*Barron's*, May 9, 1949, p. 10.)

Should the British and Americans take steps to protect their markets, as they probably would, the Germans would then be forced to rely increasingly on trade with eastern Europe, and this in turn would divide Germany still further from the Anglo-American bloc. The truth of the matter is that the apparent solidarity of world imperialism at the present time is largely due to the fact that all of Japan and the most productive parts of Germany are under the direct or indirect military control of the United States. To the extent that this control is relaxed, the latent contradictions of imperialism will come increasingly to the surface and will play an ever more important role in world politics. It goes without saying that the Russians would rather be faced by a divided than a united imperialist world. If the sacrifice of Eastern Germany would make an important contribution to splitting the imperialist powers, they might well be prepared to pay the price.

That Soviet thinking runs along these lines has been proved again and again in the past — most dramatically, of course, in the case of the Soviet-German pact of 1939. The latest evidence is to be found in the controversy which took place among Soviet economists late last year over the views of the well-known theorist, Eugen Varga. One of the points for which Varga was severely and repeatedly condemned was his underestimation of the contradictions of imperialism. According to K. V. Ostrovityanov, Director of the Economics Institute of the Academy of Sciences of the USSR,

we must reject decisively Comrade Varga's attempt to revise the basic proposition of the Leninist-Stalinist theory of imperialism, on the inevitability of war between the imperialist powers, stemming from the sharpening of the uneven economic and political development of capitalism in the period of imperialism and of the general crisis of capitalism. (*Current Digest of the Soviet Press*, April 19, 1949, p. 19.)

Clearly, the Soviet leaders believe in the reality and depth of the contradictions of world imperialism. If they should base their foreign policy to an increasing extent on this belief, it ought neither to surprise nor to shock anyone who is familiar with the history of the last three decades. And if the Russians were to decide, as they did once before, that if there is to be another war they will do their best to see that it is not an anti-Soviet war, who, in all conscience, could blame them?

What all this adds up to is really very simple — and very important. The German problem can be solved only by Germany's becoming a socialist country. The Russians would welcome such a solution, but if they can't get it there is no reason to expect them to stand idly by while Germany is transformed into the war head of a great anti-Soviet coalition. The rulers of America have willed it that German imperialism shall be revived and once again play a role in world politics. They may find that, like the sorcerer, they have conjured up forces from the nether world which they can no longer control. It happened before, after World War I. It can happen again, after World War II.

Sordid power politics? Of course. We shall continue to live in a world of sordid power politics until mankind, or at least a decisive majority of it, learns to control the forces of society as it has already learned to control the forces of nature — until socialism has been victorious in the major countries of the world, including the United States of America.

18

National Socialism

This review of Franz Neumann's *Behemoth: The Structure and Practice of National Socialism* (New York, 1942) appeared in *Science & Society*, Summer 1942.

NATIONAL Socialism, in its basic aspects, is not a peculiarly German phenomenon; it is a manifestation of a worldwide tendency to reaction which, for a variety of historical reasons, has reached its most developed and dangerous form in Germany. This fact lends to the study of National Socialism a significance which far transcends the immediate period of armed conflict. In spite of the enormous importance of understanding the nature and workings of National Socialism it cannot be said that there have been more than a handful of genuinely scientific contributions to the subject. Not that there has been any shortage of books on Germany in recent years; the trouble is that very few have been written by authors equipped with a technique of social analysis which enables them to arrive at sensible and useful answers to the really crucial questions, namely, where National Socialism comes from, why it operates as it does, and where it is leading. Some studies have thrown light on certain aspects of these questions, but the great majority have been based on an acceptance, however unconscious, of the Nazis' own thesis that they are building a new form of society which obeys the will of an omnipotent leader rather than objective laws of social development. Under the circumstances it is a source of gratification and pleasure to be able to report the publication of a full-length study of National Socialism which meets every test of scientific scholarship. Franz Neumann's *Behemoth* is unquestionably the best work on the subject that has yet appeared, and it sets a very high standard for future writers to live up to.

Neumann has excellent qualifications for the task which he has undertaken in this book. As a lawyer for the German trade unions in the days of the Weimar Republic, he acquired an extensive firsthand knowledge of the workings of the German economy; his erudition in the fields of legal and political theory is impressive both in its extent and thoroughness; since 1933 he has painstakingly followed the course of Nazi thought and policies in the original sources. But perhaps most important of all, he has the advantage of a thorough Marxist grounding in the social sciences which enables him at once to grasp the interrelations of theory and practice and to avoid a one-sided overemphasis on the subjects which he happens to know most about from his own experience and research.

Behemoth opens with a brief but excellent introduction on the collapse of the Republic. The Weimar constitution represented an attempt on the part of liberals and reformist socialists to provide a framework of class compromise. Unfortunately it left the basic antagonisms of capitalism untouched, and in this circumstance is to be found its fatal weakness. The main outlines of the story are well known, but Neumann tells it in a fresh and convincing manner.

Part One deals with "The Political Pattern of National Socialism" and contains Neumann's most original and significant work. Three chapters describe the historical background and structure of the totalitarian state, including the role and interrelation of party, bureaucracy, and leader. A chapter on the roots and social functions of Nazi racial doctrines is excellently calculated to refute the foolish notion that racism in the modern world can be combated merely by demonstrating that it is nonsense from the standpoint of biology and anthropology. Finally the last two chapters in this part constitute a brilliant discussion of the relation between "geopolitical" and racial ideology on the one hand and the necessities of capitalist economy on the other. Geopolitics, the pseudo-science of space, is shown to be merely a rationalization of Germany's annexationist drive; while racism in this connection serves at once to justify German conquest and to win the masses to a policy which, objectively considered, is contrary to all their interests. At a time when similar doctrines are beginning to attract considerable attention in America it is of greatest urgency that progressives should be able to interpret and expose them for what they are. A careful study of these chapters will prove of inestimable assistance in this task.

Part Two is entitled "Totalitarian Monopolistic Economy" and describes in elaborate detail the institutional characteristics of the Nazi economy. The general picture here is better known to English and American readers through the works of Brady and others, but Neumann fills in many blank spaces and presents much material for the first time in English. The treatment is qualitative and descriptive rather than quantitative and statistical. An introductory chapter discusses several theories which have been put forward concerning the nature of the Nazi economy, and it seems to me that here Neumann tends to concede somewhat too much to the "new order" viewpoint. On the whole, however, he understands that National Socialism has succeeded only in changing the form in which the contradictions of capitalism manifest themselves and not in eliminating the contradictions as such. This is one of the most difficult problems of economics today, and it has been so inadequately dealt with by economists that one can hardly blame Neumann for certain weaknesses in his argument. It is interesting to note that most of the theories about a "new" economic order are the creation of refugees and foreigners, not of the Nazis themselves. This is in striking contrast to the Nazis' inventiveness in the fields of political and social theory. The difference is probably to be accounted for in terms of the more crucial ideological role of political and social theories as compared to economic theories, under conditions of fascism. The fact that popular attention has to be directed away from economic problems as much as possible is also a factor of great importance.

Chapter II of Part Two on the organization of business gives a thorough account, perhaps somewhat overlaid with detail, of the role of manufacturers' associations and chambers of commerce, while Chapter III deals with cartels and corporations. The extent to which monopoly capital has grown and extended its power at the expense of all and sundry is made very clear. These chapters should make interesting reading for those stalwarts who never tire of writing obituaries for German capitalism. Chapter IV deals with the economic role of the Nazi Party and the state, but instead of giving it a straightforward title which would indicate the subject matter, Neumann has chosen to call it "The Command Economy." This title is, to say the least, unfortunate since it gives the quite erroneous impression that alongside "The Monopolistic Economy" there is a second, distinct, and rival economic system in Germany under the control of the authorities. Actually the chapter discusses such diverse phenomena as the extent of nationalized production (which has diminished under the Nazis), the combines like the Goering Works which have been put together by a new group which might best be described as the "party industrialists," and the various types of price, production, and investment controls which are, of course, a feature of every capitalist war economy. To deal with these quite different subjects under the single heading "The Command Economy" serves no scientific purpose and merely creates confusion where clarity is particularly needed. Fortunately Neumann's analysis is not subject to the same strictures. He clearly recognizes the nature of the party industrialists as conforming to "the familiar pattern of American gangsters, who, after having accumulated money by blackmail and 'protection,' realize their dreams of becoming honorable by entering into legitimate business." (Pp. 298-299.) He might have pointed out that nothing that has happened under the Nazis shows more strikingly the capitalist character of the regime. The desideratum of every capitalist is to get control over the largest possible aggregate of capital. Messrs. Goering and Co. are certainly not the most gentlemanly players, but it is crystal clear that they are playing the same old game. The superficiality of our "new order" theorists appears most obviously in their attempts to palm off the Goering Works episode as proof of the noncapitalist character of the German regime. Neumann's treatment of governmental controls is on the whole satisfactory, and he correctly stresses their relation to the preparation for and waging of imperialist war. It is necessary to insist, however, that government controls are an integral part of the monopolistic economy and not in the least evidence of a distinct and rival system. It is especially important that Americans, brought up on popularizations of classical *laissez-faire* economics, should once and for all rid themselves of the false idea that government intervention in economic life is a sign of the weakening or disappearance of monopoly capitalism.

Part Three consists of two chapters, one on the ruling class and one on the ruled classes. There is much in the chapter on the ruling class with which I cannot agree. It seems to me that in placing the ministerial bureaucracy, the party, the army, and the industrialists on a par, as sectors of the ruling class, Neumann is falling into one of the commonest errors of liberal political science, and it is all the more surprising that he should do so since his own analysis provides ample evidence against this particular categorization. The ministerial bureaucracy and the army are in no sense independent historical forces; Neumann himself presents more than enough material to prove that they willingly backed the

Nazi regime because it is reactionary, antidemocratic, and expansionist. Naturally this does not mean that in a crisis they may not try to save their skins by shifting their allegiance to another regime, but in this they would only be following a well-known tradition of bureaucracies and armies. Only one proviso needs to be added, and it is very revealing concerning the role of these organizations, namely, that they will not and cannot adapt themselves to the genuinely socialist order which is now the only way out of their difficulties for the overwhelming mass of the German people. As to the Nazi Party, the case is certainly less clear. In one sense it undoubtedly possesses enormous power, but that power cannot be used just any way the party leaders choose. They are irrevocably committed to a course of aggression and exploitation, and in this respect they are the instruments of a social system which cannot continue to live without aggression and exploitation: monopoly capitalism. The real ruling class in Germany is therefore made up of the representatives and beneficiaries of monopoly capital. This, of course, does not exclude party members; on the contrary, the decisive circles in the party are thoroughly integrated into the structure of monopoly capital — Goering is merely the outstanding example — but it does mean that Nazis are members of the ruling class not by virtue of their membership in the party but because of their position in the structure of productive relations. The chief disappointment in Neumann's interpretation of the ruling class is that it represents a step backward as compared to the preceding analysis of Nazi politics and Nazi economics. Bureaucracy, party, army, and industrialists are all, of course, important, but the crucial questions are precisely what are the relations among them and what role do they play in the developmental tendencies of National Socialism. To lump them together as coordinate rulers of Germany avoids these questions; it does not answer them.

The chapter on the ruled classes is excellent. Neumann

shows convincingly that labor power has not lost its commodity character under National Socialism, but that the laborer has been completely deprived of the capacity to influence the terms and conditions of the labor contract. This is very important: it demonstrates on the one hand that the regime is capitalist and yet on the other hand that it differs in certain key respects from liberal capitalism in which the worker participates through collective bargaining in the determination of the labor contract. The techniques of Nazi domination are discussed with particular reference to the role of violence and terror. This chapter should be required reading for those who are duped by the propaganda of "Vansittartism," that is, the doctrine that all Germans are behind the Nazi leadership and equally guilty of its crimes. If all Germans, or even a large majority of Germans, approve of and support the Nazi leadership, it is quite incomprehensible that the regime should be obliged to use terror systematically and on an unprecedented scale against its own subjects.

The final section of the book, which bears the main title "Behemoth," is a brief attempt to characterize National Socialism in terms of the traditional categories of political science. Neumann believes, and I think rightly, that it is hopeless to try to discover in Nazi political writings an expression of any consistent set of principles. The Nazis borrow from all manner of sources and concoct theories to suit the needs of the moment. Whether one wants to conclude from this, as Neumann does, "that National Socialism has no political theory of its own, and that the ideologies it uses or discards are mere *arcana dominationis*, techniques of domination" (p. 467), or whether one prefers to say that Nazi political theory is unprincipled and opportunistic is perhaps a matter of taste. I do not think, however, that the same can be said about the answer given to the question, "Is Germany a State?" The name Behemoth is taken from Hobbes, who applied it to the English Long Parliament of the seventeenth century; to Hobbes, Behemoth was the negation of the state, the reign of lawlessness and chaos. Since Neumann believes that Germany under the Nazis is headed in this direction, he finds it apt to characterize National Socialism as Behemoth, the non-state. All this is perhaps intelligible enough, and may even be enlightening, to the expert in political theory who can readily distinguish from the context the special meanings which are assigned to such terms as "state" and "law." But to the majority of social scientists, not to speak of the layman, it is more than likely to be confusing. Throughout the greater part of the book, Neumann speaks of the state in the straightforward sense of the public apparatus of coercion (army, police, S.S., Gestapo), which has grown to unheard-of dimensions under the Nazi regime. That this apparatus does not operate according to "law" in the special sense of rational and predictable norms of conduct is quite true, and Neumann has performed a real service in proving the point by a detailed examination of Nazi "justice." But does this mean that one is justified in concluding that this apparatus is not a state in spite of the fact that it has been called a state all along? I must confess that I cannot see what ends are served by presenting conclusions in this paradoxical form. Moreover, and this is an important point, the disappearance of the state has a well-recognized meaning in socialist literature which, of course, has nothing in common with the sense in which the state may be said to have disappeared in Nazi Germany. This is an additional reason why Neumann's usage is unfortunate.

The criticisms which have been expressed in this review touch largely upon matters of form and presentation, and they should not be allowed to obscure the general excellence of *Behemoth*. Neumann has given us the first genuinely scientific interpretation of Nazi ideology in terms of the antagonisms and compulsions of the system as a whole. This is a great achievement which ought to have the effect of placing the study of National Socialism on a new and higher

NATIONAL SOCIALISM

level. Moreover, *Behemoth* shows us the essentially transitory character of National Socialism and gives us every reason to be confident that the German people, once the Nazi regime has been smashed, will be able to take their rightful place in leading the world into a new period of peaceful socialist construction.

19

Post Mortem

This is a review of Samuel Lurie, *Private Investment in a Controlled Economy: Germany, 1933-1939* (New York, 1947). It appeared in *The Journal of Political Economy*, April 1948.

THIS is a valuable addition to the literature on the Nazi economy. It surveys very carefully — and with a wealth of statistical and factual detail — the course of private investment from the accession of Hitler to power up to the outbreak of the war. Dr. Lurie's main conclusions may be summarized as follows: (a) under the Nazis, "the principle of production and investment in terms of private entrepreneurial motivation, and the corollary functional economic relationships had been essentially maintained"; (b) at the same time the economy was guided by the state in such a way as to favor rather than injure the private interests of the biggest capitalists; (c) a fiscal policy dominated by war preparations ran up the Reich debt to unprecedented heights; (d) individual savings were channeled through savings banks and life insurance companies into financing this public debt; (e) heavy public spending increased the liquidity of private business and allowed corporations to pay off their debts and reduce their interest burdens; (f) a general policy of freezing wages (and, to a lesser extent, prices) at levels reached during the depth of the depression permitted corporate business to make large profits as the utilization of capacity improved; and (g) corporations were encouraged in many ways to use their profits for direct expansion, especially in lines important for the war economy.

This brief summary, of course, does much less than justice to the careful workmanship with which Lurie has handled and evaluated his materials; but it may give an idea of the number of highly interesting and important problems which he has tackled and, for the most part, solved. At the same time it must be said that a considerable part of the book is substantially repetition of what has already been quite adequately covered in a number of earlier studies of the Nazi economy. Thus Chapters II and III, which constitute a sort of general picture of the Nazi economy, have little new material in them and could easily have been left out of anything but a Ph.D. thesis. The material in Chapter IV on external financing of private investment is presented at greater length than it deserves; the relevant conclusions could have been set out and convincingly documented in ten instead of fifty pages. But the three chapters dealing with internal financing are full of significant and, in many cases, original contributions to our understanding of Nazism. Here we can only be thankful for Lurie's full exposition and detailed documentation.

Lurie has for the most part avoided comments on the significance of his findings, and one may at least conclude from this that he did not undertake the study with the aim of supporting some preconceived theory. On the other hand, it is unfortunate in that it tends to conceal what are unquestionably extremely important implications concerning the nature of fascism. In the reviewer's opinion, no other book refutes the all too popular theory that fascism is some sort of a non- or anti-capitalist society more thoroughly than this one. And, conversely, no other book provides stronger evidence in support of the Marxian theory that fascism is run by and for the dominant elements of monopoly capital. But that is the reviewer's interpretation of Lurie's findings, and it would certainly be valuable to have the author's own opinion about the relation of his work to these highly important questions.

20

Resurrection?

This review of Saul K. Padover, *Experiment in Germany* (New York, 1946), and Julian Bach, Jr., *An Account of the Occupation* (New York, 1946) was published in *The New Republic*, April 22, 1946. Let me call the reader's attention to the brief account of the Antifa movement which sprang up all over Germany as Nazi rule collapsed. It is still true, so far as I am aware, that "the American public knows nothing about [this] proto-revolutionary movement" which was promptly suppressed in Western Germany by the occupation authorities.

THESE two books, taken together, give a reasonably comprehensive picture of the first year of the German occupation. Padover, whose job was to investigate German civilian attitudes for the Psychological Warfare Division of SHAEF, entered Germany in the wake of combat troops, spent nearly six months in the narrow strip of the Rhineland which was occupied in the autumn of 1944, followed the American spring offensive to the Elbe and its junction with the Russians, and finally crossed the German border westward-bound on V-E Day. Bach, on the other hand, left his infantry regiment in Belgium after V-E Day and served in Germany during the summer, autumn, and early winter as a roving correspondent for the Army periodical, *Army Talks*. Between them, therefore, they are able to present an account, divided into two clearly defined chapters, of what went on in Germany from the very beginning right up to the end of 1945.

In terms of their preconceptions and attitudes, Padover and Bach are much alike. Neither likes Germany, and both feel strongly that all Germans share the guilt of the Nazi regime. This is one side of the coin; the other is a friendly attitude toward America's allies and Germany's victims and a pessimistic view of the future of the Reich. Here, however, the similarity between the two books ceases. *Experiment in Germany* is the work of a professional historian, familiar with the language and background of the country, who derives practically all his information from a painstaking study of indigenous sources. Bach, on the other hand, an American journalist by profession, appears to have no knowledge of the German language — to judge by the numerous mistakes he makes in transcribing names and phrases — and relies almost wholly on Military Government sources. Thus, while Padover's book will retain its value to students of the occupation, Bach's may best be regarded as an extended magazine article which is useful for its topicality but will rapidly depreciate in value.

Experiment in Germany is written in straightforward, lucid prose; it holds the reader's attention throughout; at times it is exciting, at others moving. For example, the description of Sachsenhausen, as told by the little Luxembourg chauffeur, Jean Chaussy, is a controlled and horrifying account of the infamies of the concentration camps. Or, to take another example, the portrait of the German Communist Josef Mohren, who de-mined Wuerselen "to show a little bit of gratitude to the American liberators," is perhaps somewhat overdrawn, but it conveys better than chapters of general analysis the important truth that not all Germans bowed down or broke before the Hitlerite juggernaut. Finally, Padover has a fine appreciation of (and a deep contempt for) that spirit of Philistinism which has made the German *Kleinbürger* by turns an arrogant conqueror and a whining bootlicker.

The reader of Padover's book, however, should constantly

bear in mind that it deals almost entirely with a small section of the Rhineland in the earliest phase of the occupation. The region had been heavily bombed and fought over, and much of its population had been compulsorily evacuated into the interior. Those who, like the present reviewer, were charged with following German political and economic developments throughout this period as well as in the months after V-E Day, soon found that experience in the Aachen district was not an altogether reliable guide to what would happen in Germany as a whole: the pattern of German behavior, about which something will be said below, changed as the front moved eastward from the Rhine; and the MG — partly, it is fair to add, as the result of the report on Aachen submitted by Padover and his colleagues in the PWD — learned to avoid some of the worst of its early blunders. Moreover, the reader should be cautioned against accepting at face value the estimates and conclusions which Padover sometimes builds on the basis of very meager data. His estimate that German military dead for the whole war period amount to less than 2.4 million, and that therefore "the conclusion is inescapable that, in terms of human life, Germany fought a cheap war," is way off the mark. Latest Washington estimates of German casualties, based on records which have become available since V-E Day, place the figure of military dead (excluding air raid victims) at slightly over five million. It is similarly misleading to present without critical evaluation an account of the conspiracy of July 20, 1944, which was given early in 1945 by a person who was only slightly involved. It is too bad that Padover did not check these early impressions, which had their value at the time they were formed, against the much more complete and reliable information that later became available.

America's Germany is neither very well written nor very profound. At the same time, however, it faithfully reflects the views of moderate and intelligent MG officers on the spot; it should help to correct certain misconceptions which sections of the American press have done much to foster; and its observations on the behavior and attitudes of the American occupying forces are on the whole sound and useful.

Bach does well to stress the vast bomb damage in German cities and the sharp decline which productive activity has suffered. There have certainly been too many sensational reports suggesting that German industry is practically intact and ready to supply the materials for a new war of conquest. And yet when he says that "the most significant fact about German industry is that it no longer exists," he is certainly going too far in the other direction. There is still plenty of productive capacity in Germany; the chief obstacles to its fuller utilization are shortages of fuel and transport and the division of the country into four more or less watertight compartments. These obstacles are analyzed by Bach, but he apparently fails to appreciate that they are of a kind which, under favorable conditions, could be largely overcome in a matter of three or four years. It is therefore quite incorrect to say that "the possibility of German industry recovering to a point where it would be a new threat to peace is at present too remote for serious consideration." The British are already giving every indication of a strong interest in the rebuilding of German industrial strength, a move which would be the necessary first step in an effort to restore the old balance of power in European politics. It may be too early to worry, but it would surely be more prudent to hang up a few danger signals than to lull the American people into a false sense of security.

In its treatment of the various activities of the MG — in the fields of justice, education, press and radio, denazification, and so on — *America's Germany* reflects and supports the official view that a pretty good job has been done if due account is taken of the difficult conditions which have prevailed. And yet it is precisely such an apologia which, disposing — often successfully — of the common run of criticisms of the MG, brings out most clearly the essential aimlessness of American policy. It was already true long before World War I that monopoly capitalism had reached a stage of development in Germany which was no longer compatible with the social health of the German people or with the peace of the world. The revolution of 1918 failed to effect the necessary structural changes, and the result was Hitler and World War II. History has now posed the same problems again and has given the United States an opportunity to share directly in their solution. To read *America's Germany* is to realize that those who formulate and execute American policy have no sense of their responsibility, to say nothing of plans for discharging it.

It may well be asked whether the objective possibility of pursuing a bold and constructive policy has at any time existed in Germany. Is there the German human material to work on and through? It appears that both Padover and Bach would answer this question with an emphatic negative. And yet, in the opinion of this reviewer, this is a profoundly mistaken opinion. It is a curious fact, which certainly reflects on the adequacy of press reporting of the occupation, that the American public knows nothing about the proto-revolutionary movement which sprang up in city after city as the Allied armies swept eastward from the Rhine. Organizationally, this movement took the form of antifascist committees led in most cases by Communists or left-wing Social Democrats. These committees had a variety of local titles (in Bremen *Kampfgemeinschaft gegen den Faschismus*, in Leipzig *Nationalkomitee Freies Deutschland*, and the like), but they soon became widely known under the generic name of Antifa (for antifascist). In many cases they undertook direct action against Nazis, arresting notorious local bosses, confiscating food hoards, and evicting party members from their houses in favor of the bombed-out. This reviewer attended a meeting in Bremen two weeks after the fall of the city at which were gathered some seventy or eighty representatives of district groups with a total membership of several thousand. Most of those present were workingmen with pre-1933 political experience; anyone listening to their impassioned discussion could not doubt for a moment that their hatred of Nazism was much more personal and profound than that of Americans who have never experienced it and yet find it so easy to moralize about the guilt of all the German people.

But the Antifa movement never got a chance to develop. Direct action against Nazis was, in the view of the MG, "illegal" and subversive of law and order. Buildings which had been seized for headquarters (in Bremen the building which had belonged to the Labor Front) were taken over by the MG. In many cases the organizations were suppressed out of hand; American (and British) officers weren't going to have anyone telling *them* how to run their business; and besides, how could you be sure that these weren't Nazi outfits in disguise? The result was that within a month or so most of the Antifas, deprived of the possibility of functioning openly and being in principle opposed to the formation of an underground movement against the Allies, dropped out of the picture. When political activity was once again permitted, it ran for the most part into the old party channels. It is this reviewer's considered judgment that the Antifas represented the beginnings of a genuine revival of working-class revolutionary activity, and that their strangulation gave the played-out politicos of the Weimar period a new opportunity to divide the workers and to reinstate themselves in party and trade-union bureaucracies. The result is that America's Germany, as seen by such observers as Bach, appears to be politically apathetic and quite incapable of following a constructive path. Even meager reports from the Soviet zone, however, suggest that the Russians have followed a different policy from that of the Western powers; when the full story of Russia's Germany is told, it may well turn out that there is more vitality and energy in the country than Americans have suspected.

One complaint in conclusion: Padover's book has no chapter headings, no table of contents, and no index. It could be a valuable reference book; but as it stands, no one who hasn't read it can tell what's in it, and even one who has read it can't find what he knows is there.

Part V

Thinkers and Theories

21

John Maynard Keynes

This obituary appraisal was first published in *Science & Society*, Fall 1946. It was reprinted in Seymour E. Harris, editor, *The New Economics: Keynes' Influence on Theory and Public Policy* (New York, 1947).

LORD KEYNES, who died at the age of sixty-two on April 21, 1946, was unquestionably the most famous and controversial of contemporary economists. Moreover, like the great figures of the classical school — Adam Smith, David Ricardo, and John Stuart Mill[1] — he was no narrow specialist working in the seclusion of an academic ivory tower. Both as critic and as participant, he played a very important and certainly a unique role in the public life of Britain in the period of the two world wars; as a patron of the arts, he was a power in the cultural life of his country; as head of a great insurance company and as Bursar of King's College, Cambridge, he proved that the economic theorist can be a highly successful businessman; while his noneconomic writings range from the standard (literary as opposed to mathematical) *Treatise on Probability* to the incisive *Essays in Biography*. Keynes was, in short, one of the most brilliant and versatile geniuses of our time; and one can be sure that

---

[1] Keynes himself used the term "classical economists" to include the subjective value theorists — especially Marshall and his followers in the Cambridge group — of the late nineteenth and twentieth centuries. For reasons which should be clarified by the subsequent discussion, this practice seems to me to be misleading. It is preferable to regard John Stuart Mill as the last of the classical economists and to label the Marshallians the "neoclassical" school.

his place in history — not only doctrinal economic history — will be a subject of discussion and controversy for an indefinite period to come. It would be presumptuous at this early date to attempt anything in the way of definitive judgments, and in writing this brief communication I am far from entertaining any such intentions. I think it should be possible nevertheless to set out some of the factors in Keynes's work and in his influence on others which will have to be taken into account in any evaluation of the man, present or future.

In order to understand Keynes one must first understand where he stood in relation to other economists and schools of economic thought; for, as we shall see, it was what might be called an accident of location which accounts for much of the influence as well as for many of the shortcomings of his work. Modern economics — the economics of industrial capitalism and of the world market — had its origins in the later decades of the seventeenth century. During the next hundred and fifty years England was the home of the most important advances on both the industrial and the theoretical fronts; and by the time of Ricardo (1772-1823), English political economy enjoyed a degree of authority and prestige throughout the Western world which has never been equaled before or since. In the second half of the nineteenth century, the unity of the classical tradition was broken; what had been a single trunk with only minor offshoots divided itself into two great branches, each with its own sub-branches, which have on the whole been growing apart ever since. These two branches may be called the socialist or Marxian and the neoclassical respectively. To vary our metaphor, each can and does claim to be the legitimate child of classical political economy, but it must be said that for brothers they have had remarkably little to do with each other. This striking fact is due to a variety of reasons: for one thing, the two schools have diverged in their manner of selecting and discarding elements of the classical theory; for another, they have (openly in the case of Marxism, under cover of a pretended scientific neutrality in the case of neoclassicism) become intellectual weapons on opposite sides of a bitter class struggle; and, finally, Marxism — partly no doubt as a result of the historical accident of Marx's own German nationality — took root on the continent of Europe but failed for many years to win a significant following in the English-speaking world. Thus the two schools, despite their common origin, became intellectually, politically, and geographically estranged. Such contacts as they had, which were almost entirely outside Britain and the United States, were the contacts of battle and produced intolerance rather than understanding.

When Keynes took up the study of economics about the turn of the century, neoclassicism was in undisputed possession of the field in the English-speaking countries; dissent was regarded as a sign of incompetence or depravity. Keynes himself accepted the prevailing doctrines unquestioningly and soon came to be rated as a brilliant but essentially orthodox representative of the neoclassical school. There is no evidence that he was ever seriously influenced by conflicting or incompatible intellectual trends. He borrowed occasionally from foreign authors,[2] and when his own ideas had finally taken shape he was generous in giving credit for having anticipated them to a long line of heretics and dissenters; but these were essentially adventitious elements in Keynes's thought. By training he was a strict neoclassicist, and he never really felt at home except in argument with his neoclassical colleagues. In fact, one would be perfectly justified in saying that Keynes is both the most important and the most illustrious product of the neoclassical school.

This points, I think, to the true nature of Keynes's achievement. His mission was to reform neoclassical economics, to bring it back into contact with the real world from which it

---

[2] For example, the concept of a "natural rate of interest" which plays an important part in *A Treatise on Money* (1930) was taken from the Swedish economist Knut Wicksell (1851-1926). Wicksell himself, however, was essentially a neoclassicist.

had wandered farther and farther since the break with the classical tradition in the nineteenth century; and it was precisely because he was one of them and not an outsider that Keynes could exercise such a profound influence on his colleagues. The very same reasons, however, account for the fact that, as we shall see below, Keynes could never transcend the limitations of the neoclassical approach which conceives of economic life in abstraction from its historical setting and hence is inherently incapable of providing a scientific guide to social action.

Keynes's magnum opus, called *The General Theory of Employment, Interest, and Money* (1936), opens with an attack on what he calls orthodox economics — neoclassical economics, in the terminology of this article — and sustains it almost continuously to the end. The gist of this Keynesian criticism can be summed up simply as a flat rejection and denial of what has come to be known as Say's law of markets[3] which, despite all assertions to the contrary by orthodox apologists, did run like a red thread through the entire body of classical and neoclassical theory. It is almost impossible to exaggerate either the hold which Say's law exercised on professional economists or its importance as an obstacle to realistic analysis. The Keynesian attacks, though they appear to be directed against a variety of specific theories, all fall to the ground if the validity of Say's law is assumed.

Having once got hold of the essential truth that Say's law is a fraud and a delusion, Keynes was obliged to search the neoclassical theoretical structure from top to bottom to

---

[3] Say's law in effect denies that there can ever be a shortage of demand in relation to production. Ricardo expressed it as follows: "No man produces but with a view to consume or sell, and he never sells but with an intention to purchase some other commodity which may be useful to him, or which may contribute to future production. By producing then, he necessarily becomes either the consumer of his own goods, or the purchaser and consumer of the goods of some other person. . . . Productions are always bought by productions, or by services; money is only the medium by which the exchange is effected." *Principles of Political Economy* (Gonner ed.), pp. 273, 275.

separate those propositions which depend upon it from those which are valid regardless of its truth or falsity. The result of this search, as it appears in *The General Theory*, is almost incomprehensible to anyone but an adept in neoclassical economics. As Keynes himself says in the preface, "the composition of this book has been for the author a long struggle of escape, and so must the reading of it be for most readers if the author's assault upon them is to be successful" — obviously implying that he expects the readers to have the same type of training and the same general background as his own. And then he adds, with refreshing candor, "the ideas which are here expressed so laboriously are extremely simple and should be obvious. The difficulty lies, not in the new ideas, but in escaping from the old ones, which ramify, for those brought up as most of us have been, into every corner of our minds."

Keynes undoubtedly exaggerates the simplicity of his own contribution — it is noteworthy that pride in theoretical virtuosity was utterly foreign to his nature — but I think that almost all teachers will agree that it is easier to get his essential ideas across to a beginner than to a student who has already been steeped in the doctrines of the neoclassical school. Historians fifty years from now may record that Keynes's greatest achievement was the liberation of Anglo-American economics from a tyrannical dogma, and they may even conclude that this was essentially a work of negation unmatched by comparable positive achievements. Even if Keynes were to receive credit for nothing else (which is most unlikely), his title to fame would be secure. He opened up new vistas and new pathways to a whole generation of economists; he will justly share the credit for their accomplishments.[4]

---

[4] Probably only those who (like the present writer) were trained in the academic tradition of economic thinking in the period before 1936 can fully appreciate the sense of liberation and the intellectual stimulus which *The General Theory* immediately produced among younger teachers and students in all the leading British and American universities.

I have tried to show that the opportunity to which Keynes responded was essentially a crisis in traditional economics, a crisis which was both accentuated and laid bare by the Great Depression. He was able to demonstrate that his fellow economists, by their unthinking acceptance of Say's law, were in effect asserting the impossibility of what was actually happening.[5] From this starting point he was able to go on to a penetrating analysis of the capitalist economy which shows that depression and unemployment, far from being impossible, are the norms to which that economy tends, and which explodes once and for all the myth of a harmony between private and public interests which was the cornerstone of nineteenth-century liberalism. But Keynes stopped here in his critique of existing society. Our troubles, he believed, are due to a failure of intelligence and not to the breakdown of a social system. "The problem of want and poverty and the economic struggle between classes and nations," he wrote in 1931, "is nothing but a frightful muddle, a transitory and unnecessary muddle."[6]

That Keynes held this view was, of course, no accident. He could reject Say's law and the economic conclusions based on it because he thought they were largely responsible for the muddle; but it never occurred to him to question, still less to try to escape from, the broader philosophical and social tradition in which he was reared. The major unspoken premise of that tradition is that capitalism

---

[5] Apologists for the orthodox view are always ready with quotations to prove that economists were never such fools as this would imply. Keynes's answer, I think, is correct and convincing: "Contemporary thought," he wrote, "is still deeply steeped in the notion that if people do not spend their money in one way they will spend it in another. Post-war economists seldom, indeed, succeed in maintaining this standpoint *consistently;* for their thought today is too much permeated with the contrary tendency and with facts of experience too obviously inconsistent with their former view. But they have not drawn sufficiently far-reaching consequences; and have not revised their fundamental theory." *General Theory,* p. 20.

[6] *Essays in Persuasion,* p. vii.

is the only possible form of civilized society. Hence Keynes, exactly like the economists he criticized, never viewed the system as a whole; never studied the economy in its historical setting; never appreciated the interconnectedness of economic phenomena on the one hand and technological, political, and cultural phenomena on the other. Moreover, he was apparently quite ignorant of the fact that there was a serious body of economic thought, as closely related to the classical school as the doctrines on which he himself was brought up, which attempted to do these things. In Keynes's eyes, Marx inhabited a theoretical underworld along with such dubious characters as Silvio Gesell and Major Douglas;[7] and there is no evidence that he ever thought of any of Marx's followers as anything but propagandists and agitators.

This is not the place for a review of Marxian economics.[8] I raise the issue only in order to show that the school of thought to which Keynes belongs is rather isolated and one-sided, that some of his most important discoveries were taken for granted by socialist economists at least a generation before Keynes began to write, and that many of the most vital problems of the capitalist system are completely ignored in *The General Theory*. Marx rejected Say's law from the outset;[9] already before 1900 his followers were carrying on a spirited debate among themselves not only on the subject of periodic crises but also on the question whether capitalism could be expected to run into a period of permanent or chronic depression.[10] Keynes ignores technological change and technological unemployment, problems which

---

[7] *General Theory*, p. 32.

[8] I have tried to provide such a review in *The Theory of Capitalist Development* (1942).

[9] Marx remarked, in connection with the passage from Ricardo quoted in Note 3 above, that "this is the childish babbling of a Say, but unworthy of Ricardo." *Theorien über den Mehrwert*, Vol. II, pt. 2, p. 277.

[10] See *The Theory of Capitalist Development*, Chapter XI, "The Breakdown Controversy."

figure as an integral part of the Marxian theoretical structure. Keynes treats unemployment as a symptom of a technical fault in the capitalist mechanism, while Marx regards it as the indispensable means by which capitalists maintain their control over the labor market. Keynes completely ignores the problems of monopoly, its distorting effect on the distribution of income and the utilization of resources, the huge parasitic apparatus of distribution and advertising which it foists upon the economy. A socialist can only blink his eyes in astonishment when he reads that there is "no reason to suppose that the existing system seriously misemploys the factors of production which are in use. . . . When 9,000,000 men are employed out of 10,000,000 willing and able to work, there is no evidence that the labor of these 9,000,000 men is misdirected."[11] Many other examples of the insularity and comparative narrowness of the Keynesian approach could be cited. But perhaps most striking of all is Keynes's habit of treating the state as a *deus ex machina* to be invoked whenever his human actors, behaving according to the rules of the capitalist game, get themselves into a dilemma from which there is apparently no escape. Naturally, this Olympian interventionist resolves everything in a manner satisfactory to the author and presumably to the audience. The only trouble is — as every Marxist knows — that the state is not a god but one of the actors who has a part to play just like all the other actors.

Nothing that has been said should be taken as belittling the importance of Keynes's work. Moreover, there has been no intention to imply that Marxists "know it all" and have

[11] *General Theory*, p. 379. It is only fair to point out that Keynes's neglect of monopoly is not characteristic of present-day academic economics. It remains true, however, that the neoclassical treatment of the subject overconcentrates on the problems of the individual firm and has not done very much to relate monopoly to the functioning of the economy as a whole. In the latter field it would be hard to name a book even today which rivals *Das Finanzkapital* written by the Marxist economist Rudolf Hilferding in the first decade of the present century.

nothing to learn from Keynes and his followers. I have no doubt that Keynes is the greatest British (or American) economist since Ricardo, and I think the work of his school sheds a flood of light on the functioning of the capitalist economy. I think there is a great deal in Marx — especially in the unfinished later volumes of *Capital* and in the *Theorien über den Mehrwert* — which takes on a new meaning and fits into its proper place when read in the light of the Keynesian contributions. Moreover, at least in Britain and the United States, the Keynesians are as a group far better trained and equipped technically (for instance in the very important sphere of gathering and interpreting statistical data) than Marxist economists;[12] and as matters stand now there is no doubt which group can learn more from the other.

But while it is right to recognize the great importance of Keynes, it is no less essential to recognize his shortcomings. They are for the most part the shortcomings of bourgeois thought in general: the unwillingness to view the economy as an integral part of a social whole; the inability to see the present as history, to understand that the disasters and catastrophes amidst which we live are not simply a "frightful muddle" but are the direct and inevitable product of a social system which has exhausted its creative powers, but whose beneficiaries are determined to hang on regardless of the cost. Keynes himself, of course, could never have recognized, let alone transcended, the limitations of the society and the class of which he was so thoroughly a part. But the same cannot be said of many of his followers. They did not grow up in the complacent atmosphere of Victorian England. They were born into a world of war, and depression, and fascism. Some, no doubt, treading in the footsteps of the master, will seek to preserve their comforting liberal illusions as long as humanly possible. Some, in all probability, will range themselves on the side of the existing order and will sell their skill as economists to the highest bidder. But

---

[12] How few there are who really deserve the name!

still others, while retaining what is valid and sound in Keynes, will take their place in the growing ranks of those who realize that patching up the present system is not enough, that only a profound change in the structure of social relations can set the stage for a new advance in the material and cultural conditions of the human race.

This last group, I think, will inevitably be attracted to Marxism as the only genuine and comprehensive science of history and society. Perhaps the clearest indication that this is so is to be found in Joan Robinson's little book *An Essay on Marxian Economics* published in England early in the war. Mrs. Robinson, a member of the inner Keynesian circle, is one of perhaps half a dozen top-flight British economic theorists. Marxists will not be able to agree with everything she says, but they will find in her a sympathetic critic ready and anxious to discuss problems with them in a sober and scientific spirit. Can it be pure accident that one of the most prominent followers of Keynes should be the author of the first honest work on Marxism ever to be written by a non-Marxist British economist?

22

Pigou and the Case for Socialism

This piece combines, while omitting duplication, two reviews of A. C. Pigou, Socialism Versus Capitalism (London, 1937). The reviews appeared in The Nation, February 5, 1938, and Plan Age, March 1938.

IF ACADEMIC economists were asked to name the outstanding representative of their profession, it is a fair guess that Professor A. C. Pigou, of Cambridge, would carry off the honors. He is a direct descendant in the English classical tradition of Adam Smith, David Ricardo, John Stuart Mill, and Alfred Marshall. His *Economics of Welfare* ranks with the half dozen greatest works of bourgeois economics. Anything he has to say on the issue of "socialism versus capitalism" is evidently important.

It would be a great mistake, however, to assume that the significance of this work is due to the reputation of its author. Professor Pigou has written a book characterized by intellectual honesty, courage, and logical clarity. No future discussion of the economic merits of the rival systems of society can afford to neglect his cogently marshaled arguments; and fortunately, since the book is addressed to the general reader, no such discussion need neglect them.

In passing judgment on the book it is necessary to remember that Professor Pigou operates within the narrow framework of orthodox economics, a framework which on principle excludes the consideration of the effects of economic forces on the social and political complexion of society. Professor

Pigou's work, like that of his predecessors and contemporaries in the orthodox tradition, is essentially static and taxonomic. This approach, I think, is an unfortunate one, and yet when carried out honestly it has a curious result.

Capitalism is presented in a very favorable light considering the plain facts about inequality, unemployment, monopolistic restriction, and so forth, none of which does Professor Pigou attempt to gloss over. This is possible because the connections between capitalism as an economic system and the ugliest phenomena of the modern world — imperialist conflict and class brutality — are regarded as no concern of the economist. Yet in spite of this favorable presentation of the case for capitalism, Professor Pigou inevitably finds that socialism, regarded merely from the point of view of economic technique, is superior on nearly every count examined. For, whatever may be said of war and class oppression, there can be no doubt that inequality, unemployment, monopolistic restriction, and cyclical fluctuations are endemic to the capitalist system. And there can be just as little doubt that these things are no part of the logic of socialism.

In many ways the first chapter, entitled "Definition and Description," is the best in the book. The distinction between the *fact of profit* as the organizing principle of capitalism, and *the profit motive*, meaning simply the desire for personal gain, is an extremely valuable one. When this distinction is clearly grasped, it becomes obvious that "it is . . . correct to say . . . that to substitute socialism for capitalism would eliminate profit, but incorrect to say that it would eliminate the profit motive." This one simple point cuts the ground from under most of the arguments against socialism of the you-can't-change-human-nature variety. It also demonstrates that the Soviet Union is not returning to capitalism simply because it appeals to the desire for personal gain as an incentive to accomplishment.

Professor Pigou does not bother specifically to refute the Mises school of antisocialism, according to which it is a priori impossible to plan rationally the economic life of the community as a whole. Possibly this is because the job has been done so often and so thoroughly in the technical literature that he regarded it as unnecessary to go over the ground again. This must be accounted unfortunate in view of two recent events: the publication of Mises' magnum opus in English (under the title *Socialism*), and Walter Lippmann's belated discovery of this latter-day champion of vulgar Manchesterism. Since Lippmann rests his case against socialism largely on Mises, it would be valuable to have a specific exposé of the latter from so authoritative a pen as that of Professor Pigou. Still, Chapters VII and VIII are so plainly an implicit refutation of the whole Mises doctrine that Lippmann can ignore them only at the expense of branding himself as an open propagandist for the *status quo*.

Not the least interesting part of *Socialism Versus Capitalism* is the concluding chapter, in which Professor Pigou makes what he calls "a confession of faith." His reasons for doing so should be read and pondered over by those "impartial" intellectuals who pride themselves on their refusal to espouse any program of social change.

The fact that we are without the data and the instruments of thought necessary for assured judgment does not entitle us to sit back with folded hands. For to sit so is itself to take a decision; to make the great refusal, to declare ourselves in advance opponents of any change. . . . we must use these imperfect data as best we may, and take the plunge, and *judge*. There is no other way.

Professor Pigou declares in effect for gradual socialization — a Fabian among Fabians. If capitalism were really what he supposes it to be, his advice could be wholeheartedly accepted. As it is, the events of the past twenty-five years must be regarded as grave confirmation of the counter-arguments, which are as old as the doctrine of gradualism itself. Even for the Fabians, however, Professor Pigou has wise counsel, and underneath his calm language is veiled a stinging rebuke. "Gradualness," he says with conspicuous emphasis, "implies action, and is not a polite name for standing still."

23

Hansen and the Crisis of Capitalism

Part I is a review of Alvin H. Hansen, *Full Recovery or Stagnation?* (New York, 1938), which appeared in *The Nation*, November 19, 1938; Part II is a review of Hansen's *Fiscal Policy and Business Cycles* (New York, 1941) which appeared also in *The Nation*, September 27, 1941.

I

IT WILL scarcely be questioned by anyone that the fundamental problems which America faces today are economic. Nor will it be denied that a successful solution of those problems requires as a first condition a clear understanding of their nature. It is for this reason that Professor Hansen's new book must be regarded as one of the most important to come from the pen of an American economist in recent years. By this I do not mean to imply that Professor Hansen has produced a learned treatise dealing with every aspect of the current economic scene, for he has not. What he has done is perhaps more important: he has set down in a form intelligible to the nonprofessional reader ideas which go to the root of many of our difficulties and ought to help us to lay intelligent plans for overcoming them.

Professor Hansen's central thesis may be summarized somewhat as follows. In a society such as ours, in which there is at all times a certain amount of more or less automatic saving going on, there must be an amount of expenditure on additions to the community's real capital at least equal to the amount of saving out of current income. If there is not, this saving simply reduces the amount of current consumption and hence indirectly the need for investment. In other words, there must be outlets for new capital investment adequate to absorb what the community wants to save if we are not to have a permanent depression. But the trend of events in the last few decades has been extremely unfavorable in this respect. New territories are no longer open for settlement and exploitation; population is now practically stable and may soon begin to decline in various Western countries; no innovations in industrial technique which would require vast amounts of capital are in sight. In short, the era of economic expansion has come to an end, a fact which enormously aggravates the difficulty of finding a sufficient volume of investment outlets. These are hard facts which have to be reckoned with. As Professor Hansen says, "Many of us do not like the current trends in economic life. But in every age there is something more or less inevitable about the stream of historical events."

The implications of these facts for public policy are fundamental. It is extremely unlikely that capital expenditures by businessmen in search of profits will ever again approach a figure adequate to support a satisfactory national income. That they ever were adequate may be doubted. Professor Hansen shows that the prosperity of the twenties rested to an amazing extent on capital expenditures of a nonbusiness nature, for example, residential construction and road building. But if nonbusiness expenditures were necessary even in earlier times, how much more true is this today when the field for business expansion has been radically curtailed. "When one views the problem in this manner," Professor Hansen says, "the role of public debt and of governmental expenditures, and indeed the whole question of taxation, takes on quite a different aspect from what it had in the nineteenth century." This, I think, is the very least that can be said.

If Professor Hansen's analysis is brilliant and profound,

his proposals for policy are disappointing. The fault does not lie with him as an individual but with the tradition of thought — orthodox economics — with which he is identified. The economic system, according to the orthodox way of looking at things, can be analyzed and its ills prescribed for in complete abstraction from the kind of society to which it gives rise. Whether capitalism will survive, says Professor Hansen, "is not so much a question of class struggle; it is rather a question of the inherent workability of the system." But the basis of the system is a set of property relationships which carries with it a set of power relationships which, in turn, inevitably gives rise to the class struggle. Here again it is not a question of whether we like it or not; to attempt to understand capitalism in abstraction from class struggle is to miss the nub of the problem as it exists in the real world.

This does not mean that orthodox economics is not capable of contributing extremely valuable partial analyses: Professor Hansen's book is living proof to the contrary. It does mean, however, that these partial analyses fail to carry with them suggestions for ultimately successful action. I think this point is so important that I should like to illustrate what I mean by a specific example from Professor Hansen's book.

In his essay "Economic Bases of Peace," Professor Hansen gives an admirably clear analysis of one of the economic forces which drive the aggressor nations to seek new territory, namely, their urgent need for basic raw materials. The usual liberal answer is: Well, then, let them buy raw materials; the price is the same to them as to everyone else. But, as Professor Hansen shows, the trouble is not the price but the simple fact that they have no money to pay with. And as long as restrictions on trade are such that they cannot export, it is clear that they cannot acquire the necessary money. From this Professor Hansen concludes that the remedy is a return, as far and as fast as possible, in the direction of free trade. The conclusion is as logical as it is futile. It completely ignores the fact that the ruling classes (or, in

Veblenian terminology, the vested interests) in each country have erected the barriers to trade in order to monopolize the home market. To preach free trade to those who live on protection is like preaching suicide to a healthy man. The aggressions of today are a sufficient commentary on similar preachments of yesterday.

But I suppose it is too much to ask an orthodox economist to be more than a very good orthodox economist; and *Full Recovery or Stagnation?* shows that Professor Hansen is all of that. Anyone who will cast aside his preconceptions and prejudices and study this book carefully will gain greatly in understanding of the world's problems even if he may still be left wondering how they can be solved.

II

After more than a hundred years of devotion to superficial apologetics and elegant irrelevancies, bourgeois political economy has, in the last decade, experienced a genuine renaissance. The world crisis of capitalism, which has already extended over a full quarter century of war, revolution, and profound economic disturbance, and which is even now approaching a climax in the Second World War, has forced economists to come forward with a critical appraisal of the operation of the society in which they live. No American has contributed more to this rebirth of scientific economics than Professor Alvin H. Hansen; his latest, and in many ways his most important, book deserves therefore the utmost attention of every student of world affairs.

Fiscal Policy and Business Cycles, like several earlier works by the same author, is not an integrated treatise, nor is it for the most part written exclusively for the economic specialist. It is rather a series of related but nevertheless independent essays covering a wide range of topics, sometimes impressionistically, occasionally with all the paraphernalia of formal theory, but always originally and suggestively. The essential independence of the parts enforces a considerable amount of repetition of important principles, which, however, is in no sense to be accounted a weakness. The style throughout is straightforward and unpretentious; what is lacking in grace is made up in intelligibility and compactness.

Part One is an attempt to place the depression and partial recovery of the 1930s in proper historical perspective. Many of the ideas are already familiar to those who have studied Hansen's well-known TNEC testimony, but they are here set out in greater detail and with more supporting factual evidence. Chapters IV and V are of particular value in dispelling widely held popular misconceptions. In the former, Hansen shows that the fiscal policy of the New Deal was compounded very largely of "salvaging" operations and had little in common with constructive economic planning; in the latter, he properly underlines the special and very probably nonrecurring factors which accounted for the mildness of depression and the extent of recovery in Great Britain — such factors as accumulated shortages from the relatively depressed twenties, the abandonment of free trade, the availability of very cheap imports from hard-hit agricultural countries, and so on.

Part Two is devoted to "The Changing Role of Fiscal Policy." The American tax structure comes in for severe criticism on precisely the right grounds, namely, the colossal drag which it constitutes on the level of consumption. The vital role which public debt has played since the very beginnings of capitalism is given full weight; in this connection the supporting data will come as a revelation to those who derive their picture of reality from the distorted mirror of the modern press. The United States national debt of today, about which until recently we heard so much clamor, is little more than half of our national income; by contrast, the English debt of 1818, after the Napoleonic wars, and again in 1923, after the World War, stood at a figure twice the national income.

Part Three contains the most difficult theoretical chapters.

Here the interrelation of income, consumption, and investment is subjected to searching theoretical and empirical analysis. Hansen senses the profound bias of our present economic order: in favor of expanding capital and against expanding consumption. Moreover, he makes of this the foundation stone of his explanation of our present economic dilemma, and he sees much more clearly than any other bourgeois writer that this difficulty would by no means be removed by that eternal panacea of the vulgar economist, a freely competitive price system. Chapter XV should be required reading for all those who plan to save the world à la Thurman Arnold. The upshot of this part is that we must have ever more investment, if not by business then by government, if we are to avoid a state of chronic depression in the future.

Part Four examines "Investment Incentives, Past and Present," and comes to the conclusion that the role of government will in all likelihood be much greater in the future than it has been in the past.

Part Five, on problems of defense, is more topical than the rest of the book; it is also less substantial and, on a long view, less important.

What is to be said in criticism of this stimulating book is less a matter of detail than of fundamental approach. (The details can be safely left to that large number of professional economists who will doubtless find Hansen too bold and outspoken for their taste.) Hansen understands very well *what* is wrong with our present-day economy, and that is all to the good. But ask the question of this book: *why* have matters turned out as they have? You will not find much by way of answer. The modern world is very complex; rapid adjustments are needed, but certain habits and institutional patterns stand in the way. To deal with these problems we need "bold social engineering," and this will be possible only if we have the requisite "vision and courage." In the final analysis, therefore, the present world crisis is a crisis of intelligence. This is the inevitable implication of Hansen's position.

What Hansen does *not* see, and in this he is of course by no means peculiar, is that the economic troubles which he so skillfully describes and analyzes are manifestations of the real nature of the capitalist system itself. Capital, the dominant force in society, seeks its own self-expansion and cares not a hang for a smoothly working economy or for the consumption of the masses if they stand in the way. There is perhaps little in Hansen's analysis which is actually inconsistent with this interpretation, but what a difference it makes to the conclusion! There is no lack of intelligence in the world; the trouble is that too much of it can be bought by people whose ends are entirely different from those which Hansen too easily takes for granted. There is no lack of courage and vision in the world; the trouble is that too much of it is betrayed into fighting on the side of that economic frustration which Hansen rightly accounts the fundamental evil of our time. In reality the future is both brighter and darker than he will admit: brighter because he underestimates the resourcefulness of the human race; darker because he underestimates the power of capital. On balance, however, his is surely the less cheerful outlook, for there is little evidence that the intelligence of the human race has changed for several thousand years, while the power of capital is at most a few hundred years old.

24

Schumpeter's Theory of Innovation

This article appeared under the title "Professor Schumpeter's Theory of Innovation," in the February 1943 issue of *The Review of Economic Statistics* (now *The Review of Economics and Statistics*), a special number to commemorate Schumpeter's sixtieth birthday.

PROFESSOR Schumpeter is known primarily as a business cycle theorist, but his fundamental interest is much broader than this reputation would suggest. A careful reading of his works clearly shows that the objective is nothing less than to lay bare the anatomy of economic change in a capitalist society. English and American economics, on the other hand, has traditionally been content to confine its attention to what may be called the normal functioning of the capitalist economy. Such an approach, of course, does not exclude treatment of the business cycle, but it does exclude the larger problems of change and development which are customarily regarded as lying within the province of the economic historian. The most important part of Professor Schumpeter's theory of economic development which falls within the traditional scope of Anglo-American economics is that which is concerned with business cycles. Now I do not mean to suggest that there is any objection to regarding Professor Schumpeter as a business cycle theorist, for he is certainly one of the most distinguished contributors to this branch of economics; but the circumstance should not be allowed, as it too frequently has been, to obscure his no less distinguished and important achievements in clarifying the processes of economic change. In this paper I shall ignore business cycle problems and attempt to bring into sharp relief Professor Schumpeter's views on the mechanism of economic change in the capitalist economy.

Professor Schumpeter's starting point is an economy from which change (though not growth) is assumed to be absent.[1] In other words, the specific factor that causes change is abstracted. The resulting economic system is called the "circular flow" because it is found to run on, year in and year out, in essentially the same channels. The circular flow is in no sense conceived as an *unrealistic* construction; rather, it is an *abstract* construction which is intended to portray the consequences of a limited number of very real economic forces. From this point, the procedure is comprised of three steps: first, the causative factor of change — the entrepreneur or innovator — is analyzed as a pure type in abstraction from its economic environment; second, the factor of change is inserted into the model of the circular flow; and third, the interaction of the innovator with the forces at work in the circular flow is subjected to exhaustive analysis. What emerges is a process of development which displays the specific wavelike form of the business cycle.

This simplified version of Professor Schumpeter's method is intended to focus attention upon certain questions which are of crucial importance in any final evaluation of his theory. Has he really isolated and abstracted for analysis the *primum mobile* of change? Is the picture of the circular flow fully satisfactory? Is the result of joining the two elements a correct representation of the essentials of capitalist reality?

The causative factor in change, according to Professor Schumpeter, is "innovation," which is defined as "doing things differently in the realm of economic life."[2] If this were interpreted to mean no more than that "the cause of change

---

[1] For the distinction between change (or development) and growth, see his *Theory of Economic Development* (Cambridge, Massachusetts, 1934), Chapter II.

[2] *Business Cycles* (New York, 1939), Vol. I, p. 84.

is change," it would, of course, be a mere *petitio principii;* but such an interpretation would be a misreading of Professor Schumpeter's meaning. Innovation is the activity or function of a particular set of individuals called entrepreneurs. The entrepreneur is a sociological type that can be isolated and investigated independently of the consequences which follow from the actions of the entrepreneur. Hence any suspicion of circular reasoning is unfounded. What are the characteristics of the entrepreneur? First, of course, the ability to appreciate the possibilities of an innovation; whether or not he is also the discoverer or "inventor" of the innovation is a matter of minor consequence. But even more important, the entrepreneur must be able to overcome the psychological and social resistances which stand in the way of doing new things; he must, in short, have the qualities of leadership. Thus the entrepreneur is not a social type *sui generis;* he is rather a *leader* whose energies happen for one reason or another to be directed into economic channels. This conception of the entrepreneur leads Professor Schumpeter to locate the source of economic change in the personality traits of a certain group of men, a group which is in principle drawn from all strata and classes of the population.

The plausibility of this diagnosis depends in large measure on Professor Schumpeter's analysis of the circular flow. The conception of the circular flow is arrived at by simply abstracting entrepreneurs from the economic environment. We must not fall into the error of supposing that by taking away entrepreneurs we *ipso facto* eliminate change from the economy. The problem is precisely to show that by eliminating a certain type of individual we thereby eliminate the significant forces making for change. If this can be successfully proved, it is clear that we shall be left with the conclusion that entrepreneurs *are* the source of change: in short, the theory will be vindicated. If, on the other hand, the economy without entrepreneurs, that is, without a certain type of person, still displays tendencies to change, then we shall have to re-examine our initial assumptions. Professor Schumpeter's analysis is therefore designed to show that without entrepreneurs we have a stationary economy.

Professor Schumpeter's idea of the circular flow is in most particulars similar to the Walrasian state of general equilibrium, or, what comes to much the same thing, Marshall's conception of long-run equilibrium, which, though usually discussed with reference to a particular firm or industry, really implies an equilibrium of the system as a whole. Consumption motives dominate the economic subjects — this does not, of course, imply the acceptance of philosophic hedonism — and determine the allocation of resources to different branches of production. In one respect, however, Professor Schumpeter goes further than his predecessors in that he denies the existence, in the circular flow, of surpluses in the form of interest and profit. Land is privately owned and yields a rent, but in the absence of a positive rate of interest there is no basis for valuing land: on a capitalized earning-power basis its value is theoretically "infinite," which is only another way of saying that there is no market for land in the circular flow. The denial that surpluses (other than rent) exist in the circular flow has given rise to much controversy; many critics have suspected that there is something wrong with Professor Schumpeter's reasoning at this point. This opinion seems to me to be in error: it is not the reasoning but the implicit assumptions on which it is based that account for the disappearance of the surpluses. For in effect Professor Schumpeter assumes that in the circular flow there is no special class of capitalists. Society is divided into two classes: landlords and others. Everyone has equal access to "capital." Under these circumstances, clearly, no surpluses can accrue to employers of labor; for if they did, the laborers would themselves turn employers and compete the surplus away. Hence all income flows to landlords or laborers, and there is no special employing function outside of the simple details of bookkeeping and disbursing incomes on paydays.

The assumptions underlying the circular flow are certainly sufficient to produce a stationary economy, and, moreover, one in which income is entirely consumed with nothing left over for saving and accumulation. (The absence of saving follows from the assumption of the primacy of consumption motives. Where this assumption is made, one must insert the further postulate of time preference in the Böhm-Bawerkian sense, in order to explain saving. Professor Schumpeter rightly rejects this conception of time preference as arbitrary and unfounded.) If this were indeed the appropriate conception of the capitalist economy *sans* entrepreneur, then we should have to agree with Professor Schumpeter that the entrepreneur is the true source of change and, along with it, of the most characteristic features of capitalist reality, such as profits, interest, and business cycles. Thus, unlike many of his critics, I have no fault to find with the logic of Professor Schumpeter's argument; on the contrary, it appears to me indisputable that on its own assumptions his theory of the mechanism of economic change is unassailable.

When we turn from the logic of the theory to its assumptions, however, there appears to be more room for doubt. For example, Professor Schumpeter's conception of the circular flow obviously is not the only possible picture of an economy from which the entrepreneur has been eliminated. We may start from a situation in which there are not only landlords but also capitalists, in other words a special class of individuals having exclusive control over the means of production other than land. (The capitalists may also be landlords, of course.) For institutional reasons, laborers find it impossible to gain control over means of production and hence are unable themselves to become employers. Under this assumption, a surplus in the form of profit and/or interest is a logical corollary. By adhering to the assumption of the primacy of consumption motives, we can still have a stationary economy that is in many respects similar to Professor Schumpeter's circular flow, but the justification for this assumption seems much less clear in this case than in Professor Schumpeter's. Let us examine the problem more closely.

It is extremely plausible to suppose that in a society based on the postulates of the circular flow the primary motive for all economic behavior would be the satisfaction of consumers' wants. The only class division is that between landlords and laborers. Moreover, since there is no market for land, the owners of land would constitute an hereditary aristocracy to which wealth as such would not be a ticket of admission. Differences in incomes between laborers would be based solely on differences in productive efficiency, since savings could not provide a source of income. Under these conditions the accumulation of wealth would appear to have little attraction: it would serve neither as a badge of social prestige nor as a source of income. Hence Professor Schumpeter is undoubtedly right to exclude saving and accumulation as significant factors from the circular flow and to treat them as phenomena which are the consequence of change rather than its cause.

On the other hand, if we take as our starting point a society with a class structure different from that underlying the circular flow, then the case for excluding saving and accumulation is very much weaker. Where there is a distinct employing class based on ownership of capital, in addition to landlords and laborers, a strong motive to accumulate wealth exists quite apart from any doubtful ideas about time preference. No longer can it be argued that social power and prestige are the monopoly of an hereditary aristocracy; in fact, since along with a rate of interest goes the marketability of land, it is possible for anyone with enough money to buy his way into the landlord class. But even more important is the fact that employers likewise constitute an upper class, which is based directly upon the possession of accumulated wealth. Furthermore, since this kind of wealth is measurable in abstract value units, it follows that the relative status of the members of the upper class can be exactly calculated. Under such circumstances the way to social preferment and success is evidently to be sought by way of wealth accumulation; and, considering the fact that social status is essentially a matter of one man's position relative to others, there is no limit to the amount of wealth which it is rational to want to accumulate. It follows that in the kind of economy which we are now investigating there exist not only the surpluses from which it is possible to accumulate but also plenty of motives to accumulate: in one sense, indeed, it is not incorrect to say that the surpluses provide both the possibility of and the incentive to accumulation.

Professor Schumpeter's ordering of cause and effect may now be reversed. Instead of regarding surpluses and accumulation as the effect of change, we can look upon them as exercising a profound and steady pressure in the direction of economic change. The reasons for this may be briefly indicated.

First, accumulation in the absence of change tends to wipe out the surplus and hence to threaten the social position of the capitalist class; needless to say, no class tamely submits to its own extermination. Second, the individual capitalist who introduces new methods makes a larger surplus and hence can get ahead more rapidly than his fellows. Finally, the capitalist who refuses to enter the race for new and improved methods stands in danger of being eliminated by his more alert competitors.[3] Thus we see that in a society with a capitalist class structure by no means all social pressures stand opposed to "doing things differently in the realm of social life"; on the contrary, the capitalist must adjust himself to a life of continuous change or run the risk of losing everything which gives him social prestige and power.

---

[3] For a fuller exposition of the relation between accumulation and change, see my book *The Theory of Capitalist Development* (New York, 1942), Chapter V.

We see that the construction, on what seem quite reasonable assumptions, of an alternative starting point to the circular flow is possible. This economy can be made stationary for purposes of analysis by abstracting the *primum mobile* of change, namely, the accumulation of capital, just as Professor Schumpeter renders his economy stationary by abstracting the entrepreneur. But in our case it is clear that, in order to produce change, we do not require the insertion of a special sociological type which has the specific characteristic and function of being able to overcome resistances to innovation. There is no need to deny the existence of such resistances, but there is equally no reason to suppose that they are always, or on balance, stronger than the pressures to innovate which are generated by a capitalist class structure. This becomes particularly clear in the case of a modern large-scale corporation or combine in which the process of innovation becomes highly institutionalized in the hands of staffs of research scientists, cost accountants, and the like, and in which it might be extremely difficult if not impossible to find a Schumpeterian entrepreneur.

While the view of the innovation mechanism which has been suggested here differs in important respects from that adopted by Professor Schumpeter, it should not be supposed that the two are mutually exclusive. There is plenty of room for entrepreneurs of his type in the capitalist class economy, and, obviously, any satisfactory theory must make a place for them. The rise of new firms and new fortunes, which was such a common feature of the capitalist economy of a generation or two ago, is probably best accounted for along the lines of his theory. But nowadays, when the appearance of important new firms is a rare event and when innovation is carried out largely by existing enterprises almost as a part of their regular routine, reliance on the volitional and spontaneous activity of the entrepreneur as an explanatory principle seems less and less safe. Professor Schumpeter himself might possibly agree with this conclusion, at least in part, since all his major works include suggestions that he regards his theory as more suitable to conditions of competitive than what he calls "trustified" capitalism.[4] Of course in saying this I have no intention of imputing to him agreement with the alternative view of the innovation process which has been sketched in this paper.

In conclusion, let me attempt to sum up as concisely as possible what I conceive to be the essential point of this analysis of Professor Schumpeter's theory of economic change. I see no reason to find fault with his conception of innovation as a central feature of economic development; I should go further and say that anyone who denied this part of his theory would be flying in the face of an overwhelming mass of obvious and indisputable facts. But his selection of the entrepreneur, a special sociological type, as the *primum mobile* of change can be called into question. We may instead regard the typical innovator as the tool of the social relations in which he is enmeshed and which *force* him to innovate on pain of elimination. This approach implies a different view of profits and accumulation from that of Professor Schumpeter. For him profits *result* from the innovating process, and hence accumulation is a derivative phenomenon. The alternative view maintains that profits exist in a society with a capitalist class structure even in the absence of innovation. From this standpoint, the form of the profit-making process itself produces the pressure to accumulate, and accumulation generates innovation as a means of preserving the profit-making mechanism and the class structure on which it rests. A different view of the business cycle is also implied, but, as noted earlier, that subject lies outside the scope of the present article.

---

[4] See, for example, "The Instability of Capitalism," *Economic Journal*, Vol. XXXVIII (1928), pp. 384-385. An even stronger statement to this effect occurs in Professor Schumpeter's latest work, *Capitalism, Socialism, and Democracy* (New York, 1942), pp. 132-134, which appeared only after the completion of the present article.

25

Hayek's Road to Serfdom

This review of F. A. Hayek's well-known antisocialist tract, *The Road to Serfdom* (London, 1944, Chicago, 1945), was published under a pen name in Britain during the war (in the *Left News*, organ of the Left Book Club, for September 1944). The reason for anonymity was that I was then attached to the Research and Analysis Branch of the Office of Strategic Services in London and was of course subject to restrictions on writing for publication. Whether book reviewing came under the ban or not I neither knew nor thought it worth while to ascertain — very likely no one else knew either, and if the question had been raised it might have become the subject of memoranda, conferences, cables to Washington, and heaven knows what. People had other things to do in those days, and the use of a pen name seemed simpler.

THE intellectual attack on socialism takes two main forms. Either socialism won't work, and any attempt to make it work will result in chaos and universal impoverishment. Or socialism may work, but it must inevitably lead to a vicious form of totalitarianism. Professor Hayek is one of the few versatile critics who work both sides of the street with equal diligence and enthusiasm. In some of his earlier writings, he proved, to the satisfaction of himself and a few other stalwart rugged individualists, that economic planning is impossible and a sure road to economic ruin. In *The Road to Serfdom* he dons the garb of the political philosopher to warn his contemporaries of the terrible totalitarian dangers that lurk behind the fair promises of the socialist planners.

Briefly, Professor Hayek's case is somewhat as follows. Back in the nineteenth century the world was a fine place. Private property, competition, and liberty were marching forward triumphantly, bringing wealth and culture in their wake. This was due to the spread of liberal ideas, from England as the center, which began with the growth of commerce in early modern times. Some time about 1870, for some obscure reason which Professor Hayek does not reveal, the liberal tide reached its flood and began to recede. A new movement of ideas, this time generated in Germany, began to sweep the Western world. The watchwords of this new intellectual movement were "socialism" and "organization." Most of Europe, including of course Germany and Russia, succumbed. Ever since 1931, England herself, the homeland of liberalism, has been hastening along the road to ruin, and all signs point to an acceleration of the pace in the years immediately ahead. Unless . . . well, unless the English decide, presumably by an act of will ("human will has made the world what it is"), to renounce all these ideas of planning and organization and to install an economy of free and atomistic competition.

It would be interesting to have a coherent account of the theory of historical causation which underlies this thesis. Professor Hayek admits that modern ideas of individualism and liberalism owe their origin and development to the spread of commerce. This would have been a valuable clue to follow up. It might have led him to associate more recent shifts in ideology with fundamental economic trends. And this, in turn, would have forced him to look at what has been happening in the world in the last hundred years or so, and to put the intellectual history of the period into some sort of meaningful context. But Professor Hayek appears to believe that during the nineteenth century there occurred a complete reversal of the role of ideas in the historical process. Ideas began to emerge full-blown, like Minerva from the head of Jove, and to exercise a decisive influence on the course of historical development. From Professor Hayek's point of view, it seems to have been just bad luck that the ideas that really counted were all anti-individualistic, because these were the ideas that persuaded "us" to adopt policies which stifled competition — and the only alternative to competition is totalitarianism. The present state of the world is thus "the result of genuine error on our own part." One is reminded of the epitaph:

> Here lie I and my three daughters,
> Died of drinking Cheltenham waters.
> If we had stuck to Epsom Salts,
> We wouldn't be lying in these here vaults.

But it must not be thought that all this can be written off as harmless nonsense. As a matter of fact it is this "theory" which underlies Professor Hayek's most misleading and mischievous doctrine. The choice of liberalism — in the sense of individualism and competition — as the standard of judgment, deviation from which is to be regarded as error, permits him to lump all anti-individualist thought and policy together as simply totalitarian. It follows that socialism and fascism, Bolshevism and Nazism, are all "the same," that is, they are all anti-individualist. Professor Hayek could have saved himself the embarrassing attempts to prove these propositions — for example, by quoting such authorities as Max Eastman, F. A. Voigt, and Peter Drucker! — since in fact they follow logically from his basic preconceptions.

It is easy to see that this doctrine, by setting up false and irrelevant antitheses, slurs over or actually denies the decisive conflicts of the present historical period. Individualism and competition are simply not important issues, and no amount of assertion from Professor Hayek or anyone else will make them so. The real question is whether the productive forces of modern industry are to be controlled and organized in the interests of capital, which means to make profits and expand investments, or whether they are to be controlled and organized in the interests, as Marx expressed it, of "expanding the life process of the society of producers." The former way leads to crises, international anarchy, frustration, and ultimately war; the latter leads to rising standards of life and culture, cooperation among peoples, and eventually to a degree of freedom such as none but a few at the top of the social pyramid enjoyed even during the heyday of nineteenth-century liberalism. The impending defeat of Nazi Germany, the victorious emergence of the socialist Soviet Union from trials such as no other country has ever survived, and the stirring of the people all over the continent of Europe — these are the concrete proofs that history is approaching a decisive turning point and that the world will soon be face to face with unprecedented opportunities.

Professor Hayek is, of course, completely blind to the magnificent perspective which is now opening out before us. To him — though he never quite dares to say it openly — the Soviet Union is just as bad as Nazi Germany. The inspiring demonstration which socialism has given that a multitude of races and nationalities can live together in an atmosphere of harmony and mutual assistance is completely lost on him. He even goes so far as to compare Nazi anti-Semitism with the liquidation of the kulak in the USSR. The two things, of course, have absolutely nothing in common. The Jew remains a Jew; the kulak could, and most of them did, become a collective farmer on exactly the same terms as his fellows.[1] The sacrifices and sufferings which the

---

[1] This comparison is very revealing and would repay careful examination. By making it, Professor Hayek in effect declares that a given structure of social classes is as much a part of the order of nature as a given pattern of biological races—the fact that there is really no such thing as a Jewish race does not affect the character of the argument since modern anti-Semitism assumes that there is a Jewish race. This is, of course, a basic tenet of bourgeois thought in general. The reasons advanced — by Hayek and others — for disbelieving in the possibility of democratic socialism arise largely from the (often unconscious) conviction that the class structure of capitalism is natural, permanent, and inevitable. What capitalist will ever agree to the planning of production in the interests of the people? Obviously, the argument runs, they will have to be forcibly repressed. It never

people of the Soviet Union have lived through in order to build the foundations of socialism and to protect it against the constant threat of outside aggression — these are merely indications to Professor Hayek that the Soviet citizen is as much a slave as the German under the brutal and destructive Nazi regime. But it is hardly necessary to labor the point at greater length; fortunately, few of the people of Britain are likely now, or at any time in the calculable future, to believe that there is much similarity between Nazi Germany which tried to enslave them and Soviet Russia which is doing a very large and efficient part of the job of stamping out Nazism once and for all.

Besides the general argument from history, Professor Hayek has a number of more specific objections to socialism and socialists. It may be worth while to examine several of these.

Professor Hayek chides socialists with promulgating the myth of "potential plenty." According to this expert economist, "the reader may take it that whoever talks about potential plenty is either dishonest or does not know what he is talking about. Yet it is this false hope as much as anything which drives us along the road to planning." This argument is supported by a trick which does less than credit to the objectivity of its author. Potential plenty is identified with a state of things in which there is no economic problem, in which everyone can have everything he wants and there is no need to choose among alternatives. This is, quite properly, said to be out of the question. And the conclusion is then drawn that poverty is inevitable! Of course, socialists have never thought of potential plenty in any such abstract and irrelevant terms. What they have meant is a decent livelihood for everyone — and that is a perfectly realizable goal. Let Professor Hayek ponder the fact that wartime national

---

occurs to these people that we can do very nicely without capitalists and that we don't need to shoot all of them to get rid of them. What we have to do is take their capital away. Show me a capitalist without any capital!

income in the United States is enough to provide an average family income (assuming four members to each family) of well over £1000 per annum. How many people in the world would object to that as a standard of potential plenty? And is there any reason why they can't have it — not tomorrow, to be sure, but when we have had time to organize a rational utilization of the world's productive resources?

Another objection to socialism, which Professor Hayek repeats again and again, is that economic planning requires that everyone subject to it should have exactly the same set of ethical principles and values. Without it, they will disagree upon the ends of planning, and in the absence of agreed ends planning is impossible. Since people do not in fact have identical values it follows that planning can be put into practice only by forcing them to conform, only by strict regimentation.

There is, of course, a grain of truth in this argument. Socialist planning will be directed to the end of raising the material and cultural level of *all* the people. If a substantial number object to this with sufficient vehemence they will have to be restrained. No one can deny that the early phases of socialism may involve a considerable amount of regimentation of the former capitalists and their beneficiaries. This is certainly unfortunate, but it is a strictly transitional problem, and the ex-capitalists will certainly be given a chance to re-educate themselves and thus to escape regimentation. This is all there is to Professor Hayek's thesis. The assertion that everyone will have to agree down to the last detail on what they want is nonsense. Economic plans are built up on statistical aggregates, not on individual tastes. Individuals can differ widely and change their tastes at will without affecting the essential stability of social demands. If this were not true, capitalism would be just as impossible as socialism. Moreover, for the benefit of Professor Hayek, we may as well confess that socialist planners will sometimes make mistakes. They might, for example, overestimate the birth rate and order the production of too many baby carriages. But we can assure him that they will not at once decree a step-up in procreative activity because something has happened "for which the plan does not provide." There is a much simpler remedy — add the surplus baby carriages to stock and reduce production by the required amount next year.

Professor Hayek, as must by now be expected, views the extension of planning into the international sphere with grave misgivings. Will not the people of poorer countries be jealous of the people of wealthier countries? Is it not a "consistent and inevitable development of socialist doctrine that class strife would become a struggle between the working classes of the different countries"? Professor Hayek, the good liberal, seems to have forgotten the venerable doctrine of comparative advantage. All parties can gain through the rational exchange of goods and services. International socialist planning will make possible such a general all-round advance. Compared to this, the difference in absolute levels as between the various countries is a secondary question; the good sense of the common man, when it gets a chance to express itself in economic policy, can be trusted to prefer steady improvement to the universal impoverishment of a war undertaken in pursuit of an abstract goal of equality. Moreover, there is every reason to suppose that the more backward nations can look forward to more rapid advance than the wealthier nations. This is very clearly demonstrated in the case of the Soviet Union, where the greatest relative progress since the Revolution has been made in what had been the most backward parts of the USSR. Has Professor Hayek heard of a "class struggle" between the peoples of the Central Asian Soviet Republics and the people of Great Russia? Does he imagine that if Britain were to play a genuinely progressive role in India the Indian people would so resent the higher standards of the British worker as to refuse to cooperate?

In conclusion, I cannot refrain from quoting one sentence which I think deserves the widest possible reading public.

Discussing "the alleged suppression of useful patents," Professor Hayek has the following to say (the italics are his): "The conditions in which it would be profitable to put into cold storage a patent *which in the social interest ought to be used* are so exceptional that it is more than doubtful whether this has happened in any important instance."

26

Rosa Luxemburg and the Theory of Capitalism

This review of Rosa Luxemburg, *The Accumulation of Capital*, English translation by Agnes Schwarzschild, introduction by Joan Robinson (London and New Haven, 1951), appeared in *The New Statesman and Nation*, June 2, 1951.

ROSA Luxemburg is one of the really big figures in the history of the international socialist movement, and *The Accumulation of Capital* is unquestionably her magnum opus. That the work should now be made available in English, and in an excellent translation, too, is all to the good.

To understand *The Accumulation of Capital* one must "place" it in the socialist literature of the late nineteenth and early twentieth centuries. This was the period of the great debate between the "orthodox" Marxists and the "revisionists," a debate which, on the purely analytical plane, turned around the question: could capitalism go on expanding indefinitely, or must it sooner or later break down from its own inherent economic contradictions? The revisionists championed a theory of indefinite expansibility and drew from it the conclusion that there was no rush about socialism and no need to prepare for emergencies — everything could be arranged quietly and gradually. The "orthodox" were unanimous in rejecting this theory but very far from unanimous about what they thought to be the correct theory. It was in effect this problem that Rosa Luxemburg undertook to solve in *The Accumulation of Capital*. The title indicates where she found the core of the problem and conveys, as accurately as a brief title can, the subject matter with which the whole book is concerned.

Rosa Luxemburg's theory is original and ingenious. She starts by examining Marx's famous reproduction schemes in Volume II of *Capital*, and concludes that he did not succeed in demonstrating the possibility of accumulation in a closed capitalist system. Accumulation, she held, can take place only if capitalists can turn their surplus value into money, and this presupposes the existence of an effective demand of the right kind and magnitude. But where is this demand to come from? According to Rosa Luxemburg, Marx had no answer. She next sets off in search of an answer in the works of other economists — Sismondi, the Ricardians, Malthus, Rodbertus, Bulgakov, and Tugan-Baranowsky are the chief ones covered — but finds that all of them failed to provide it. She now gives her own explanation of this apparent paradox: no economist has ever been able to demonstrate the possibility of accumulation within a closed capitalist system because in truth no such possibility exists. Capitalism can live and expand only in a noncapitalist environment which provides the effective demand for the capitalists' surplus value and thus enables them to accumulate. But in expanding, capitalism uses up and destroys its noncapitalist living space and eventually must make its own further existence impossible. In the meantime its course is one of merciless encroachment upon any and all noncapitalist strata and nations. All the latest phenomena of imperialism are brought into the framework of this theory: nowhere is there to be found a more impassioned and sustained denunciation of the horrors of imperialism than in the closing chapters of *The Accumulation of Capital*. But this theory did more than account for what was happening in the capitalist world; it also pointed to the inevitable breakdown facing capitalism when the noncapitalist environment is at length exhausted, and it warned socialists to be ready to take over — when the final debacle comes, at the latest, but preferably long before, in order to put an end to the dreadful agonies which capitalism inflicts upon the human race.

There is something very impressive about the unity and power of Rosa Luxemburg's argument. Indeed, seen as a whole and in the context of the debate over revisionism, it stands out as a remarkable achievement — and this in spite of numerous analytical errors which entirely invalidate the central economic thesis. A series of critics — all, as far as I know, Marxists of one sort or another — have demonstrated the confusion which lies at the basis of Rosa Luxemburg's theory. There is no a priori impossiblity of capital accumulation in a closed capitalist system; and if there were, the noncapitalist environment would in no way help matters. What Rosa Luxemburg really does is to examine the problem of accumulation with the premises of "simple reproduction" (from which accumulation is excluded) and then call in the noncapitalist environment as a sort of *deus ex machina* to get her out of the resulting muddle. But confused as her economic theory is, Rosa Luxemburg had the kind of inspired grasp of historical realities which enabled her to transcend all her illogicalities and to produce a work which lives on as one of the classics of socialist literature.

Of all this, it should be said, there is hardly a trace in Joan Robinson's introduction to the English translation of *The Accumulation of Capital*. Mrs. Robinson's interests lie elsewhere, in finding similarities and analogies between the ideas of Rosa Luxemburg and those of latter-day academic economists, especially Keynes and his followers. With this in mind, Mrs. Robinson cheerfully ignores or brushes aside arguments which Rosa Luxemburg would have insisted upon as the very heart of her theory; in their place Mrs. Robinson puts her own interpretations, which are certainly closer to Keynesian doctrine but which, one suspects, would hardly have evoked the enthusiasm of Rosa Luxemburg. In the eyes of the Keynesians there is no greater honor than that of having been in some sort a forerunner of the master. An old socialist fighter like Rosa Luxemburg would doubtless have declined the honor without thanks.

There is one serious criticism to be made of this edition of *The Accumulation of Capital*. The work was originally published in 1912, and was immediately subjected to a storm of criticism in the German and Austrian movements (essentially aimed, it ought to be added, at its revolutionary conclusions rather than at its economic theory). While in prison during World War I, Rosa Luxemburg wrote an answer which was published after the war under the title *The Accumulation of Capital, or What the Epigones Have Made of Marxian Theory*. This reply to her critics is valuable not only from the standpoint of doctrinal history but also because it contains the simplest and most concise statement of Rosa Luxemburg's own theory. It is a great pity that it was not included in the English edition.

27

Thorstein Veblen: Strengths and Weaknesses

This review of the 1946 reprint of Veblen's *The Nature of Peace* (first edition, New York, 1917) appeared in *The New Republic*, February 25, 1946.

VEBLEN'S *The Nature of Peace*, which first appeared early in 1917, has now very appropriately been reissued. In it, he set down his thoughts on the war which was raging about him and on the prospects of the peace to come. The work as a whole, however, is not dated by the particular circumstances of the day; Veblen was really writing about a whole historical period from which we are only now beginning to emerge, and the reader today will find the book as stimulating and absorbing as he would have on the morrow of its publication.

The historical period about which Veblen was writing began roughly in the last quarter of the nineteenth century with the emergence of Germany and Japan as unified imperial states. He saw clearly that these two nations, preserving intact their feudal-dynastic political institutions and appropriating the most modern techniques of production and warfare, had come to dominate the international scene, and that they would continue to do so until their entire social structure had been radically and permanently transformed. "The upshot of all this recital of considerations," he says at one point, and the idea frequently recurs, "appears to be that a neutral peace compact may, or it may not, be practicable in the absence of such dynastic states as Germany and Japan; whereas it has no chance in the presence of these enterprising national establishments." This analysis led Veblen to advocate — usually he wrote specifically of Germany with an addendum to the effect that the same applies to Japan, "only more so" — the "disestablishment of the Imperial dynasty and the abrogation of all feudalistic remnants of privilege in the Fatherland and its allies, together with the reduction of those countries to the status of commonwealths made up of ungraded men." Thereafter, there would have to be a long period of surveillance during which the defeated country would be kept strictly disarmed — a period, he warned, much longer than the time required to prepare a new campaign of conquest. Eventually, however, he believed the German people would slough off their aggressive inclinations and acquire the matter-of-fact and essentially peaceful outlook which is fostered by the discipline of modern machine industry.

Generally speaking, Veblen was not very sanguine about the Allies' willingness to go as far as this, and the German revolution of 1918, which accomplished at one stroke much of what he advocated, must have come as a pleasant surprise to him. Nevertheless, his pessimism turned out in the long run to be fully justified. The German revolution, unlike its Russian counterpart, failed to make a clean sweep of the old order; the forces of reaction simply bided their time and eventually, with Allied connivance, returned to power in the doubly vicious and aggressive form of the Hitler dictatorship. Had he lived to see it, Veblen would undoubtedly have been profoundly depressed, for he would have immediately understood the full meaning of the event. At the same time, however, it can hardly be maintained that he would have been surprised.

Reading Veblen's book today, and with the bitter experience of the interwar years fresh in mind, one finds oneself continually asking: Has the lesson been learned? Will the Allies see it through this time? Has the period about which Veblen wrote with so much insight and understanding really come to a close? Sometimes one cannot help doubting — when, for example, one reads that the American Military Government has given its blessing to a Bavarian royalist party; or when one reads that the British (under a Labor government, too) are already, long before there is conclusive evidence of the destruction of Nazism, arguing for the restoration at a high level of German heavy industry; or when one realizes that the American authorities in Japan have let six months go by without laying the ax to the economic roots of Japanese imperialism. There are plenty of disturbing signs; and yet there are two factors in the situation which are both relatively new and entirely favorable. For one thing, the USSR, which has suffered most from German and Japanese aggression and which has no inherited tenderness for predatory ruling classes, is this time one of the leading Allies and can be counted upon to throw its full influence against the recovery of reaction in Germany and Japan. And, for another thing, the underlying population (to use a favorite phrase of Veblen's) is everywhere fed up with war and realizes more clearly than ever that the greatest danger comes from the countries which have just plunged the world into the most destructive war of all time. The issue has not yet been finally decided, but on balance there is no ground for discouragement.

While history has fully vindicated Veblen's analysis of the role of Germany and Japan, I think one must nevertheless adopt a critical attitude toward much of the reasoning which underlies that analysis and which has a direct relevance to a wide range of vital problems of the day. (In this connection, one must not be misled into supposing that a correct conclusion proves the correctness of the reasoning by which it is reached.) Veblen takes his departure from a theory of nationalism or patriotism — he uses the terms interchangeably — which is very one-sided and, despite appearances to the contrary, unhistorical. According to this theory, the prehistoric forerunner of modern patriotism was a sense of group solidarity which served the utilitarian purposes of survival. Later on, however, when society had become differentiated into classes, there were no longer interests common to the group at large. Nevertheless, the ruling classes fostered the traditional sense of group solidarity which now became essentially a device for hiding real conflicts of interest within the group. During feudal times, this sense of group solidarity became fixed in the form of the loyalty of the subject to his ruler, and it is in this form that it has come down to modern times. In the case of such countries as imperial Germany and Japan, Veblen considers the relationship to be direct and obvious, while in the case of the democratic countries he asserts that their "patriotism" or "national spirit" is "after all and at best an attenuated and impersonalized remnant of dynastic loyalty."

Now of course there is much truth in the view that patriotism, especially in its more extreme forms, provides a cover for class, as opposed to general, interests. But to suggest, as Veblen does, that nationalism is nothing but a hangover from feudal times, and that it constitutes a purely negative and destructive force in the modern world, is to leave out one whole epoch of history and to forget that we are passing through another. In the formative stages of modern society, it was bourgeois nationalism which carried the banner against feudal separatism and obscurantism; and in the very country which Veblen often picks out as the only one devoid of a spirit of patriotism — China — we have been witnessing the growth of a nationalism that extends to nearly all classes and basically reflects a desire for independence and social reform. Similarly, in the Soviet Union a new sense of patriotism has grown up in recent years which embraces not only Great Russians, in whose case it might be supposed to be a carry-over from prerevolutionary times, but also peoples who were previously among the most backward in the world. Thus one cannot avoid the conclusion that Veblen's theory, while it happens to work well in the case of contemporary Germany and Japan, is at best a half-truth which can easily lead to false diagnoses of existing social situations.

The treatment of nationalism is only one example of theoretical inadequacy in Veblen's work. Despite the fact that he is commonly rated as an economist, it must be said that his economic analysis is usually weak and often misleading. He regards capitalism — for which he has a variety of designations, among the most frequent of which are "business enterprise" and "the price system" — in a wholly negative light and thus sees only one side, historically the least important side, of its nature. In Veblen's view, the capitalist operates purely in the realm of finance, and his only relation to production is one of sabotage and obstruction; his object is to mulct the underlying population to the maximum possible degree and to waste the proceeds in ostentatious display. Meanwhile, despite the obstruction of capitalists, mechanical industry expands and becomes increasingly productive. This view leads Veblen to regard the industrial engineer as the truly progressive factor in the modern economy and to postulate the existence of a basic conflict between the capitalist and the engineer. There are four main weaknesses in this theory: (1) it ignores, or at best slurs over, the capitalist's fundamental urge to add to his wealth as distinct from consuming it; (2) it entirely fails to see that accumulation by the capitalist can take place only through the steady expansion of the means of production and employment of more labor; (3) consequently it fails to see that the capitalist in effect calls into existence the industrial engineer, pays him, and gives direction to his work; and finally, (4) it inverts the relationship of engineer to capitalist, which is in reality one of dependence of the former on the latter, and makes it appear as a relation of conflict. It is not hard to understand how this theory of Veblen's became the basis of a variety of crackpot and even semifascist schemes in the hands of "followers" who totally lacked his deep historical knowledge and insight.

But the theory also had unfortunate consequences for Veblen's own work. Because he ignored the accumulation process — what modern economists would call the problem of savings and investment — he was debarred from developing an adequate theory of employment and of business fluctuations in general. (What he had to say on these subjects, chiefly in *The Theory of Business Enterprise,* is obscure and seems to center largely on expansion and contraction of the debt structure.) And without such a theory, his views on the economic functions and policies of the state were necessarily one-sided and frequently have a strong air of unreality about them. Indeed, what Veblen wrote on these questions often seems as though it could have come from the pen of a nineteenth-century Manchester liberal who had acquired his economics at second hand from Adam Smith. Tariffs, encouragement of exports, conquest of colonies, and so on, are all lumped together as patent economic absurdities which benefit only a few people directly concerned and cause damage and loss to everyone else. In a world of full employment and extreme mobility of productive resources, this would be largely true; but this is just another way of saying how far from true it was in the real world about which Veblen was writing. Since Veblen regarded practically all government economic policies as absurd and harmful, he was forced to assume that they must be linked up with the competitive struggle for prestige which, like its twin brother patriotism, is a carry-over from the feudal period. Thus in Veblen's treatment, many of the most important phenomena of modern social life have the character of an elaborate make-believe centering around the beliefs and customs of the feudal period and having nothing whatever to do with the real interests of living people.

The weaknesses of Veblen's economic analysis show

through repeatedly in the book under review, but most clearly in the final chapter entitled "Peace and the Price System." This chapter may be taken as typical of most of Veblen's economic writings: full of brilliant perceptions and insights but based on a theory which is always threatening to put him off the track and not infrequently leads up a blind alley.

For all the criticisms that can be made against it, however — and there are many that cannot be included in a brief review — it must nevertheless be said that *The Nature of Peace* is a great book which stands head and shoulders above the innumerable contributions to the subject which have flowed in a steady stream from the pens of respectable authorities during the period of the two world wars. That is because Veblen, unlike the respectable authorities, had a profound understanding of history and was able to see the present not as an epoch of anarchy and unreason but as a stage in a long-run process of social change.

Here we have the key, I think, to one of the most puzzling things about Veblen, namely, that the so-called "institutionalist" school which he inspired disintegrated rapidly and never produced anything of lasting value. He was a great man, and he attracted followers because of it. But he was greater than his own theories; and unfortunately greatness cannot be passed on, while theories can.

Part VI

Some Problems in Political Economy

28

Marxian and Orthodox Economics

This is the text of a talk to the John Reed Society of Harvard, March 24, 1947. It was published in Science & Society, *Summer 1947.*

I WOULD probably not be justified in assuming on the part of even so interested an audience as this a working knowledge of the principles of Marxian social thought. It is a paradox which is worth pondering that though Marxism is entirely a product of that "Western civilization" which our universities talk so much about preserving and though Marx was, as one wholly un-Marxian economist recently said, "the most influential figure of the nineteenth century,"[1] still our universities devote less attention to Marx and Marxism than to any one of a dozen secondary intellectual movements. Hence I would like to begin with a very brief sketch of Marxian economics which will serve as a basis for what I shall have to say later.

I

Marxian economics can only be understood as a part of a general theory of society and history. This general theory starts from a conception — itself derived from a study of historical facts — of human societies as being in a constant state of flux and change. This perpetual motion, sometimes slow and sometimes rapid, is of course the outcome of the activity of innumerable human beings. Their activity, how-

[1] Alexander Gray, *The Socialist Tradition* (London, 1946), p. 331.

ever, is neither arbitrary nor inexplicable; rather it is the product of the concrete circumstances in which they live, circumstances which include especially their physical environment, the methods which they use to manipulate that environment, and their relations with one another. At any given time and place, those who are similarly circumstanced tend to have a common outlook and common interests and hence to act in a similar fashion; those who are differently circumstanced tend to come into conflict. Groups which are determined and delimited in this way are called classes, and their opposition is called class struggle. On the stage of history it is classes — or, if one prefers, individuals grouped into classes — which are the chief actors. It is their strivings and their struggles with one another which constitute the motor forces of social change and social development.

According to this theory, if one wants to understand what happened in a particular part of the world during some specified segment of historical time one must first investigate the circumstances which determined the behavior of the people concerned. In other words, one must investigate the environment and resources, the technical means, and above all the class structure of the society (or societies) which existed in the place and at the time under review. One must then proceed to formulate a specific theory of the functioning of the particular society in question. This specific theory will concern itself first with the fundamental problems of the organization of production and distribution on the one hand, and the developmental tendencies to which these arrangements give rise on the other. In other words, it will start with a theory of the economy of the society in question and will build up on this foundation theories of politics, law, religion, culture, and the like. This theory, or rather these interrelated theories, can then be used as a guide to the study and ordering of such facts as the historian may be able to extract from the sources which are available to him.

This approach can be applied to the present as well as to

the past. In fact it acquires its greatest significance as a method of dealing with the present, for it enables us to see contemporary events in proper perspective and to understand the forces which are shaping the future. As applied to the present, therefore, it is not only a canon of interpretation; it is also a guide to action which looks to the creation of a better society.

It was, above all, the problem of the present and its relation to the future which interested Marx; and for this reason he devoted the greater part of his life to working out a theory of the society in which he lived. He did not complete the job; he did not even complete the first part of the job, which was to develop a theory of the economy of contemporary society. But he showed the way; and in *Capital*, incomplete though it is, he built the foundations of a genuinely scientific understanding of the social order under which we in this country and much of the rest of the world are still living.

Let us attempt to set down the broad outlines of Marxian economics conceived as the basis of a comprehensive theory of the contemporary social system. In order to do this it is, of course, first necessary to specify the decisive characteristics of this system. These are: (1) That production is typically organized by private individuals with a view to sale rather than use. (In Marxian terminology: products take the form of commodities; the system is one of commodity production.) (2) That the means of production are monopolized by a small minority of the total population. (3) Therefore, that the vast majority is forced to work for the minority in order to gain the means of subsistence. (In Marxian terminology: labor power is itself a commodity.) Under these circumstances, economic relations are essentially relations of purchase and sale which find a quantitative expression in terms of exchange value. It is for this reason that economics must start with the theory of value, which, however, is only the beginning and not the end of the science.

We need not go into Marx's value theory except to point out that it is essentially the classical (Ricardian) theory which he took over and adapted to his own purposes. The same can be said of the theory of surplus value which asserts that the value of the worker's product exceeds the value of his means of subsistence (wages) and that the difference goes to the owners of the means of production in the form of profit, rent, and interest. As developed by Marx, the theories of value and surplus value provide the means of translating the dominant social relations of capitalist society into quantitative terms which will be suitable for rigorous theoretical treatment. At the same time, they provide a path by which one can return at any time from the abstract realm of quantity to the underlying realm of social relations.

It is clear that the capitalist occupies the central position in the economy which has been briefly characterized. It is he who hires laborers, organizes production, and markets commodities. The very form of the process imposes upon the capitalist the aim of acquiring surplus value. This becomes the dominant motive of his activities, and he pursues it in every way open to him. This means on the one hand that he attempts to maximize the rate of return on a given range of operations and on the other hand that he continually extends the range of his operations by adding a part of his surplus value to capital — in other words, by accumulating capital. Thus capitalism is by its very nature a highly dynamic economy which involves ever new revolutions in technique and a restless expansion of production.

This process of development, however, contains a whole series of what Marxists call contradictions. The investigation of these contradictions and their implications constitutes the central core of Marxian economics, and it is obviously impossible to go into the subject in a brief summary. We must be content to set down the most important ones. First, technological change under the direction of capitalists creates unemployment (Marx's "reserve army of labor") which in turn holds wages in check and depresses the consuming power of the working class. It is in this sense that unemployment is an essential and integral part of the capitalist system; without it capitalists would be in danger of losing their control over the labor market. Second, as capital accumulates, the rate of profit tends to fall. A falling rate of profit causes capitalists at a certain stage to interrupt the accumulation process, and this in turn produces economic crises and depressions. Third, as a capitalist country grows wealthier it tends to devote an ever larger share of its resources to increasing its powers of production. But the power of the working class to consume plus the willingness of capitalists to consume by no means keeps pace with this growth of production potential. The result is that to an ever greater extent the latter remains unutilized; in place of actual economic expansion there at length sets in stagnation and even contraction. Finally, both capital accumulation and technological change favor the growth of the scale of production and the centralization of capital under the control of great trusts and monopolies. The development of monopoly not only accentuates the other contradictions of capitalism; it also adds new ones of its own making, such as a vastly inflated and wasteful apparatus for distributing and selling commodities.

In order to overcome these contradictions, capitalists make use of the state power over which they have ultimate control. To a certain extent they make concessions to the workers in order to keep them from developing in a revolutionary, anticapitalist direction. But their main objective is always to use the state as a means of improving their own position and the functioning of their particular segment of world capitalism at the expense of all other countries, including both those which are and those which are not capitalist. This leads to trade wars, empire building, exploitation of backward peoples — in short, to all the phenomena which are generally known under the name of imperialism — and finally to war itself.

II

This outline of Marxian economics is sketchy and no doubt very imperfect. Nevertheless, I hope it will serve to bring into clear focus certain points which in the past have often been neglected even by trained Marxists. I shall try to state these points as simply as possible and to avoid the intricate problems of methodology which their full elaboration would necessarily involve.

In the first place, we see that what is usually called "Marxian economics" is in reality *a part of the theory of the functioning of a particular social system,* namely, capitalism. In principle, much more could be included. There could be Marxian economics of feudalism, Marxian economics of socialism — in short, Marxian economics of every distinct social system. Something, indeed, has been done by Marxists toward clarifying the economics of social systems other than capitalism, but my impression is that it is still not much more than a beginning. There is an enormous amount of fruitful work yet to be done, work which I think will make possible revolutionary advances in historiography. But in the meanwhile there can be no doubt that what we understand by "Marxian economics" applies exclusively to capitalism, an historically specific and essentially transitory social system which made its appearance in western Europe between the sixteenth and the nineteenth centuries, achieved a dominating position in the civilized world during the nineteenth and early twentieth centuries, and entered its final phase with the Russian Revolution of 1917. Orthodox economics — the kind you study in your textbooks and courses — is more ambitious in its objectives: it sets out to explain man's economic behavior regardless of time and place. Its interest in social systems is purely incidental, its relation to the understanding of history no concern of the economist qua economist. In sharp contrast, Marxian economics is always based on the postulates of a given social system and has no purpose other than understanding some phase of history, including the present regarded (as it should be) as an integral part of history.

In the second place — and this point is related to the preceding one — Marxism (and hence, of course, Marxian economics) implies a very definite, though still inadequately spelled out, theory of social psychology. This theory begins with the premise that one cannot analyze social behavior by starting with individuals and adding them up (this is the traditional method of orthodox economics) but one must instead start with the structure and form of society and work back to individuals, or, rather, characteristic groups of individuals. Thus the objectives which the individual seeks to attain and to a very large degree the motives which drive him on are, in the Marxian view, not derived from "human nature" or "instincts" or any other supposed but essentially indefinable causal constants. They have their roots in a certain social order, a definite class structure, a determined historical background. It follows that *the intelligent analysis of human behavior can never be separated from the question of the social system and its past history.* I believe that modern psychologists and anthropologists are gradually coming to a realization of this fact, but I wonder how often the idea has been presented to you in your reading or in your classes.

There is one more point about Marxian economics which I want to emphasize, namely, that it assumes as a matter of course in any class society economic power and political power are in the hands of the same class and in general will be used for the same ends. (During periods of transition there may be exceptions to this rule, but this is a refinement which does not affect its general validity.) It follows, of course, that in reality *there is no clear dividing line between the "economic" and the "political" elements in social life,* even though it may be convenient and even necessary to separate them for analytical purposes. In dealing with problems of the real world, as distinct from problems of abstract theory, it is therefore almost never permissible to treat economic or political factors in isolation. And yet this is exactly what orthodox economists are always doing. Some of them regard the government as a sort of devil responsible for any and all economic troubles; others regard the government as a *deus ex machina* which can rescue the economy from any difficulties it may get into. Neither group bothers to investigate the real relation between the economy and the state. That, after all, would be getting outside the field of economics, and your orthodox economist is nothing if not a scrupulous observer of jurisdictional lines.

III

I should like now to analyze somewhat more specifically the views of the Keynesians — by all odds the most important school of capitalist economists — toward the issues which have been raised in the preceding section.

If the Keynesians have any coherent theory of history they have certainly been successful in preventing it from obtruding itself into their economic writings. Perhaps they would explain this by saying that the two subjects, history and economics, are mutually irrelevant, or that history has something to learn from economics, but not vice versa. More likely, most of them have never given the subject a thought and would regard it as a waste of time to do so.

The consequences of this neglect of history are interesting. It leads the Keynesians to ignore the differences between social systems, which comes to the same thing in practice as denying the existence or possibility of different social systems. From this it is a natural step for the Keynesians to treat the particular form of capitalism with which they happen to be familiar as though it were the inevitable and eternal form of society. Thus we are not surprised to find that Keynes himself had no hesitation in applying his theory of public works, developed in Great Britain of the 1930s, to pyramid-building in ancient Egypt or cathedral-building in medieval Europe. Both are presumably examples of projects financed by budgetary deficits which create employment and banish depression! One is perhaps justified in suspecting that the pharaohs and bishops would have been more than a little puzzled by this interpretation of their soul-saving undertakings.

If this were all, it would perhaps be a small matter which one could afford to overlook. But a much more serious consequence of regarding capitalism as inevitable and eternal is that it prevents the learned economist from seeing what is becoming obvious to a rapidly increasing proportion of the world's population, that capitalism is breaking down under the weight of its own contradictions. To Keynes this tremendous historical drama through which we are passing appeared to be "nothing but a frightful muddle, a transitory and unnecessary muddle."[2] In general, indeed, one can say that to the Keynesians the crisis of capitalism appears as a crisis of intelligence. What is needed, according to their view, is not a redefinition of social relations but a liberal dose of Keynesian wisdom in higher places.

Let us now turn to the question of the kind of social psychology which is implicit in the Keynesian theoretical system. Here we find just what we would expect, that Keynesians treat behavior patterns which are characteristic of capitalist society as though they were manifestations of innate "propensities," "animal instincts," and so on. Let us look at what is perhaps the most important of these "propensities," namely, the "propensity to consume" or — what is but the other side of the same coin — the "propensity to save." We have already remarked above in outlining Marxian economics that under capitalism those who are in control of the means of production, the capitalists, are motivated in their economic behavior by a drive to accumulate capital.

[2] *Essays in Persuasion* (London, 1931), p. vii.

In other words, capitalists typically do not consume all of their incomes; they devote a share which generally increases with the size of their incomes to expanding the scope of their productive operations. Workers, on the other hand, behave very differently. When they are able to do so they save out of their wages, but the purpose of such savings is not, as in the case of the capitalists, to build up their wealth, power, and prestige; rather it is to provide a reserve against unemployment or old age, to finance the education of their children, or to promote some similar aim. In other words, capitalists accumulate for the sake of accumulation and the advantages it brings, while workers save at one time in order to be able to spend at another. It goes without saying that these modes of behavior have nothing to do with the nature of the human psyche; they simply reflect different objective positions in a particular complex of human relations. Now what do the Keynesians make of all this? In the first place, they lump capitalists and workers together into a category which they like to call "the public." Next, they observe, quite correctly, that when the national income goes up more is saved and when it goes down less is saved. Finally, they conclude from this that human beings are endowed with a certain "propensity to save" which governs the way they dispose of their incomes. Of course this is not the whole story; it is recognized that the distribution of income, as well as various other factors, play a part in determining the outcome for the economy as a whole. But it is an important part of the story, and it illustrates admirably the total inability of the Keynesians to relate behavior patterns to the social context from which they emerge. Not only do they treat the behavior of people under capitalism as though it were universal; they also fail to see that even under capitalism patterns of class behavior can be extremely diverse.

When we turn to the question of the relation between economics and politics, we shall find that the Keynesians hold a *deus ex machina* theory of the state. They are not all agreed on what the state should do, but each has his own recipe for full employment, higher living standards, and lasting prosperity. These programs for the most part are logically consistent and highly persuasive. They make the task of social betterment sound easy, or if not easy at any rate uncomplicated. What is needed is education (naturally along Keynesian lines), for when people — at least the right people — come to understand what is the matter and how it can be remedied, can there be any doubt about the outcome? What the Keynesians overlook, or at least completely miss the implications of, is that every one of these schemes which deserves to be taken seriously would involve redistributing income in favor of the poor, curtailing the power of capital, and enhancing the power of labor. It is simply Utopian to expect the state in a society where all the levers of control are in the hands of the capitalist class to embark upon such a course. "Where," Lenin asked in *Imperialism*, "except in the imagination of sentimental reformists, are there any trusts capable of interesting themselves in the conditions of the masses instead of in the conquest of colonies?" Until the Keynesians can answer this question, we shall, I am afraid, have to put them in the unflattering category of "sentimental reformists."

I have not been concerned in this talk to assess the value of orthodox economics in clarifying the functioning of the capitalist mechanism. Personally, I think that in the case of the Keynesian brand it is considerable and that everyone — Marxists included — has much to learn from the work of Keynes and his followers. But I have tried to show that their deserved reputation in a particular branch of economics is no reason for taking them seriously when it comes to the crucial problems of historical interpretation and social diagnosis. It is on the solution to these problems that we must rely for guidance in the field of action. Here Marxism, and Marxism alone, provides us with a comprehensive, integrated science of society and social change. Keynesism, perhaps to a greater extent than the various brands of economics which preceded it, lights up a part of the picture. But when the Keynesians try to do more — as unfortunately they persistently do — they simply purvey the stale prejudices and superficialities of bourgeois common sense.

29

Fabian Political Economy

This review of the Jubilee Edition of the famous Fabian Essays *(London, 1948) appeared in* The Journal of Political Economy, *June 1949.*

MARXISM is the accepted theoretical foundation of a large part of the present-day world socialist movement, a part which includes not only Communists and the recently unified working-class parties in eastern Europe but also left-wing socialist groups and parties of varying size and importance in many other countries (for example, the Nenni Socialists in Italy and the newly formed Parti Socialiste Unitaire in France). But what, it may be asked, is the theoretical foundation of the rest of the world socialist movement, including the Labor parties of Great Britain and several of the Dominions, the Socialist parties of western Europe, and a variety of smaller parties elsewhere which display a spiritual kinship to British and western European Social Democracy?

There are probably many who would maintain that this second branch of the world socialist movement has no systematic theory in the sense that Marxism is a systematic theory. Strictly speaking, this contention is no doubt justified. There are still some Social Democrats who pay lip service to Marxism; but even this is becoming an increasingly rare phenomenon, and it is clear that none of the Social Democratic parties can properly be regarded as Marxist. Furthermore, no generally accepted body of doctrine plays the same role in Social Democracy that Marxism does in the Communist and left-wing socialist movements. But it would be a mistake, I think, to conclude from these undoubted facts that Social Democracy has *no* coherent theoretical foundation whatever. Its world view, its methods of economic and political analysis, its conceptions of strategy and tactics, are all far too uniform and persistent to permit such an interpretation. A theoretical foundation — what is usually called an "ideology" nowadays — can exist without ever having been formulated as such. A situation of this kind is an obvious challenge to the social scientist. To make explicit what has hitherto been implicit is always an important step on the road to comprehension and evaluation.

If anyone should decide to accept this challenge, he would certainly be obliged to examine materials from a wide variety of sources going back more than a hundred years in time and covering at least the major western European countries. But I think he would almost inevitably start with Britain, the home of, by all odds, the largest and most important Social Democratic party. Having selected Britain, he would soon be led to the Fabian Society; and, having once taken up the Fabian Society, he would find himself committed to an exhaustive study of its most famous publication — *Fabian Essays in Socialism*, first published in 1889 under the editorship of George Bernard Shaw and now reissued (for the fifth time) in a jubilee edition with a 25-page postscript by the original editor himself.[1] The *Fabian Essays*, I venture to assert, constitute the most important single source for understanding the theoretical foundations of the present-day British socialist movement. The following notes are intended to help our hypothetical investigator

---

[1] *Fabian Essays*, by Bernard Shaw, the Right Honorable Lord Passfield (Sidney Webb), Graham Wallas, Lord Olivier, William Clarke, Annie Besant, Hubert Bland: With a Postscript by the Original Editor, Bernard Shaw, entitled "Sixty Years of Fabianism" (London, 1948).

(who, I hope, will not remain forever hypothetical) to a proper appreciation of the meaning and significance of these *Essays*. But since the space at my disposal is strictly limited, I shall not attempt to cover all aspects of the *Essays* but rather shall confine my remarks to the political economy of the Fabians.

Before proceeding to an analysis of Fabian political economy, however, I should like to point out what is, I think, inadequately understood, that Fabianism is by no means a peculiarly British phenomenon. On the contrary, it appeared slightly later on the Continent of Europe; but there it wore a somewhat different guise. To explain this difference we must recall that, when the Fabian Society was formed (1883), organized socialism was much stronger on the Continent than in Britain and, moreover, that the Continental movement had, for the most part, officially embraced Marxism. The Fabians had a relatively clear road, while their opposite numbers on the Continent had to make their way in the face of a firmly intrenched socialist ideology. Hence when Fabianism appeared on the Continent, it called itself "revisionism," that is, a movement based on an alleged "revision" of Marxism. But as regards content, Fabianism and revisionism are blood brothers — or perhaps I should say "father and son," because both the priority of Fabianism and the direct relation between Fabianism and revisionism are demonstrable facts. E. R. Pease, the historian of the Fabian Society, boasts, with reason, that the Fabians led an *international* revolt against Marxism. So far as the Continent was concerned, Pease tells us,

the revolt came from England in the person of Edward Bernstein, who, exiled by Bismarck, took refuge in London, and was for years intimately acquainted with the Fabian Society and its leaders. Soon after his return to Germany he published in 1899 a volume criticizing Marxism and thence grew up the Revisionist movement for free thought in Socialism which has attracted all the younger men, and before the war [World War I] had virtually, if not actually, obtained control over the Social Democratic Party. In England, and in Germany through Bernstein, I think the Fabian Society may claim to have led the revolt.[2]

Here Bernstein's work is correctly characterized as being an *attack* on, rather than a *revision* of, Marxism; and the priority of the Fabians is given its due recognition.

Let us now turn to the *Essays*. There are eight in all (two by Shaw and one each by the other six), divided into three groups. The first group is headed "The Basis of Socialism" and contains an "Economic" essay by Shaw, a "Historic" essay by Sidney Webb, an "Industrial" essay by William Clarke, and a "Moral" essay by Sydney Olivier. The second group, entitled "The Organization of Society," contains "Property under Socialism" by Graham Wallas and "Industry under Socialism" by Annie Besant. The third and last group, entitled "The Transition to Social Democracy," consists of "Transition" by Shaw and "The Outlook" by Hubert Bland. The most important essays, of course, are by Shaw and Webb, who had already achieved intellectual leadership in the Fabian Society and, together with Beatrice Webb, who joined two years later, were to dominate its development for many years to come. If I had to rank the others in descending order of importance, I think I should put Clarke at the top of the list, followed by Wallas, Bland, Olivier, and Besant. The Besant essay is by far the weakest, representing a lapse into a kind of insipid Utopianism which is not generally characteristic of the Fabians.

In his valuable introduction to the 1920 reprint of *Fabian Essays*, Sidney Webb expressed the opinion that the part of the book which had stood up best was the economic analysis:

> I think it is not merely the partiality of friendship that finds in the first essay [by Shaw] a survey of the economic evolution of society which, for terse comprehensiveness and brilliant gen-

---

[2] *The History of the Fabian Society* (London, 1916), p. 239.

eralization, has not since been excelled in any language. But throughout the whole book what is distinctively economic is, in my judgment, as incisive and accurate today as it was when it was written. Tested by a whole generation of further experience and criticism, I conclude that, in 1889, we knew our Political Economy, and that our Political Economy was sound. (P. xviii.)

What, then, was the political economy of the Fabians in 1889 and apparently for at least the next three decades?

The various influences which went into the Fabian synthesis are clearly recognizable in Shaw's essay. In the background and dominating the whole is Ricardo — not, however, the real historical Ricardo but a thoroughly "Henry-Georgeified" Ricardo. The labor theory of value, with its correlative theory of profit, is missing, while the classical theories of rent and population stand out all the more boldly for having been lifted out of their total context. In place of the Ricardian theory of value, Shaw substitutes the Jevonian theory, complete with all the characteristic Jevonian terminology.[3] In place of the Ricardian theory of profit, Shaw substitutes . . . what? I find it quite impossible to give a clear-cut answer to this question. A "rent of ability" theory is occasionally in evidence (e.g. p. 9), though how much importance Shaw attaches to it is not clear. Sometimes profit appears to be a sort of super-rent, "a payment for the privilege of using land at all — for access to that which is now a close monopoly." (P. 10.) Sometimes, incongruously, profit is represented as arising, in the manner of the Marxian theory, from the capacity of the proletarian to produce a surplus over and above his subsistence. (P. 11.) Sometimes

[3] Shaw had originally adhered to the Marxian theory of value but was converted to the utility school as the result of a debate with Wicksteed in 1884 in the pages of the socialist magazine, *Today*. Wicksteed's critique of the Marxian theory is one of the earliest and also one of the best from the point of view of the subjective value theory. It is reproduced, along with Shaw's reply, in the 1933 edition of *The Commonsense of Political Economy*. (Vol. II, pp. 705 ff.)

profit seems to disappear altogether, as in the statement that "all men will cease producing when the value of their product falls below its cost of production, whether in labor or in labor *plus rent*." (P. 17.) And sometimes profit (or at least interest) seems to be merely rent under another name, as when it is asserted that "colloquially, one property with a farm on it is said to be land yielding rent; whilst another, with a railway on it, is called capital yielding interest." (P. 19.)

One might suppose that this confusion about the theory of profit would prove fatal to a specifically socialist political economy. But Shaw, I imagine, would have brushed the criticism aside even if he could have been persuaded of its correctness. For him, rent was overwhelmingly the dominant form of unearned income, profit a phenomenon of secondary importance. "The socialization of rent," he tells us, "would mean the socialization of the sources of production by the expropriation of the present private proprietors, and the transfer of their property to the entire nation. This transfer, then, is the subject matter of the transition to Socialism." (P. 167.) And the same idea recurs again and again in the arguments of all the essayists. If this were the case, it would follow, of course, that no amount of confusion regarding profit could affect the essential soundness of the Fabian scheme of political economy.

Needless to say, Shaw's theory of economic development is constructed in such a way as to place landed property and rent in the center of the picture. The dynamic factor is population growth, which drives the margin of cultivation further and further down, forcing the unfortunate proletarians to accept an ever lower standard of living and pouring a constantly growing stream of wealth into the pockets of the idle landlord class. There is no mention of the problem of capital accumulation.

The Jevonian theory of value is not an integral part of this scheme. Even without it, the structure would remain standing, just as a column will continue to do its work without the volutes which decorate the capital. The only positive conclusion which rests on the Jevonian theory is the ingenious but unconvincing one that the existence of unemployed workers proves that labor is really valueless, since "by the law of indifference, nobody will buy men at a price when he can obtain equally serviceable men for nothing." (P. 18.) Of course, the unemployed will not work for nothing, and neither will the employed workers whom they might replace. But this does not prove that the workers have a value: "Their wage is not the price of themselves: for they are worth nothing: it is only their keep." (P. 18.) It seems that Shaw would have done better to stick to the less paradoxical but more logical classical theory according to which their keep *is* their value.[4]

It is possible to find numerous passages in the volume as a whole that are hardly consistent with the abstract theory of political economy set forth in the opening essay. Particularly in discussing the history of nineteenth-century Britain, the Fabians showed themselves to be fully aware that the victory of free trade was merely the reflection in the political sphere of the economic triumph of the mill-owning capitalists over the landowning aristocracy.[5] But they never followed up the theoretical implications of this awareness. If they had,

---

[4] Nevertheless, it must not be overlooked that Shaw was here grappling with a very real problem toward the solution of which neither the classical nor the marginal-utility economists had the slightest contribution to make. That problem is simply this: how to account for the persistence of unemployment. Shaw's attempt to solve the problem in terms of the marginal utility theory leads to a flat contradiction; but this is hardly a sign of inferiority to economists who never even recognized the existence of the problem. He could have found a way out by returning to Marx. His latter-day successors in the British labor movement have been saved this painful alternative by the providential (from their point of view) intervention of Keynes.

[5] Note, for example, the statement of Clarke: "The triumph of Free Trade therefore signifies economically the decay of the old landlord class pure and simple, and the victory of capitalism." (P. 75.)

they would have been forced to concern themselves with the problems of capital accumulation, and they would perhaps have come to a recognition of the fact that the development of capitalism can lead, via technological advance and the opening of the world market, to a rise instead of a fall in the margin of cultivation. With this recognition there would surely have come another, that the whole Shavian structure of political economy was a house built on sand. And then? Is it too much to suppose that Marx might at least have been given a more respectful hearing?

But this is to indulge in unfruitful speculation. As a matter of fact, the ideas of the Fabians remained under the domination of a Shavianized Henry-Georgian version of the classical theories of rent and population; and this fact can, I believe, be directly related to another aspect of Fabian doctrine which has had a much more lasting and fateful influence on British socialism than has Fabian political economy itself. I refer to the famous theory of "gradualism," which is often — and not without reason — considered to be the very essence of Fabianism.

One can find in the *Essays* support for two different versions of the theory of gradualism. On the one hand, there is the idea, expressed in numerous passages, that society is *automatically* socializing itself, that "the economic history of the [nineteenth] century is an almost continuous record of the progress of Socialism" (Webb, p. 29), and that "there will never be a point at which a society crosses from Individualism to Socialism. The change is ever going forward; and our society is well on the way to Socialism." (Besant, p. 141.) According to this theory, socialism irresistibly permeates all classes and parties ("we are all socialists now," in the famous words of the Liberal politician, Sir William Harcourt), and the only function of the conscious socialist is to help the process along; there is no need for a separate socialist political party with a program and strategy of its own. The second conception of gradualism holds that the underlying economic development of society favors the growth of socialism but that the actual introduction of socialism can come about only as a result of the conscious actions of a separately organized party which carries on a continuous political struggle against all bourgeois parties. The strategy of this socialist party must or ought to be (both views can be found in the *Essays*) one of piecemeal reform which will yield full-fledged socialism only as the outcome of a protracted process. This conception of gradualism finds its clearest expression in the concluding essay of Hubert Bland, who gives short shrift to the permeationist school of thought.

Despite the coexistence in the *Essays* of these two ideas of gradualism, I think there can be no doubt that in practice Fabianism promoted the independent political-action type. Sidney Webb, in his 1920 introduction, is emphatic on this point; and, though it seems to me that he underestimates the strength of permeationism in the *Essays* themselves, I see no reason not to accept his judgment. It is clearly this conception of gradualism which was embraced by the Labor Party in 1919 (when a definitely socialist constitution was for the first time adopted) and which has been the party's leading political tenet ever since. How is gradualism in this sense related to the Fabian theory of political economy, which we have already examined?

To answer this question, we must keep in mind that the gradualist strategy implies not only an assumption about what is desirable but also an assumption about what is possible. It obviously presupposes that the property-owning classes will confine their opposition to socialism to the arena of constitutional politics and will accept defeat with a good grace. If this assumption is not made — if it is assumed, instead, that at some stage the property-owning classes will not hesitate to throw over the constitution and use violence in defense of their privileges — then to preach unconditional gradualism is simply to disarm the socialist movement in advance and to invite ultimate disaster. What, then, was the basis of the Fabians' estimate of the probable behavior of the British ruling class? No small part of the answer, I think, lies in their obsessive concern over rent and the land question. The landed aristocracy had submitted to defeat in 1832 without raising the standard of revolt: it was manifestly parasitic and lacking in vigor. If the achievement of socialism was essentially a matter of nationalizing the land, as the essayists repeatedly assert, then indeed it was reasonable to assume that "moral force" (to use the expression which had been popularized a half century earlier by the peaceful wing of the Chartist movement) would suffice to carry the day.

That this was, in fact, the perspective of the Fabians could be demonstrated by numerous quotations, but two or three from scattered parts of the *Essays* will illustrate the point. Clarke speaks of taking up "the threads when they fall from the weak hands of a useless possessing class." (P. 95.) Besant emphasizes "the success of capitalism bringing about a position which is at once intolerable to the majority, and easy to capture by them." (P. 141.) Shaw explicitly states that "we need not seriously anticipate that the landlords will actually fight" (p. 179) and holds out the hope that "much of that process [of transition] as sketched here may be anticipated by sections of the proprietary class successively capitulating, as the net closes about their special interests, on such terms as they may be able to stand out for before their power is entirely broken." (P. 185.)

All this makes good sense if we think in terms of a class of idle rentiers; but how relevant is it when applied to the capitalist class which made Britain into the "workshop of the world" and built up the largest empire known to history without scrupling to use force whenever it served its purpose to do so? Are we not entitled to assume that the political vision of the Fabians was seriously distorted by a peculiarly rigid and unrealistic theory of political economy?

One further aspect of Fabian political economy seems to me to call for particular notice. As is well known, Marxian theory divides the history (past, present, and future) of Europe since the fall of the Roman Empire into three stages, each designated by the name of a dominant social system: feudalism, capitalism, and socialism. In Sidney Webb's "Historic" essay, three analogous stages appear, but with different names: the Old Synthesis, the Period of Anarchy, and the New Synthesis. It is not stretching a point unduly to equate the Old Synthesis with feudalism and the New Synthesis with socialism, but a Marxist would never agree that capitalism is appropriately characterized as the Period of Anarchy. The contrast in names here indicates a profound difference in viewpoint.

In the Marxian view, capitalism is a social *order* which can be understood only in terms of its internal laws of cohesion and its overall laws of development. The key to the internal laws is what Marx called the "law of value," which I have elsewhere characterized as "a theory of general equilibrium developed in the first instance with reference to simple commodity production and later on adapted to capitalism";[6] the laws of development derive from the phenomena of capital accumulation. These ideas have no counterpart in the Fabian system. As we have already seen, the Jevonian theory of value does not play an essential role in Fabian political economy;[7] and the motive force of capitalist development — population growth — seems in the Fabian view to be naturally rather than socially conditioned. Since there is no conscious, purposive direction of society under capitalism, it appears to be not a social *order* at all but mere *disorder* —

---
[6] *The Theory of Capitalist Development* (New York, 1942), p. 53.
[7] This may be partly due to the fact that Jevons, unlike his contemporaries in the Lausanne school, conspicuously failed to develop a theory of general equilibrium. Subjective value theory as such throws no light whatever on the nature of capitalism as a *system* of society, and it is only by means of a general equilibrium theory that the coordinating role of prices and markets is brought into sharp focus.

lawless, chaotic, and inherently unsusceptible to rational analysis. This view is succinctly expressed by Hubert Bland in his admiring appraisal of Sidney Webb's contribution to the *Essays*: "His paper was an inductive demonstration of the failure of anarchy to meet the needs of real concrete men and women — a proof from history that the world moves from system, through disorder, back again to system." (P. 188.) There is no indication in the whole volume that the Fabians had ever given thought to the problem of how productive resources get distributed among various industries under capitalism or how it happens that, without any central direction, a steady flow of materials through the productive process is kept up and consumers' goods emerge in quantities sufficient to maintain the life processes of society.

This gap in Fabian theory had a peculiar corollary which I think is still making itself felt in the British socialist movement. Never having pondered the problem of allocation of resources under capitalism, the Fabians failed to recognize the existence of the problem at all. As a consequence, they had nothing to say about its solution under socialism. I should emphasize that I am not referring here to the abstract and largely unreal debate which arose after World War I, about whether it would be theoretically *possible* for socialism to solve this problem. I am talking rather about the implications of the problem and the *method* of solving it for the form and structure of socialist society. The most striking evidence in this connection is that, so far as I can recall, the word "planning" does not once occur in the whole volume; nor is there any discussion of the role of the central government under socialism beyond such general assertions as that it will run large-scale industries of national importance. The essays which deal with the organization of socialist society (Wallas's, Besant's, and Shaw's second) put the main emphasis on the municipalization of the means of production and never even hint that the activities of the various municipalities would in some way or other have to be coordinated with one another.

Thus, while Marxists have always been fully aware that socialism must be a centrally planned society, British socialist thought, following in the footsteps of the Fabians (and somewhat later of the Guild Socialists, who in this respect showed a close affinity to the Fabians), has always been vague and obscure on this crucially important question. I think that anyone who sets out to discover what the present Labor government in Britain means by "planning" will soon become painfully conscious of this long-standing weakness in British socialist thought.[8]

I conclude that Fabian political economy, as expounded in the *Essays*, was far from being the "incisive and accurate" weapon of analysis which Sidney Webb's confident statement of 1920 asserted it to be. Perhaps the Fabians could, after all, have learned something from the "old-fashioned" Marxian theory. And it is just possible that there is a lesson in this even for the British socialist movement of today.

---
[8] See, for example, the White Paper entitled *Economic Survey for 1947* (reprinted in the *Federal Reserve Bulletin*, April 1947), which devotes more than a quarter of its length to a section headed "Economic Planning."

30

Science, Marxism, and Democracy

I participated, along with many scholars from this and other countries, in an inquiry into the meanings of the concept of "democracy" which was undertaken by UNESCO in 1948 and which issued in the volume edited by Richard McKeon, *Democracy in a World of Tensions* (Chicago, 1951). In the course of this inquiry I prepared a number of memoranda dealing with special topics. This piece is one of them.

THESE notes are directed to Karl Popper's three articles which appeared in *Economica* (May 1944, August 1944, and May 1945) under the title "The Poverty of Historicism."[1] I conclude with a few remarks on the relevance of these articles to the subject of democracy and social science.

It is clear that Popper regards Marxism as a variety of historicism, and in so far as I deal with his arguments I shall do so on the assumption that they are intended to apply to Marxism. This may not be so in all cases, but it is impossible for the reader to divide the arguments which are intended to apply to Marxism from those which are not. I want to make it quite plain that I do not deny that much of what Popper says is justified and valid as applied to certain theories, for example, the culture cycle theories of such writers as Spengler and Toynbee.

---

[1] Popper's book, *The Open Society and Its Enemies* (2 vols., London, 1945), in which the ideas expounded in the *Economica* articles were greatly elaborated, was not available to me when I wrote this memorandum. With regard to the problems discussed, however, the book introduced no significant changes.

Let us first consider what Popper has to say about the historicist view of the role of generalization in social science:

> The possibility of generalization and its success in the physical sciences rests, according to historicism, on the general uniformity of nature; upon the observation — better perhaps described as an assumption — that in similar circumstances similar events will happen. This principle, which is taken to be valid throughout space and time, is said to underlie the method of physics. Historicism insists that this principle is necessarily useless in sociology. Similar circumstances only arise within a single historical period, and do not persist from one period to another. (*Economica*, May 1944, p. 87.)

In my opinion, this is not at all true of Marxism, which insists on the possibility and necessity of generalization in precisely the sense here described. Nevertheless it is not difficult to see why Popper might come to a different, and therefore erroneous, conclusion. Marxism does maintain that, so far as the most important problems of the social sciences are concerned, similar circumstances exist only in similar social systems, and it also generally adopts a scheme of periodization based on the prevalence in a fairly well defined region of a given social system. Hence Marxists frequently speak of the laws and tendencies of a certain *social system* as though they were the laws and tendencies peculiar to a certain *period of history*. This may be, and indeed often is, justifiable; but it may also tend to obscure the fact that the concern of Marxism is with social systems and never with such mystical entities as *Zeitgeiste* and the like. Marxism would never think of denying, for example, that different social systems can coexist and that a given segment of history can be understood only in terms of their interaction.

Let us now turn to the problem of prediction. Popper says that he agrees with historicism's inclination to stress the "importance of prediction as a task of science" but immediately adds that he does not believe in historical prediction. (May 1944, p. 89.) His meaning can perhaps be made clear as follows: physics can predict that if you strike a match you will get fire, but physics cannot predict when a match will be struck in such a way as to burn down a city block. In other words, the predictions of physics can be described as conditional predictions but never as concrete historical predictions. Historicism, on the other hand, is said to be interested in unconditional "prophecies." (May 1945, p. 77.)

It seems to me that Popper is here drawing a rigid distinction between conditional and historical prediction where none in fact exists. The statement, "If you strike a match you will get fire" (conditional), can easily become, "The child is striking a match and hence the house will burn down" (historical). The scientific knowledge involved in the two statements is exactly the same, but in the one case it is stated in general form while in the other it is applied to a concrete situation. No doubt there are conditional predictions which are not so easily transformed into historical predictions, but there are also many others which in this respect are just like the example of the match and the fire. We can state this in the form of the following theorem: a conditional prediction can become a historical prediction if the conditions which it specifies are sufficiently accurately reproduced in an actual historical situation.

As far as Marxism is concerned, it seems to me quite clear that all of its historical predictions are of this kind. The conditional predictions (which can also be called scientific laws) are of the form, "If you have capitalism you will get increasingly severe depressions culminating in a general crisis of the system"; the historical prediction (first formulated in a more or less explicit way in the *Communist Manifesto*) then takes the form, "You have capitalism in such and such countries, and as long as you do have it you will have increasingly severe depressions culminating in a general crisis of the system as a whole."

Of course, Popper can reject this prediction. But if he does so it will be because he rejects the theory of capitalism on which it is based, not because there is an unbridgeable methodological gulf between natural science and Marxism.

Popper in effect admits this himself when he says, after criticizing the historicists who attempt to discover what he calls "absolute trends":

> But what about those who see that trends depend on conditions, and who try to find these conditions and to formulate them explicitly? My answer is that I have no quarrel with them; on the contrary. That trends occur cannot be doubted. Therefore we have the difficult task of explaining them as well as we can, i.e. of determining as precisely as possible the conditions under which they persist. (May 1945, p. 78.)

I find the formulation somewhat lacking in precision here, but there can be no doubt about Popper's general intention: the statement can only mean that if Popper properly understood Marxism he would have no *methodological* quarrels with the kind of historical predictions which Marxism makes.

Another of Popper's most serious charges against historicism is what he calls its "holism." He distinguishes between two meanings of the term: "(a) the totality of all the properties or aspects of a thing, and especially of all the relations holding between its constituent parts, and (b) certain selected properties or aspects of the thing in question, namely those that make it appear as an organized structure rather than as a 'mere heap.'" (August 1944, p. 126.) Now whatever may be said of some "historicists," there can be no doubt that Marxism speaks of wholes (for example, capitalism) only in the latter sense, and Popper himself admits that "wholes in sense (b) can be studied scientifically." (August 1944, p. 127.) Hence we see that here again Popper's criticism of Marxism — and I assume that this particular stricture is supposed to apply to Marxism — is based on nothing more substantial than misunderstanding.

I do not deny that there is a very real difference between the way Marxism deals with "wholes" and the way Popper thinks social science *ought* to deal with "wholes." (In this connection, I think we may take Popper's repeated and admiring references to Hayek as a clear indication of the kind of social science he himself espouses.) Popper believes in what he calls, following Hayek, "methodological individualism," which means that "our task is to analyse our sociological models [that is, our wholes] carefully in descriptive or nominalist terms, viz., *in terms of individuals*, their attitudes, expectations, relations, etc." (May 1945, p. 80; italics in original.) In other words, we start with individuals, and especially with ourselves about whom we know most, and having found out what they are like we proceed to put them together into groups and systems. *We build up our wholes from their previously analyzed individual parts.* In this way we are supposed to get scientific knowledge which is valid for all times and places. Marxism, of course, rejects this procedure on the ground that the "attitudes, expectations, relations, etc." of individuals are very different depending on what kind of group or system they happen to belong to. The individual cannot be understood apart from a particular form of society, a particular class, and particular membership groups. Hence the correct procedure can be described as starting the analysis from the whole and working back through the parts to the individuals. In this way, we can get individuals as they really are, not some purely imaginary universal human beings, and can use them as the elements of models which will display the characteristics of real social systems. It is obviously impossible to go into this subject in detail here. I will only say that the difference between Popper and Marxism at this point seems to me to be less a question of scientific method than of an unscientific versus a scientific view of human psychology and behavior.

I have considered Popper's arguments relating to (1) generalization, (2) prediction, and (3) holism, and have found that in every case his strictures on "historicism" either do not apply to Marxism or are thought to apply to Marxism only because of a misunderstanding. It would be possible to examine the rest of his arguments in the same way and with the same results. But I think it is hardly necessary. Popper himself would surely concede that his most important criticisms come under these three headings and moreover that many of his other criticisms are closely related to those that do. Hence I think we are safe in concluding that Popper's critique as a whole in no way impugns the scientific character and validity of Marxism.

What has all this to do with the relation between democracy and social science? Are Marxists justified in concluding that because Marxism is a valid social science they would have the right — assuming that they had the power — to suppress all opposing opinions? In my judgment, the answer is "Certainly not." Just because an opinion is wrong — and regardless of whether the reason is ignorance, superstition, or learned attachment to a false theory — is no reason why it should be suppressed. It is rather a reason why the person holding the wrong opinion should be patiently shown *why* it is wrong and educated to hold what is, so far as the state of scientific knowledge permits us to know, the right opinion. And, it may be added, it will be possible to show and educate large masses of people holding wrong opinions only when the conditions which foster ignorance, superstition, and false theories have been done away with — that is to say, when society is based on the rational principle of planned production for the general welfare.

That this is the traditional attitude of Marxism can, I think, easily be shown. Take the case of religion in the sense of belief in the existence of a supernatural deity. As is well known, Marxism rejects religion in this sense. But does that mean that it is a part of the program of Marxism to suppress religious views and practices? Of course not. Marxists believe, to quote Engels, that

when society, by taking possession of all means of production and using them on a planned basis, has freed itself and all its members from the bondage in which they are now held by these means of production which they themselves have produced but which now confront them as an irresistible extraneous force; when therefore man no longer merely proposes, but also disposes — only then will the last extraneous force which is still reflected in religon vanish; and with it also will vanish the religious reflection itself, for the simple reason that then there will be nothing left to reflect. (*Anti-Dühring*, Part III, Chapter 5.)

And the Marxist attitude toward any attempt to suppress religion by force is spelled out by Engels in the next paragraph:

Herr Dühring, however, cannot wait until religion dies this natural death. He proceeds in more deep-rooted fashion. He out-Bismarcks Bismarck; he decrees sharper May laws not only against catholicism, but against all religion whatsoever; he incites his gendarmes of the future to attack religion, and thereby helps it to martyrdom and a prolonged lease of life.

It is clear, therefore, that Marxism does not claim science as a justification for suppressing opposing opinions. Unfortunately, however, this does not quite dispose of the problem. There are times, particularly revolutionary times, when opinions become so involved in social conflict that they cannot escape being treated as weapons. Now Marxists are revolutionaries (though not conspirators, as their opponents persist in believing), and whenever they succeed (as they are convinced they will succeed everywhere, sooner or later) they claim the revolutionary right to protect the new order against counter-revolution. To a varying extent, depending on specific conditions and historical backgrounds, the defense of a revolution may involve suppressing opinions. This is unfortunate, and I think all Marxists should regret it in exactly the same way that they regret the fact that people lose their lives in revolutions. They should hope and work for revolutions from which both bloodshed and the suppression of opinions are absent, and they should of course not justify suppression by self-righteous appeals to science.

This is one side of the question of the relation between social science and democracy. But there is another side, too. If, as I believe to be the case, Marxism *is* a valid social science, then certainly I, as a Marxist, cannot admit the tenability of the defense of multiparty democracy and free expression on the ground that there is no such thing as a valid social science. To do so would be absurd. Multiparty democracy and freedom of expression can be defended on many different grounds, but in my judgment they emphatically cannot be defended on the ground that we do not have or cannot achieve valid knowledge of society, its real interests, and the possible ways it can develop in the future.

31

Strategy for Socialism

This is a review of Oskar Lange and Fred M. Taylor, *On the Economic Theory of Socialism* (Benjamin E. Lippincott, editor, Minneapolis, 1938). It appeared in *The Nation*, June 25, 1938.

IN THIS little book Mr. Lippincott has brought together in readily available form two of the most important contributions to the theory of economic planning that have yet been written. The first, entitled "The Guidance of Production in a Socialist Sate," was the presidential address delivered before the American Economic Association in 1928 by the late Professor Fred Taylor of Michigan. Professor Taylor's address seems to have been promptly forgotten by his fellow economists, and its republication at a time when many of the ideas expressed in it are beginning to find their way into economic literature from other sources is an act of historical justice.

From the point of view of current controversy, however, there is no doubt that the much longer paper of Oskar Lange, from which the book takes its name, has first claim on the reader's attention. In my opinion Dr. Lange has produced the conclusive refutation of the antisocialist arguments of Mises and his followers which have recently enjoyed a revival in English-speaking countries in the writings of such authorities on socialism as Walter Lippmann. I do not wish to enter into this controversy further than to say that I wholeheartedly agree with everything Lange has to say on the subject and to recommend a careful study of his arguments to all who are seriously interested in the problem.

The most important part of Lange's paper, I think, is that in which he discusses the economic problems which have to be solved if socialism is to be attained at all. Here new ground is broken and theoretical considerations of the greatest importance brought forward. Lange argues that the functioning of capitalism is necessarily disrupted by a serious threat to the foundations of the system itself. Capitalists cannot be expected to continue to produce unless they have reasonable assurance of stability in the basic property relationships on which all their calculations are based. It follows from this that *on economic grounds alone* a socialist party which really means to introduce socialism must be prepared to put through a very large measure of socialization as the first step after taking office. For otherwise the economic chaos which is sure to follow will weaken its position and force it either to renounce its socialist objective or to undertake the struggle against its enemies under the most unfavorable conditions. "Socialism," as Lange says, "is not an economic policy for the timid."

Does this mean that a socialist party should take no part in shaping governmental policies unless it is in a position to carry out a program of rapid socialization? The answer is No. To behave in this way in a period of capitalist disintegration would clearly be playing straight into the hands of reaction. Socialists should, on the contrary, take the lead in organizing mass support behind a policy of large-scale government spending, since at the present time this is the only policy which can save democratic institutions and thus keep the way clear for eventually winning the masses to a socialist position. If this policy is successfully carried through — and there is no reason why it should not be — socialists will gain enormously in prestige and popularity.

Lange might well have cited the example of the French Popular Front as a negative confirmation of his position. The

Popular Front, though organized by Communists and Socialists, was never intended as a vehicle for the introduction of socialism; its purpose was to combat the allied enemies of depression and fascism. The timidity and at least temporary failure of the Popular Front can be traced directly to its stubborn adherence to bourgeois canons of "sound finance." A bold policy of public works coupled with devaluation of the franc and exchange control, which certainly could have been instituted by the Blum government in the first weeks after its accession to office, would have raised the national income and enormously strengthened the position of the socialist parties. The melancholy history of the last two years might well have been altogether different if this policy had been followed.

In this country, thanks to the New Deal, there is less attachment to the ruinous principles of "sound finance." Socialists ought to be the first to appreciate the great advantage which this gives them over their European colleagues. They have a lot of economics to learn from the experience of the last decade, and perhaps the greatest merit of Lange's article is that it helps to point the way to a true understanding of what has happened.

32

A Crucial Difference Between Capitalism and Socialism

The original draft of this article (written in 1952 and here published for the first time) was submitted to five economists for comment. Each had criticisms; and, except for a few that were based on misunderstanding, all the criticisms made good sense. Some I have tried to meet by changes in formulation. But the more important ones, it seemed to me, could be satisfactorily dealt with only within the framework of a different and much longer article. Since it would undoubtedly be prudent to assume that the same or similar criticisms will occur to other readers, I would like to explain in advance that this is *not* an attempt to expound a theory of industrialization. Rather, it is an attempt to throw light on what happens *after* a process of basic industrialization has been completed. In other words, what I have to say about the process of industrialization itself is by way of setting up a problem, not solving one. With regard to the main thesis of the article, my conviction both that it is valid and merits attention has been strengthened by the comments of those who read the first draft.

EVERY economically advanced society must go through a phase, which will be measured in decades rather than years, of *industrialization*, that is to say, the building of its basic industrial equipment from the ground up. This phase, to be sure, has no precise beginning and no precise ending, but it has a very real existence and importance all the same.

We can perhaps best appreciate this if we imagine ourselves in the position of central planners in a backward country whose task it is to develop an advanced industrial economy. They will first think of all the basic industries, using the term in its widest sense, that must be built up. They will realize that during this build-up period a very large part of production will have to be, as it were, plowed back and that the rate of expansion of consumption will be severely limited. And they will make at least rough estimates of when the build-up period will be over and the harvest can be reaped in the form of rapidly expanding consumption.

All this is clear enough if we think in terms of a planned economy. But most economists seem to have overlooked it in their theories of the unplanned economy, perhaps precisely because it harbors no one whose point of view corresponds to that of the central planner. At all events, I believe that the facts alluded to are important and that by explicitly taking them into account we can gain significant insights into the functioning of both unplanned (capitalist) and planned (socialist) economies.

I

Let us begin by dividing the economy into two departments. Department I produces all producers' goods, Department II all consumers' goods. The dividing line between the two departments is not clearly defined, but the distinction itself is perfectly clear and usable.[1] In order to avoid getting entangled in the problems of technological change, let us assume that we are dealing with an economically underdeveloped country which can draw on the known techniques of more advanced countries. To begin with, this country has a

---

[1] This departmental schema, of course, originated with Marx and has been extensively used by later Marxian economists. See my *Theory of Capitalist Development*, especially Chapters 5, 10, and 11. But it is not incompatible with most non-Marxian theories and does not imply acceptance of such specifically Marxian doctrines as the labor theory of value or the theory of surplus value. See Ragnar Nurkse, "The Schematic Representation of the Structure of Production," *Review of Economic Studies*, June 1935.

very small Department I, most of its economy being concentrated in Department II. We will suppose that there are no relevant shortages of natural resources or labor power. Under these conditions, the economy can expand all around, in both departments at the same time. "Saving" or, more accurately, accumulation of capital does not involve cutting down on current consumption but rather proceeds *pari passu* with an increase in consumption. This increase in consumption, in turn, can be broken down into a component due to the growth of the labor force and a component due to rising real incomes.

If we assume, as we should, that workers on the average consume the whole of their incomes, then the remainder of the demand for the output of Department II will depend on two factors: (1) the division of income between workers and capitalists, (2) the rate of capitalists' accumulation.[2]

Generally speaking, the demand for the output of Department I is made up of what we can call replacement and expansion demands of the capitalists of both departments. Let us make the simplest possible assumption about replacement demand, that is, that a given proportion of capital requires to be and is replaced each year. Then the replacement demand of each department will vary directly with the size of the department. This brings us to the key question: What determines the expansion demand of the two departments?

As to Department II, a sensible assumption would seem to be that capitalists base their investment decisions on the actually observed and experienced trend of consumption. If consumption is growing slowly, the expansion demand of Department II will be small; and conversely if consumption

---

[2] Each of these factors, of course, is extremely complicated. For example, the inflationary creation of bank credit can expand the capitalists' share of total income and at the same time raise the capitalists' rate of accumulation. I am not trying to exclude such processes, which indeed have played a crucial role in the development of all capitalist countries, but merely to subsume them under shorthand formulas.

is growing rapidly, the expansion demand of Department II will be large.

Finally, then, there is the expansion demand of Department I for the products of Department I. This, it should be noted at once, lies at the very heart of the question of industrialization. A large expansion demand from Department I is equivalent to rapid industrialization, a small expansion demand to slow industrialization.

Let us pause to note that it is not wholly obvious why there should be such an expansion demand in Department I. It could be reasoned that both departments, after all, have to be geared to the output of consumption goods; that the expansion demand of Department II therefore measures the primary requirement for more means of production; and that expansion demand in Department I could consequently be expected to be limited to what would be needed to meet slowly rising replacement demands. Such a case is certainly conceivable, but it is completely unrealistic. In practice, Department I cannot expand slowly and continuously in the wake of rising consumption. Whole industries, transport networks, communication systems, and so on, that will be absolutely essential when consumption has reached a certain level, simply do not exist at the outset, and they cannot be brought into existence bit by bit. For a long time the growth of Department I must anticipate and be largely independent of the growth of consumption. This anticipatory and independent expansion of Department I is precisely what we mean by industrialization.[3]

During this phase of development, the only limit to the

---

[3] The point can be illustrated by the growth of the American railroad system. Mileage expanded at an extremely rapid rate from the middle of the nineteenth century to about 1910, after which further expansion tapered off nearly as suddenly as it had begun. During the whole period of rapid expansion, building was ahead, and sometimes way ahead, of demand for railroad services. After the basic network had been completed, further investment (in double-tracking and the like) followed and was closely geared to traffic requirements. This is an extreme case, but the phenomenon it illustrates is typical not only of individual industries but of Department I as a whole.

size of the expansion demand of Department I — or, to put it otherwise, the only limit to the speed of industrialization — would seem to lie in the capitalists' capacity to accumulate. This, of course, is the obverse of their demand for consumers' goods and is determined by the same two factors, namely, the division of income between workers and capitalists and the capitalists' rate of accumulation.

Our main conclusions to this point can be expressed in two brief propositions. (1) The economic development of a backward society implies a period of industrialization during which the demand for the products of Department I comes to a considerable extent from Department I itself. (2) The higher the rate of profit and the stronger the capitalists' urge to accumulate, the slower the growth of consumption and the more rapid the rate of industrialization.[4]

Let us now analyze what happens as the period of industrialization approaches an end. Basic industries have been created, a railroad network is in existence, and so on. Department I, in other words, has been built up to the point where it can meet all the replacement and expansion demands of Department II. Leaving aside the question of new industries (which we shall touch upon later), Department I will no longer present a substantial expansion demand for its own products. Such expansion demand as does arise within Department I will be derived from the gradually rising replacement demands of Department II and to a much smaller extent of Department I itself. In other words, as the period of industrialization approaches an end, most of the expansion demand of Department I simply vanishes. Note that this does not imply any earlier slowing down, still less cessation, in the growth of either consumption or the expansion demand of Department II. It results from the simple fact that Department I has been built up to a point

---

[4] Note that if the rate of growth of consumption were faster, the rate of industrialization would be cut down on two separate counts: first, because the rate of accumulation would be lower, and second, because a higher proportion of accumulation would have to go into Department II.

where it can handle existing and prospective requirements for its output, and that to go on adding to it at the established rate would simply be to pile up excess capacity.

The question now arises as to whether there is anything in the mechanism of the capitalist economy which will tend to produce an offset to this falling off in the expansion demand of Department I. (We can assume that it occurs gradually, so as not to introduce the problem of sudden dislocations or immediate adjustments.) Classical and neoclassical theorists would for the most part have answered this question in the affirmative. They would have argued that the price mechanism would operate to bring about a falling rate of profit (or interest) which, in turn, would check accumulation and stimulate consumption. This would happen in one or both of two ways. First, the fall in the rate of profit might be sharp enough to lower the relative share of capitalists, or, in other words, to involve a transfer of income from accumulators to consumers. Second, the decline in the rate of profit would in any case induce capitalists to accumulate less and consume more. In terms of our two-department schema, the result would be that the gap in total demand created by the disappearance of expansion demand in Department I would be made up by an increase in consumption demand on the one hand and an increase in expansion demand in Department II on the other.[5]

---

[5] At first sight, it might appear that even so there would be trouble in Department I, since the increased expansion demand from Department II would not be enough by itself to compensate for the diminished expansion demand from Department I. But to reason in this way is to conceive the departmental schema too rigidly. Actually, a considerable part of the resources employed in Department I can be quickly shifted to Department II, and, with a changing pattern of demand such as the older theorists envisaged, this would certainly happen. For example, firms that had been constructing new factories would turn to constructing new houses, truck plants would shift to passenger cars, and so on. In other words, a smooth transition at the end of the period of industrialization — if it were possible — would involve some immediate expansion of Department II at the expense of Department I.

But it is certainly impossible today to maintain that the capitalist price system works this way. Relative shares have been shown to be remarkably resistant to change under the most diverse conditions, and very few would still argue that there is a significant relation between the mere rate of profit and capitalists' attitudes toward accumulation and consumption. In other words, there is no reason to suppose that the approach of the end of the period of industrialization would set in motion a mechanism accelerating the growth of consumption at the expense of accumulation and thus taking up the slack which the disappearance of expansion demand in Department I would otherwise cause. Other things being equal, in a capitalist system the fruits of industrialization, instead of being enjoyed in the form of rapidly increasing consumption, are dissipated in unemployment and depression.

Of course, other things do not remain equal, and new factors may intervene to take up the slack. For example, new industries generally produce an effect akin to that of industrialization, and if they are sufficiently numerous and important they may keep the system going at or near full capacity.[6] But in each case the effects are bound to wear off sooner or later. The *tendency* to collapse is always there in an industrialized capitalist society; depression or stagnation or whatever we choose to call it must be regarded as its normal condition, in precisely the same sense that the classical and neoclassical economists regarded full-employment

---

[6] New or improved methods of producing existing commodities present a more complicated problem. They may take the place of, and in an economic sense destroy, means of production already in use. To this extent, their effect is similar to that of new industries. But they may also be introduced as part of the process of replacing worn-out capital, and to this extent they do not create any expansion demand at all. If innovations of this kind are introduced by new firms, they are more likely to have the former effect; if by existing firms, the latter effect. The problem is therefore not only one of technology but also of industrial organization.

equilibrium as the normal condition of capitalist economies at every stage of their development.

II

Let us now turn to the case of a centrally planned socialist economy. Here, unlike in the capitalist case, the allocation of resources to the various departments and industries is decided upon by a central planning board; and prices and income flows are to a large extent adjusted (also by the planning board) with the object of enabling the allocation decided upon to work itself out smoothly and efficiently.[7]

We assume a planned economy in the same position we earlier assumed a capitalist economy to be in, in other words, at the beginning of the process of industrialization and handicapped by no shortages of natural resources or manpower. We also divide the economy into the same two departments.[8]

The question of how fast to industrialize — or, to put it the other way round, how much to brake the growth of consumption in the interests of accumulation — will be determined not by the distribution of income and the desire of one class in the community to increase its wealth, but by a deliberate decision of the planning authority. This basic decision will guide the allocation of resources to the two departments. In order to ensure that money demands correspond to the chosen pattern of resource allocation, the planning board will have to establish a level of consumers' goods prices in relation to workers' incomes which will leave the workers just enough real purchasing power to absorb the planned output of Department II. The more rapid

[7] Naturally this statement is subject to all sorts of qualifications, but it stresses what is important from our present point of view, namely, that socialist central planning deals fundamentally with production and relegates the price system (using the term in the broadest sense) to an essentially auxiliary role.

[8] The departmental schema, it need hardly be emphasized, is descriptive of the physical process of production, not of its social organization. It can therefore be employed in the analysis of both capitalist and socialist economies.

the industrialization decided upon, the higher will be the level of consumers' goods prices, and vice versa. The revenue accruing to the state from this price markup can be looked upon as profit, or it can take the form of a turnover tax, or some combination of these approaches can be used. For the sake of simplicity, and to facilitate comparison with the capitalist case, we will refer to it as profit. But it is important to bear in mind that profit in the socialist society is not a crucial factor in the operation of the economy in the sense that it is in the capitalist case; it merely measures what is being withheld from current consumption for purposes of accumulation.[9]

Now, during the period of industrialization, Department I, in the socialist as in the capitalist case, exercises an expansion demand for its own products which is the stronger the more rapid the rate of industrialization. And, likewise in both cases, as the period of industrialization approaches an end, this expansion demand quickly shrinks to an insignificant fraction of its former size. The question is whether this circumstance should be a source of difficulty for the socialist economy, as we have seen it to be for the capitalist economy.

The answer is surely that there is not the slightest reason why it should be. The planning board, seeing that the basic build-up of the country's industrial equipment is nearly accomplished, will shift resources to Department II as rapidly as they become available and will channel the greater part of fresh accumulation into further expanding Department II. In other words, the board will plan for a much more rapid expansion in the output of consumers' goods. And in order to ensure that this flood of consumers' goods finds a market the board need only progressively lower their prices. True, this will involve a continuous fall in the profit accruing to the state, but this will be merely a technical detail which it would never occur to anyone in a socialist society to worry

---

[9] And other public purposes too, of course, but we are abstracting from this aspect of the problem.

about. Under socialism, in other words, the end of the period of industrialization ushers in, not a period of continuous depression (actual or potential), but rather a period of genuine fulfillment.

III

The reason for the difference between capitalism and socialism disclosed by the foregoing analysis is an extremely interesting and important problem, not of pure economic theory but of what may be called economic sociology. Basically, as we have hinted, this reason lies in the wholly different character and role of profit in the two forms of society. Under capitalism, profit is the form in which the economically dominant class gets its income. It is, so to speak, the economic foundation of the very existence of this class. The vested interest which this class has in the maintenance of profit as such, as well as in the maintenance of a large volume of profit — the two are not really distinct problems in the minds of the capitalists — is by far the most powerful and passionately defended vested interest in capitalist society. Every conceivable kind of support and protection — economic, institutional, legal, and ideological[10] — is built up around profit. As near as anything can be, profit is the be-all and end-all of capitalist society. It follows that when the economic functioning of capitalism calls for a drastic and steady decline in profit and/or a use of profit which runs directly counter to the will of the capitalists, then the system is caught in a very real contradiction.[11]

---

[10] What is often called the degree of monopoly (in the economy as a whole) is little more than a reflection of capitalists' success in putting up economic, institutional, and legal fences around their profits. Ideological supports are of the most varied description, ranging all the way from the glorification of private enterprise through the reviling of the price-cutter to the ostracizing of the radical.

[11] Compare the remark in Schumpeter's forthcoming *History of Economic Analysis:* "If a system or model that correctly expresses fundamental features of the capitalist society contains contradictory equations, this would be proof of inherent hitches in the capitalist

A CRUCIAL DIFFERENCE

Capitalism may be temporarily rescued from the contradiction by new industries; it may seek, with more or less success, an escape through imperialism and militarism; it may even undertake, again with more or less success and certainly against the growing resistance of the capitalists themselves, to modify the functioning of the system through taxation and government spending. But one thing is certain: as long as it remains capitalism, it can never *abolish* the contradiction.

And this is precisely what socialism does do. Under socialism, profit is not a form of income at all. No one has a vested interest in its maintenance either as an economic category or as an economic magnitude. Whatever the smooth functioning of the system requires to be done to profit, can be done with no resistance and no fuss.

This is certainly only one of many differences between capitalism and socialism. But it is just as certainly, in my judgment, one of the most important and far-reaching in its implications.

---

system — proof of real, instead of imaginary, 'contradictions of capitalism.'" (Part IV, Chapter 7, Section 3, Note 17.) Needless to say, the reality of the contradictions does not depend upon their taking an equational form. The reason economists have generally failed to recognize the contradiction we have been discussing is simply that they have misunderstood or ignored the role of profit in capitalist society as a whole. There could be no other way of explaining, for example, Keynes's famous passage about the "euthanasia of the rentier." (*General Theory*, pp. 375-376.)

33

A Reply to Critics

The origin of this article is explained in the text itself. It appeared in the bilingual Japanese periodical, *The Economic Review* (published by Hitotsubashi University, Tokyo), April 1950.

The publication in 1952 of Stalin's *Economic Problems of Socialism in the USSR* would make possible today a more satisfactory reply to Mr. Kazahaya on the law of value under socialism (pp. 356-358 below). Briefly, Stalin's position is that the law of value still continues to operate under socialism to the extent that certain features of capitalism, particularly the operation of the price mechanism in the agricultural sector of the economy, have not yet been eliminated. Under full communism, on the other hand, the law of value will no longer apply. In the light of this explanation, which seems to me entirely sound, I should like to amend the statement which Mr. Kazahaya criticizes, by substituting "communist" for "socialist" and "communism" for "socialism." It would then read as follows: "In the economics of a communist society the theory of planning should hold the same basic position as the theory of value in the economics of a capitalist society. Value and planning are as much opposed, and for the same reasons, as capitalism and communism." This conveys my meaning more accurately than the original wording and is, I think, entirely in accord with Stalin's view.

I HAVE been invited by the editor of *The Economic Review* to comment on reviews by Professor Yoshida and Mr. Kazahaya of my book, *The Theory of Capitalist Development*. I am more than happy to accept this invitation, but I

A REPLY TO CRITICS

must explain, especially to the reviewers themselves, that my comments are based on brief digests of their reviews and not on the full texts, which are not available to me.[1] Under the circumstances, the reader will understand that I am unable to quote their exact words, and it is of course not impossible that I may have misunderstood or failed to appreciate some of their arguments. If this should be the case, I can only apologize and hope the editor will give the reviewers whatever space may be necessary for them to reply.

I

Professor Yoshida centers his critical remarks on my exposition of the theory of crises arising from underconsumption. He has, I am sure, put his finger on one of the weakest parts of the book. I was never altogether satisfied with this exposition, and if I were writing it again today I would certainly do it differently. At the same time, however, I must admit that, though I have given considerable thought to the question, I have not come to definite conclusions or formulations.

Professor Yoshida is correct that the constant ratio between stock of means of production and output of consumption goods (or output of all kinds of goods) cannot be theoretically defended. Given a rising organic composition of capital, this ratio must also rise. But I do not think this is very important from the point of view of the problem of underconsumption. The growth of constant relative to variable capital is a gradual, long-term, technically conditioned trend which certainly cannot be expected to accommodate itself to the manner in which fresh surplus value is capitalized. As a first approximation, therefore, it may be quite legitimate to postulate a constant ratio between capital and output.

I share Professor Yoshida's preference for the Marxian

---

[1] The digests, which were compiled by the editors of *The Economic Review*, are printed as an appendix to this article.

two-department scheme over the Keynesian aggregative models (whether the aggregates are net or gross), and of course a large part of my treatment of underconsumption crises is devoted to explaining and analyzing the two-department scheme under conditions of expanded reproduction. It is true, however, that my own exposition of the theory of underconsumption is couched in terms of net aggregates. It is a little hard for me to reconstruct the reasons for this, at a distance of nearly ten years. I suppose that in part it was due to the intellectual environment in which I was working; nearly everyone thought and talked in terms of aggregates, and I was naturally not unaffected by that fact. An additional reason was that my own thinking on this subject at the time I was writing the book was influenced to a considerable extent by the relevant chapter in Otto Bauer's *Zwischen Zwei Weltkriegen* (a very valuable and stimulating book which deserves to be more widely known than it is). Bauer likewise used aggregates in this connection, though I am sure this was not due to Keynesian influence. Still another reason may have been the fact that aggregative analysis lends itself much more readily to relatively simple mathematical treatment, and this presented a temptation to which I was at that time by no means immune.

But whatever the reasons, there is no doubt that in my handling of underconsumption there occurs a rather abrupt transition from departmental to aggregative analysis. It seems to me today that this is unfortunate, if not positively wrong, and if I ever prepare a revised second edition of the book I intend to try to formulate the whole chapter in terms of the departmental scheme. I have not yet done this, however, and I hope that by the time I get to it I shall have much new and valuable work, especially by younger theorists like Professor Yoshida, to draw on.

Apart from questions concerning the formal aspects of the theory, I take it from Professor Yoshida's remarks that he does not dispute the essence of the theory of underconsumption presented in *The Theory of Capitalist Development*, namely, that "capitalism has an inherent *tendency* to expand the capacity to produce consumption goods more rapidly than the demand for consumption goods" (p. 180) and that this is one of the fundamental contradictions of the system. This is, I think, an extremely important point and one which, as I tried to show, by no means all Marxian writers have accepted. I should hope that a careful working out of the theory in terms of the departmental scheme would lead to a much more substantial measure of agreement among Marxian economists than has existed heretofore.

In concluding my comments on Professor Yoshida's review, let me say that I agree with him that the kernel of the problem of crises lies in the process of accumulation and in how the disproportionate growth of investment is made possible and then subsequently becomes untenable. I would only add that under certain circumstances the underlying contradiction manifests itself in another form: the untenability of a disproportionate growth of investment is to a certain extent foreseen, with the result that the volume of investment is curtailed and the economy stagnates instead of going through a boom and a crash. Something like this, I believe, happened in the United States during the 1930s and could happen again, perhaps even in the fairly near future. It would seem to be connected with the growth of monopoly and what ironically is called "planning" in capitalist circles.

II

It seems to me that Mr. Kazahaya makes rather too much of my use of the term "theory of general equilibrium." The sentence in which the term appears (p. 53) can be omitted entirely without in the least changing or distorting the sense of the passages in which it occurs. I used it merely to try to make my meaning clearer to economists trained in the orthodox tradition and unfamiliar with Marxian ideas. Admittedly, there are difficulties, and perhaps even dangers, involved in trying to explain aspects of one theoretical system in terms of concepts peculiar to another, but if we are to communicate successfully I think we must sometimes take the risk.

With regard to the meaning of the term, it seems to me that Mr. Kazahaya goes too far in identifying the theory of general equilibrium with modern bourgeois economics. It is a theory developed by one school of economists and covers only a small part of modern bourgeois economics. Moreover, while modern bourgeois economics in general does take for granted the permanence of capitalism, the theory of general equilibrium as such is as applicable to simple commodity production as it is to capitalism and does not necessarily imply the permanence of either. The significance of the theory of general equilibrium is that it shows more clearly than any other part of bourgeois economics how and why private producers, each producing individually and with only his own interest to guide him, are tied together into a mutually interdependent *system*. In Marxian political economy, the law of value performs the same function, and it is this fact which led me to compare the two.

Of course Mr. Kazahaya may be right in his view that I have not succeeded in transcending the limitations of my own training as an orthodox economist. That is for others than myself to decide; after all, the subjective judgments of an author are not worth much in matters like this. But I do think that to support his contention he will have to do more than cite my use of the term "theory of general equilibrium."

Turning now to the problem of the role of the law of value under socialism, it seems to me undeniable that Marx used "the law of value" to designate the regulative mechanism of a *capitalist* society. The regulative mechanism of a socialist society, on the other hand, is conscious, centralized planning. These two mechanisms are not only different, they are the direct opposites of each other. It was for this reason that I wrote the passage which Mr. Kazahaya quotes: "In the economics of a socialist society the theory of planning should hold the same basic position as the theory of value in the economics of a capitalist society. Value and planning are as much opposed, and for the same reasons, as capitalism and socialism." (P. 54.)

The only work by Soviet economists bearing on this subject that I have seen is the well-known article by Leontiev and others which appeared in 1943. (Published in English translation under the title "The Teaching of Economics in the Soviet Union" in the *American Economic Review* for September 1944, the most important parts were also published in English in *Science & Society*, Spring 1944.) There is nothing in this article to induce me to change my mind about the correctness of the position taken in *The Theory of Capitalist Development*. Nor, in my judgment, is there any contradiction between that position and the *substance* of the views expressed by Leontiev and his collaborators. The *apparent* contradiction between the two arises from the fact that Leontiev and his associates give the "law of value" a different, and, as it seems to me, rather special, meaning. They use the term to designate not the regulative mechanism of an unplanned capitalist society but the apparatus of money and prices through which that mechanism works. *In this sense* it is certainly true that the law of value applies to a socialist society, for, as is obvious from two decades of Soviet experience, centralized planning also requires this apparatus to operate efficiently.

I suppose that the Soviet economists, in raising this question and in insisting that socialism cannot do without the law of value, were combating ill-considered and harmful theories to the effect that socialist economy has nothing whatever in common with capitalist economy.[2] This is cer-

---

[2] On this point, and indeed on the whole range of issues raised by the Leontiev article, see the excellent communication, "New Trends in Russian Economic Thinking?" by Paul A. Baran, *American Economic Review*, December 1944.

tainly desirable and necessary, though I am not convinced that it required them to interpret the law of value in a way which is certainly different from Marx's normal usage of the term.

However that may be, it seems to me wrong to make a great issue of principle out of this question. As society develops and socialism replaces capitalism, old terms inevitably take on new meanings, and perhaps this will be the case with the law of value. There is nothing sacred about Marx's usage, as I am sure Marx himself would have been the first to admit. At the same time, however, there is also nothing wrong about adhering to the older usage in spite of indications that a change may be in the process of developing.

III

The editor of *The Economic Review* has also asked me to comment on the article by E. D. Domar, "The Problem of Capital Accumulation" (*American Economic Review*, December 1948), in so far as this article relates to the theory expounded in my book. I can do this the more briefly since Professor Domar deals only with the aggregative analysis criticized by Professor Yoshida and since, as I have already indicated, I am not satisfied with this analysis myself.

First, let me say that *from the point of view of aggregative analysis* Professor Domar's criticisms seem to me to be on the whole well taken. If one looks only at aggregates, there is no justification for postulating a special relation between stock of capital and output of consumption goods (this is a point also made, at least by implication, by Professor Yoshida), and Professor Domar is right to substitute the relation between stock of capital and total output. Moreover, by making this change, and by a few further emendations, he shows that it is possible to obtain stronger results than I obtained in the book. There is, however, this important difference: since consumption has been merged into total output, the results obtained by Professor Domar's method can no longer be said to have any relation to the problem of underconsumption. That problem simply disappears, and what emerges from his reasoning — or it might be more accurate to say, what could be derived from his reasoning — can perhaps be called a theory of a tendency to overaccumulation.

According to this theory, genuine overaccumulation will occur only if the rate is so high as to be incapable of being sustained by available physical resources — at least I think this is a fair interpretation — and Professor Domar seems to be quite certain that this is also what my theory (of underconsumption) implies and is intended to imply. In this connection, he cites page 189 where I speak of abundant or rapidly increasing manpower and alludes to Chapter XII where the population and manpower problems are dealt with in considerable detail.

As far as my theory is concerned, Professor Domar is very wide of the mark here. In my opinion, underconsumption (and the kind of overaccumulation, or potential overaccumulation, which can always be said to be the counterpart of underconsumption) has very little to do with physical limitations on the growth of production. The problem, it seems to me, is the failure to establish and maintain tenable proportions between consumption and the other components of total production, and this failure exists and normally manifests itself in the form of crises before physical limitations put a check on the growth of total production. My emphasis on population arises not from a belief in its importance as a physical barrier to the expansion of production but rather from the belief that the rate of population growth, operating through its effect on the rate of wages and the division of newly capitalized surplus value between variable and constant capital, plays a highly important role in determining the *relative* size and rate of growth of consumption.

I thought I had made this position clear on pages 222-225,

but at the same time I can hardly blame Professor Domar if he misunderstood me. From his point of view, the interesting part of my analysis is the aggregative scheme (pp. 180 ff.), and here my attempt to bring in the consumption factor was, as I have already noted, a failure. Professor Domar, however, considered the attempt to be a slip of the pen rather than a failure — otherwise how could he write, "I hope I do not violate the spirit of Sweezy's theory by substituting 'income' for consumption"? — and he was understandably not prepared to find anything inconsistent with this interpretation in other parts of the book. The root of his misunderstanding lies in my having introduced the aggregative scheme at all. Such a scheme is not suitable for analyzing the problem of underconsumption, and I should not have attempted to make use of it.

The main lesson to be drawn from Professor Domar's paper, therefore, is much the same as the main lesson of Professor Yoshida's review, namely, the necessity to stick to departmental analysis and to work the underconsumption problem out afresh and in detail in these terms. I regard this problem as a standing challenge to Marxian economists. The first one to solve it satisfactorily will, I am convinced, be making a theoretical contribution of the greatest importance.

APPENDIX

SUMMARY OF PROFESSOR Y. YOSHIDA'S COMMENT

(1) Mr. Sweezy, in explaining "crises arising from underconsumption," tries to establish a stable relation between "stock of means of production" and "output of consumption goods." He says: "Such evidence as we have . . . strongly suggests a remarkably high degree of stability for a reasonably well-developed capitalist economy." (P. 182.) Even if the empirical evidence appears to prove this stability, it has to be shown *theoretically*. Theory must come first.

(2) So long as we assume the improvement in the method of production and the rise in the organic composition of capital, the stable ratio referred to above cannot be logically defended. Especially if we mean by the relation between stock of capital and output of consumption goods *not* the relation between stock of capital in the second department (the consumption goods department) and output of consumption goods *but* the relation between stock of capital in both departments and output of consumption goods, the stability referred to becomes all the more untenable. Mr. Sweezy does not seem to make any distinction for his theoretical purpose between capital goods in general and capital goods for the second department.

(3) One departure which Mr. Sweezy makes from Marx is the use of the Keynesian concepts of *net* aggregates instead of the two-department scheme of Marx. The two-department scheme enables us to see the possibility of producers' goods increasing more rapidly than consumption goods and yet maintaining a balance in the process of social reproduction. The basic contradiction of capitalist production which Mr. Sweezy so neatly summarizes does not show itself *directly*, as he implies, through the conflict of the two relations (the two ratios referred to on page 183), but through the process of accumulation which actually permits for a while the unbalanced development of the first department in an apparently balanced manner. The kernel of the problem of crises lies in the process of accumulation and how the disproportionate growth of investment is made possible and then subsequently becomes untenable. (Summarized from a review article in *The Economic Review*, January 1950, pp. 56-61.)

SUMMARY OF MR. Y. KAZAHAYA'S COMMENT

(1) The passage characteristic of Mr. Sweezy's theoretical position is: ". . . the law of value is essentially a theory of general equilibrium developed in the first instance with

reference to simple commodity production and later on adapted to capitalism." (P. 53.) It is true that the value theory in Marx deals with problem of equilibrium, but this does not mean that it is a "theory of general equilibrium." "Theory of general equilibrium" is another name for modern bourgeois economics which basically stands on the assumption of the permanence of the capitalist mode of production. Mr. Sweezy does not seem to have quite gotten out of the spell of the modern economic theory in which he was trained for so many years.

(2) As is clear from his passage: "In the economics of a socialist society the theory of planning should hold the same basic position as the theory of value in the economics of a capitalist society. Value and planning are as much opposed, and for the same reasons, as capitalism and socialism" (p. 54). Mr. Sweezy takes a rather stereotyped position as regards the role of the law of value in a socialist society. We should like to hear his opinion on this problem, now that the new light has been thrown upon it through the discussions started in 1943 by Soviet economists. (Summarized from a review article in the *Shiso no Kagaku*, June 1947, pp. 221-232.)

34

Peace and Prosperity

This is the text of a talk delivered before a panel of the annual convention of the National Lawyers Guild, Hotel Park Sheraton, New York City, February 21, 1953.

IT IS an honor to be able to speak before the National Convention of the Lawyers Guild. There are not many organizations that have as good a record in fighting against the growing threat of American fascism — to use milder language would be dishonest — and I salute you all for your part in making that record. I also wish you the strength and courage to keep up the good work no matter what difficulties lie ahead.

I take it that by inviting me to speak on "Governmental Policies Required for Prosperity in a Peacetime Economy" you have indicated on the one hand that you want to hear the opinion of an economist and on the other hand that you are willing to listen to a specifically socialist analysis of this question. I must warn you at the outset that I have only twenty minutes to deal with what I am sure is, in its implications and ramifications, one of the most important problems facing the American people today. Under the circumstances, I have no choice but to stick to the barest essentials — to oversimplify, some of you may think. I know of no other way to present the problem in its true proportions.

The heart of the problem is this: under conditions of full or near-full employment, the American economy, dominated as it is by a few hundred monopolistic giants, generates the enormous total of 40 to 50 billion dollars of profits. If the economy is to be kept going at this rate, these profits have to be regularly returned to the market as demand for goods and services. If they are not, the result will be a recession or depression or crash — the appropriate term depending on how large and rapid the shortfall is.

It can be taken for granted that not very much of this vast profit total is going to find its way into the market for consumers' goods. In the last few years, for example, less than 25 percent has been paid out in dividends, and most of that goes to people who are relatively well off and habitually save a large part of their incomes.

Under the present setup, therefore, the whole problem of prosperity revolves around the question of finding ways of spending the bulk of these profits on something besides consumers' goods.

In recent years an answer has been found — at least a temporary one. A large part of the profits is taxed away and spent by the government on war preparations, while the remainder is invested in building up the armaments industries (using that term in the broadest sense to include not only military end-products such as guns and tanks and planes but also the heavy industries which feed the production of these end-products).

From the point of view of the capitalists, this solution has one great disadvantage: high taxation. Everything else is in its favor. It is precisely the biggest monopolies which benefit most directly from arms spending; there is no competition, direct or indirect, with private enterprise; the atmosphere of hatred and intolerance that goes with war preparation — the witch hunts, the jingoism, the glorification of force — creates the conditions in which the propertied classes find it easiest to control the ideas and activities of workers and farmers and lower middle classes. For all this and prosperity too, the capitalists find it well worth while to accept the burden of high taxes. Despite its obvious dangers to world peace, this solution accords with the fundamental interests of the capitalists. It is folly to forget this.

Now if a large part of the spending on arms were cut out, there would clearly be two possible ways to maintain prosperity. First, some other way might be found to spend the profits. Second, some way might be found to reduce profits while simultaneously expanding the incomes of workers and other consumers. Let us consider these two possibilities in turn.

The champions of private enterprise like to argue that if arms spending and taxes were both cut, the larger profits remaining in the hands of the capitalists would be invested in expanding the capacity of the economy to produce civilian goods and services. This can safely be dismissed as nonsense. Profits are so large as to confine the growth of consumption within narrow limits, and if they were largely invested in expanding civilian capacity the result would very soon be a crisis of excess capacity and overproduction. If profits are to remain at this exorbitant level, taxes would have to be kept up and the government would have to find suitable substitutes for armament spending. That is one possibility.

The other is reducing profits while expanding the incomes of workers and other consumers. Trade union spokesmen frequently argue that this is simply a matter of raising wages. Unfortunately, this is not the case. The big monopolies regularly raise prices by enough, or more than enough, to offset wage increases. Strongly unionized workers may benefit, but it is normally at the expense of nonunionized workers and other consumers (pensioners, for example) rather than at the expense of profits. But an effective redistribution of income could, at least theoretically, be achieved in one or more of the following three ways: (1) keeping up taxes on profits and turning the proceeds over, directly or indirectly, to consumers; (2) an assault, via trust busting or some similar device, on monopoly; (3) rigorous price controls to squeeze profit margins and raise the purchasing power of consumers' incomes.

To summarize: What is required is either a vast amount of government spending for nonmilitary purposes, or effective income redistribution, or some combination of the two. As I said at the outset, it is not my intention to go into details, but I think it is clear that it would be possible to work up a program of interrelated measures which could plausibly be called the answer to our question: What governmental policies are required for prosperity in a peacetime economy?

But would it really be an answer?

I'm afraid not. The reason, put in its simplest terms, is that the capitalists would not play ball. As long as the levers of control over the basic productive apparatus of society are in capitalist hands, no economic program can hope to succeed without their consent, if not active cooperation. They have the power to sabotage policies of which they disapprove. Remember, for example, how they forced the abandonment of price controls against the will of the Truman administration in 1946. And, if necessary, they can do more than sabotage individual policies — they can literally *create* a depression. In more orthodox economic terminology, their "confidence" can be so badly shaken that buying is reduced to a hand-to-mouth basis and total demand shrinks to depression levels.

And, make no mistake about it, it is precisely this kind of opposition that the policies outlined above would face. It cannot be emphasized too often or too strongly that capitalists are dead set against each and every one of them. Nor is this mere irrationality or stupidity on their part.

Whereas, in the case of arms spending, the only drawback from a capitalist standpoint is high taxes, in this case high taxes are only one of many drawbacks and dangers.

It may be possible to spend a few billion dollars in ways that do not threaten capitalist interests, but this is certainly not so of 25 or 30 or 40 billion — and these are the relevant orders of magnitude. That is to say, it is not possible *except* on war preparations. All other forms of really large-scale government spending either involve competition with private enterprise or they confer benefits on the masses and thus indirectly undermine the authority and privileges of the capitalists and their upper-class allies and retainers.

As to a direct assault on inequality of income, it is clear that this strikes at the very heart of our social-class system and will be resisted to the end by the special beneficiaries of that system.

I am not, of course, developing an argument *against* radical economic policies — they constitute the only alternative to war or chronic depression. What I am arguing is that no program has any claim to be taken seriously unless it foresees the kind of opposition it will encounter and includes measures for overcoming it.

But I would go further. Since the opposition to the *carrying out* of the program is of precisely the same nature as the opposition to its *enactment*, it follows inescapably that combating that opposition is both a prerequisite and a postrequisite — an integral part of the program, without which it has no meaning and makes no sense.

Let us follow this line of reasoning and see where it leads.

How could we hope to get an adequate economic program enacted in the face of the determined opposition of what, following Veblen, we may appropriately call "the vested interests"? Not, of course, through the Republican Party, which is simply the party of Big Business. But neither could we hope to get it enacted through the Democratic Party. True, the Democratic Party can, as the experience of the New Deal shows, mobilize the support of the masses, and it is only this support that can ever push through a radical economic program. But the Democratic Party rallies the masses not to give them leadership and direction but to hold them in check, to keep them from making demands that might be unacceptable to the vested interests. (How it does this — by giving a virtual power of veto to the Southern reactionaries, the Catholic hierarchy, and the city bosses — is one of the great political triumphs of American capitalism, but we must pass it over here.)

No, the Democratic Party is not a political *instrument* of the masses, it is a political *strait-jacket* on the masses. The precondition of radical reform is the bursting of this strait-jacket and the forging of a real instrument of reform—which, as the experience of all industrially advanced countries shows, can only mean the formation of a labor party by the labor movement itself.

A labor party could center its program on massive government spending and income redistribution with a reasonable hope of electoral and legislative success. But that would be only the beginning of the fight. It would then have to put the program into effect and make it work against the economic power of the vested interests. To put the matter in its simplest terms, it would be a case of the political power of labor against the economic power of capital.

I do not for a moment believe that labor could win if the struggle remained on this level. Economic power has deeper roots and is more durable. It may suffer setbacks and defeats, but as long as it survives intact it will always come back and in the long run it will win. That is surely the lesson of all reform movements in American history—most recently of the New Deal, though the effort to work through the Democratic Party clearly doomed the New Deal from the outset—and there is no reason (aside from wishful thinking) to suppose that matters would be different in the future.

Does this mean that *all* reform movements are certain to fail? Of course not. What it means is that if a reform movement is to succeed, it cannot and must not rely solely on its political power to enact laws which its opponents can later repeal. *It must use its political power to acquire an ever-increasing share of economic power.* In this way, and only in this way, can the economic power of capital be weakened and eventually defeated.

Concretely, this means that a labor party will be able to achieve its historic mission, which no one can doubt is to achieve *both* peace and prosperity in the United States, only by socializing the decisive corporate monopolies. However it may regard itself at the outset, the labor party of the United States will eventually become a socialist party—or it will become nothing.

If I am right, how much better it would be for the labor party of the United States — you see I have no doubt that we shall have one sooner or later — to be a socialist party from the outset! For socialism is in a very real sense a master economic reform which does away with the need for the kind of partial economic makeshifts we have so far been considering. The $40 to $50 billion of profits which caused all the trouble under the present setup simply cease to be a problem under socialism. This is not to say that there is no such thing as an excess of receipts over costs in a socialist economy — there is. But no one has a vested interest in that excess; no class lives on it. It can be disposed of (through government investment or any other kind of government spending), or it can be reduced (through a systematic policy of lowering prices and thus raising the purchasing power of consumers' incomes) in accordance with social needs. No one is going to put up a big battle over these questions because no one has a special interest in doing so.

I conclude that ultimately it will be found that the *only* way to combine peace and prosperity is through socialism, and that it would be much better for us all if this discovery were made sooner rather than later.

Let me hasten to add that I am not advocating a sterile, sectarian policy of "socialism or nothing." As long as the American labor movement is not prepared to adopt a socialist program — and it obviously isn't and probably won't be for some time — we must of course work in and with it for more limited aims—even much more limited, I am afraid, than the kind of economic program of government spending and income redistribution that I outlined a few moments ago. But what I *am* advocating is that those of us who are convinced that in the long run socialism is the only possible answer politically, and by far the best conceivable answer economically, should begin right now to explain *why*, to everyone we work with for the realization of more limited aims.

Index

NOTE: This index does not include names of persons, organizations, authorities, etc., cited in Chapter 12, "Interest Groups in the American Economy," and also omits some other names to which the text makes only passing reference.

AACHEN, 246
Abolitionists, 197
Account of the Occupation, An (Julian Bach, Jr.), 244-250
Accumulation of capital, 279-282, 299-300, 308, 324; absent from Fabian theory, 322; and change, 280-282; and closed capitalist system, 292-293. See also Capital, Investment, Saving
Accumulation of Capital, The (Rosa Luxemburg), 93, 93n, 94, 291-294
Adams, Brooks, 199
Advanced countries, meaning of imperialism for, 85; problem of, 23-27; relations with backward countries, 82-84, 87-92, 104
Africa, 84
Alsace-Lorraine, 99
Altgeld, John Peter, 198, 200
American capitalism, and Cold War, 207-208, 211; and the depression of the 1930's, 206-207; development of, 154-157; geared to militarism and imperialism, 114; and government expenditures, 113-116; power to accumulate capital, 112; saved by World War II, 207; special characteristics of, 25-26
American Economic Association, 338; *Papers and Proceedings* (1949), 16
American Economic Review, The, 197, 199, 357, 357n, 358
American Historical Association, 79
American Historical Review, 103
American Military Government (AMG), 245-249, 297
American Railway Union, 202
American Revolution, 154
American Telephone & Telegraph Co., 132, 169-170, 185, 187-188, 191
Anarchists, 197
Antifa movement, 244, 248-250
Antioch Review, The, 189
Anti-Semitism, 143, 286, 286n
Antitrust laws, 217-218
Army, role of in Nazi Germany, 237-238
Army Talks, 244
Arnall, Ellis, 217n
Assimilation, aspiration of U. S. Negroes, 149-151
Atlantic Pact, 230

BABEUF, GRACCHUS, 4
Bach, Julian, Jr., *An Account of the Occupation*, 244-250
Backward countries, meaning of imperialism for, 85; relations with advanced countries, 82-84, 87-92, 104; unbalanced development of, 83
Bagdad railway, 101
Baker, George F., 164
Balkans, 101
Balogh, Thomas, 69
Banking Act of 1933, 164, 168n, 191
Banks, included in major interest groups, 166-167, 183
Bauer, Otto, *Zwischen Zwei Weltkriegen*, 354
Behemoth (Franz Neumann), 233-241

Belgian Congo, 88, 88n, 89
Bell Report, 88, 88n
Bergson, Herbert A., 217
Bergwerkszeitung, 48
Berle, A. A., Jr., 60n; and G. C. Means, *The Modern Corporation and Private Property*, 44-45, 159-160, 175n
Berlin blockade, 223
Bernstein, Eduard, 319-320
Besant, Annie, 318n, 320, 324, 326, 328
Big Business, growth during World War II, 117
Bismarck, Otto von, 224, 319
Bland, Hubert, 318n, 320, 328
Blum government, 340
Böhm-Bawerk, Eugen von, 278
"Bold New Program," 90
Bolshevism, 285
Boston, 131
Boston interest group, 168, 182-183, 185-187
Bourne, Randolph, 200
Brady, James ("Diamond Jim"), 135
Brady, Robert A., 235
Bremen, 248-249
Brisbane, Albert, 198
Britain, 86, 95-97; and German competition, 230; relations with Germany before 1914, 99-101; still a capitalist country, 215n. See also Labor government, Labor Party
"British Labor and Socialism" (*Monthly Review*), 215
Brown, John, 203
Buckle, H. T., *History of Civilization*, 37
Bureaucracy, role in Nazi Germany, 237-238
Burnham, James, *The Managerial Revolution*, 39-66
Business cycles, 274-275; nonexistent under socialism, 210; Veblen's theory of, 300

CAPITAL, definition of, 59; power of, 273, 368; and saving, 279. See also Accumulation of capital
Capital (Marx), 81, 141, 261, 292, 307
Capitalism, and anarchy, 327; breakdown of, 292-293, 313; case for presented by Pigou, 264-265; contradictions of, 17, 308-310, 350, 350n; crisis of and bourgeois economics, 270, 272-273; defined, 205; development of in Russia, 20; dominant Western social system, 33-34; formerly a progressive system, 220; and government intervention, 237; historically specific social system, 310; lasting power in advanced countries, 23-27; life lengthened by imperialism, 24-25; "margin of expansibility" in 19th century, 24-25; nature of, 9-11, 16-17; in Nazi Germany, 236; and non-capitalist environment, 292; and racial discrimination, 151; a system of booms and busts, 206; theory of, 97-98; Veblen's conception of, 299-300; wastefulness of, 219-220. See also American capitalism

INDEX

Capitalism and Socialism on Trial (Fritz Sternberg), 93-94, 103-107
Capitalists, absent from circular flow, 277-278; consumption of, 60n; dominant motives of, 59-60, 308; preference for militarist and imperialist expenditures, 115-116
Cartels, 226
Caste, 143-145
Catholic Church, 38, 135, 367
Celler Committee, 216n, 217, 217n
Center Party (German), 97, 100
Chamberlain, Joseph, 97
Chambers of Commerce, 132
Chartist movement, 4, 326
Chase, Stuart, "If Peace Breaks Out" (*The Nation*), 211, 211n
Chicago, 131-132
Chicago interest group, 168, 178-179, 183-185
China, 22, 84-85, 87, 106, 298
Chinese Communism and the Rise of Mao (Benjamin Schwartz), 74-76
Chinese Revolution, 22, 106
Christianity, 34-38
Circular flow, 275-279
Civil War, American, 146-147, 154-157; English, 4; Spanish, 53
Civilization, Hellenic, 32; Orthodox Christian, 36; Toynbee's conception of, 32; Western, 33
Clarke, William, 318n, 320, 323n, 326
Class, capitalist class in the U. S., 126-127; general characteristics of, 122-125; lower middle in the U. S., 126-127; new middle classes in the U. S., 126-127; structure of U. S. ruling class, 130-134; U. S. class system, 126-130; U. S. middle class defined, 128-129; U. S. ruling class defined, 128; U. S. working class defined, 128. *See also* Ruling class
Class position, defined, 136-137
Class struggle, 8-9, 15-16; and survival of capitalism, 269
Classes, under capitalism, 59-60; Warner's six U. S. classes, 127-128
Classical economics, 253n, 254-256
Classless society, evolving in USSR, 62; meaning of, 50-51, 58
Cleveland, 131-132
Cleveland interest group, 168, 180, 183, 185
Cold War, 207-208, 211
Colonialism, 80-81
Committee on Interstate and Foreign Commerce, House, 175n
Commonsense of Political Economy (Philip H. Wicksteed), 321n
Commune, Paris, 6
Communism, 106
Communist International, 74
Communist Manifesto, 3-29; criteria for judging, 5-7; general principles of, 7-23; historical importance of, 3-5; and historical prediction, 332; successive prefaces to, 6-7
Communist parties (Europe), 70
Communist Party, China, 74-76; France, 340
Communists, 13, 317-318; in Germany, 248; relations with Socialists after World War II, 70-71
Competition, 284-285; proposals to enforce, 218
Conant, Charles A., 80
Conservation, coal, 219; forests, 219

Consumption, and the circular flow, 277-279
Corporations, and internal financing, 118; nonfinancial included in major interest groups, 165-166, 183; ownership and control of, 43-46; railroad in development of, 155; 200 largest nonfinancial, 116, 165; types of control, 159-160
Cox, Oliver Cromwell, *Caste, Class, and Race*, 139-152
Crises, underconsumption theory of, 353-355, 359-360
Critics and Crusaders (Charles Madison), 197-201
Cuba, 88

DEBS, EUGENE, 198, 202-204; *Walls and Bars*, 202; *Writings and Speeches*, 202
Defense program, financing during World War II, 48n
Democracy, relation to social science, 335-337; and socialism in USSR, 51-52
Democratic Party, 137, 367-368
Denazification, 227
Depression, normal state of capitalism, 347. *See also* Crises, Great Depression
Dictatorship of the proletariat, in USSR, 52
Digger movement, 4
Dissident Economists, 197, 199
Distribution of income, under Nazis, 49-50; as U. S. problem, 208, 214-216
Domar, E. D., "The Problem of Capital Accumulation" (*American Economic Review*), 358-360
Douglas, Major C. H., 259
Du Pont family, 137, 179-180
Du Pont interest group, 168, 179-180, 183, 185-186
Dutt, R. Palme, *India Today*, 144

Economic Concentration and World War II (Smaller War Plants Corporation), 117
Economic development, Shaw's theory of, 322
Economic History Association, 79
Economic Review, The (Hitotsubashi University, Tokyo), 352, 353n, 356, 361
Economic Survey for 1947 (British White Paper), 329n
"Economic Theory of Socialism, On the" (Oskar Lange), 338-340
Economic Theory of Socialism, On the (B. E. Lippincott, ed.), 338-340
Economica, 330
Educational system, and U. S. classes, 133-134
Eells, Kenneth, with Warner and Meeker, *Social Class in America*, 123
Elbe, 244
Encyclopedists, 37
Engels, Friedrich, 3-29, 52, 64, 225; *Anti-Dühring*, 28, 235-236
Engineers, relation to capitalists, 299
England. *See* Britain
Entrepreneur, 275-276, 278, 281-282
Experiment in Germany (Saul K. Padover), 244-250
Export-Import Bank, 98

Fabian Essays (Bernard Shaw, ed.), Jubilee Edition, 317-329
Fabian Society, 318-320
Fabianism, 317-329
Fabians, 265
Fair Deal, 89, 135

INDEX

Family, and control of corporations, 194; and ruling-class ideology, 133; and social class, 123
Fascism, 285; German, 46-50; relation to capitalism, 243; threat of in U. S., 363. *See also* National Socialism, Nazism
Federal Communications Commission, *American Telephone and Telegraph Company*, 170n, 188n
Federal Trade Commission, *Report . . . on the Merger Movement* (1948), 117
Feis, Herbert, *Europe, the World's Banker: 1870-1914*, 83
Feudal carry-overs, in Veblen's theory, 298, 300
Feudalism, 327
Finance capital, 155-157
Fiscal Policy and Business Cycles (Alvin H. Hansen), 270-273
Five-Year Plan (India), 87
Force and violence, 204
Fortune, 40, 40n, 45, 160
Foster, William Z., "Marxism and American Exceptionalism" (*Political Affairs*), 25
Fourier, Charles, 4
France, 95, 99
Free trade, 269, 323
French Revolution, 4
Full Recovery or Stagnation? (Alvin H. Hansen), 267-270
Fuller, Margaret, 198

GEOPOLITICS, 235
George, Henry, 199, 321, 324
German General Staff, 96
German problem, defined, 224-226; solution of, 229, 232
Germany, 46-50, 86, 95-97, 194, 223-250; bomb damage, 247; casualties in World War II, 246; character of working-class movement, 225-226; as competitor for markets, 230; foreign policy before 1914, 98-101; and managerial revolution, 41-42; under Military Government, 247-249; policies in Soviet Zone, 228; revival of imperialism in, 227; revolution of 1848 in, 13-14; Social Democratic Party of, 225-226, 320; under U. S. occupation, 227; and the USSR, 228-232; Veblen's analysis of, 295-297; weakness of liberalism in, 224-225. *See also* Denazification, German problem, National Socialism, Nazism
Geschichte und Klassenbewusstsein (Georg Lukacs), i, vi
Gesell, Silvio, 259
Goering, Hermann, 61, 237
Goering Works, 48, 236-237
Goldsmith, Raymond W., and others, *The Distribution of Ownership in the 200 Largest Non-financial Corporations* (TNEC Monograph No. 29), 44n
Goldsmith, Selma F., "Statistical Information on the Distribution of Income . . ." (*Papers and Proceedings*, American Economic Association, 1949), 214
Government investment, 213
Government spending, 113-116, 207, 211, 268, 339-340, 364-368
Gradualism, 324-326
Granby, Helene, *Survey of Shareholdings in 1,710 Corporations* (TNEC Monograph No. 30), 44n
Gray, Alexander, *The Socialist Tradition*, 305

Great Britain. *See* Britain
Great Depression, 64, 111-113, 211, 258, 271
"Guidance of Production in a Socialist State, The" (Fred M. Taylor), 338
Guild Socialists, 329

HACKER, LOUIS M., *The Triumph of American Capitalism*, 153-157
Hallgarten, G. W. F., *Imperialismus vor 1914*, 80-82, 93-104
Hansen, Alvin H., 111; *Fiscal Policy and Business Cycles*, 270-273; *Full Recovery or Stagnation?* 267-270
Harcourt, Sir William, 324
Harris, Seymour E., ed., *The New Economics: Keynes' Influence on Theory and Public Policy*, 253
Hayek, F. A., 334; *The Road to Serfdom*, 283-290
Hellenic civilization, 32, 36
Herz, John, "The Fiasco of Denazification in Germany" (*Political Science Quarterly*), 227
Hilferding, Rudolf, *Das Finanzkapital*, 65-66, 81, 98n, 260n
Hillman, Sidney, 135
Historical materialism, 8, 14-15; applied to U. S. history, 154
Historicism, 330-335
Hitler, Adolf, 242, 248
Hobbes, Thomas, 239
Hobson, John A., 80-81
Holy Roman Empire, 36
Housing, as outlet for government spending, 212
Huberman, Leo, 3; "Socialism and American Labor" (*Monthly Review*), 26
Humanitarianism, and socialism, 202-204

IMPERIALISM, concept broadened by Lenin, 81; contradictions of, 231-232; criteria of, 82-84; denotes specific social system, 82; economic impact on backward countries, 82-84; and European capitalism, 104-105; explained by Rosa Luxemburg, 292; and finance capital, 81; and the German problem, 224, 226-227; ideology of, 64-66; impact on colonial countries, 104; and Nazism, 47; original meaning of, 80; pattern of in "classic" period, 84-85; pattern of in interwar period, 85; relation to the life of capitalism, 24-25; as solution to America's problems, 73; theory of, 97-98; after World War II, 85-86
Imperialismus vor 1914 (G. W. F. Hallgarten), 80-82, 93-103
Income distribution, measure of inequality of, 214n; relation to classes, 51
India, 84, 86-87
Individualism, 285
Indonesia, 86
Industrialization, process of analyzed, 341-350
Industrials, included in major interest groups, 165-166, 183
Inequality, in capitalism and socialism, 264
Innovation, defined by Schumpeter, 275-276
Interest, absent from circular flow, 277; as share of national income, 214-215
Interest groups, 158-188; defined, 160-161; eight major groups identified, 167-168

INDEX

Interests, as motivating force of social action, 96-97
Interlocking directorates, 161-163
Internal financing, growing importance in U. S., 192; in Nazi Germany, 243
International Bank for Reconstruction and Development, 89
Internationalism, and the USSR, 53-54
Interstate Commerce Commission, 176n, 217
Investment, in Nazi Germany, 242-243; private vs. public, 272; in relation to saving, 267-268
Investment banker, and corporate control, 161; decline of, 189-196; historic role of, 189-190
Investment banking, and railroads, 155-157
Italy, 194

JAPAN, 85-86, 194, 224, 231; Veblen's analysis of, 295-297
Jevonian theory of value, 321-323, 327
Jews, 286, 286n. See also Anti-Semitism
John Reed Society (Harvard), 305
Journal of Economic History, 93
Journal of Political Economy, 74, 202, 242, 317
Judiciary Committee, House, 216n, 217
July 20, 1944, conspiracy of, 246
Junkers, 224, 228

Kampfgemeinschaft gegen den Faschismus, 248
Kapital, Das. See *Capital*
Kautsky, Karl, 65
Kazahaya, Y., 352-353, 355-358, 361-362
Kehr, Eckart, 98; *Schlachtflottenbau und Parteipolitik, 1894-1901*, 98n
Keynes, John Maynard, 111, 210, 253-262, 293-294, 323; *Essays in Biography*, 253; *Essays in Persuasion*, 258, 258n, 313n; *The General Theory of Employment, Interest, and Money*, 256-257, 257n, 258n, 259, 259n, 260n, 351n; *A Treatise on Money*, 255n; *Treatise on Probability*, 253
Keynesian theory, economic, 312-316; of the state, 315
Keynesians, 111, 210-212, 293-294
Krupp, House of, 101
Kuhn, Loeb & Co., 163, 175-177
Kuhn, Loeb interest group, 168, 175-177, 183, 185, 187
Kulaks, 286
Kuomintang, 74

LABOR GOVERNMENT (Britain), 215, 215n, 229, 297
Labor Party (Britain), 39, 70, 317-318, 325
Labor party, historic mission in U. S., 368; need for in U. S., 368; in U. S. must become socialist, 368
La Follette, Robert, Sr., 200
Laissez faire, relation to capitalism, 63-64
Lange, Oskar, "On the Economic Theory of Socialism," 338-340
Langer, William L., 103; *The Diplomacy of Imperialism, 1890-1902*, 102n; *European Alliances and Alignments*, 102n
Lattimore, Owen, *Inner Asian Frontiers of China*, 35
Lausanne school, 327n
Lawyers Guild, 363
Lebensraum, 47
Left Book Club, 283
Left News, 283

Lenin, V. I., 24, 64-65, 75, 81-82, 84-85
Leontiev, L. A., and others, "The Teaching of Economics in the Soviet Union" (*American Economic Review; Science & Society*), 357, 357n
Lewis, John L., 135
Ley, Robert, 61
Liberalism, 284-286; relation to capitalism, 63-64; weakness in Germany, 224-225
Lippincott, Benjamin E., ed., *On the Economic Theory of Socialism*, 338-340
Lippmann, Walter, 68, 265, 338
Lukacs, Georg, *Geschichte und Klassenbewusstsein*, i, vi
Lundberg, Ferdinand, *America's Sixty Families*, 122
Lurie, Samuel, *Private Investment in a Controlled Economy: Germany, 1933-1939*, 242-243
Luxemburg, Rosa, 65; *The Accumulation of Capital*, 93, 93n, 94, 291-294; *Antikritik*, 94, 294
Lynching, 148-149
Lynd, Robert S. and Helen M., *Middletown*, 121

MCKEON, RICHARD, ED., *Democracy in a World of Tensions*, 330
McNamara Case, 204
Madison, Charles, *Critics and Crusaders*, 197-201
Managerial revolution, classified as a theory, 40; theory summarized, 41-43
Managerial Revolution, The (James Burnham), 39-66
Managers, defined by Burnham, 42; their subordination to capitalists, 45-46
Manchester school, 37
Manchesterism, 265
Manufactures, investment in, 156
Mao Tse-tung, 74
Maoism, 74
Marshall, Alfred, 253n, 263, 277
Marshall Plan, 67-73, 113
Marx, Karl, 3-29, 58-60, 120, 144, 225, 259-262, 285, 305, 307-308, 323n, 324, 327, 342n, 358, 361-362; *Capital*, 81, 141, 261, 292, 307; *Critique of the Gotha Program*, 51; *Theorien über den Mehrwert*, 259n, 261
Marxian economics, 254-255, 305-312
Marxism, 262; essence of, 76; in the Far East, 74-76; and historicism, 330-335; orthodox versus revisionism, 291-292; quality of Debs's, 203; and religion, 335-336; and writing of history, 153-154
Mass unemployment, relation to capitalism and Nazism, 46-47
Mayer, Gustav, *Friedrich Engels*, 14
M-C-M', 60n
Means, G. C., 60n; and A. A. Berle, Jr., *The Modern Corporation and Private Property*, 44-45, 159-160, 175n
Mediterranean, importance to Roman Empire, 36
Meeker, Marchia, with Warner and Eells, *Social Class in America*, 123
Mellon family, 137, 177
Mellon interest group, 168, 177-178, 183-184, 186-187
Mercantilism, character of, 54-55
Merger movement, 117-118
Middle East, 101
Militant Liberals, 197-200
Militarism, as solution to America's problems, 73

INDEX

Military Government (MG), 245-249, 297
Mill, John Stuart, 253, 253n, 263
Miquel, Johannes von, 100
Mises, Ludwig von, 264-265, 338
Monopoly, degree of, 350n; development in Germany, 225; neglected by Keynes, 260, 260n; relation to ideology of capitalism, 63-64; relation to profits in U. S., 365; as U. S. problem, 208, 216-218
Monroe Doctrine, 88
Monthly Review, 3, 26, 67, 79, 92, 111, 119-120, 138-139, 223
Monthly Review Pamphlet, 205
More, Thomas, *Utopia*, 4
Morgan, J. P., 118, 135, 189
Morgan, J. P. & Co., 162-164, 168n, 170, 173, 176-177, 191-193
Morgan-First National interest group, 168, 174, 183-185
Morocco, 89
Mussolini, Benito, 135
Myrdal, Gunnar, *An American Dilemma*, 145-146

Nation, The, 30, 263, 267
National Association of Manufacturers, 132
National debt, of U. S. and U. K. compared, 271
National Income and Expenditure (British White Paper), 215
National Lawyers Guild, 363
National Resources Committee, 158
National Resources Planning Board, 116
National Socialism, 233-241. See also Denazification, Germany, Nazism
National University Extension Association, Debate Handbook, *Welfare State*, 205
Nationalism, 297-299; and U. S. Negroes, 149-150
Nationalkomitee Freies Deutschland, 248
Natural rate of interest, 255n
Natural resources, as U. S. problem, 208, 218-219
Nature of Peace, The (Veblen), 295-301
Nazi economy, 235, 242-243
Nazi Germany, compared to Soviet Union, 286-287
Nazi Party, relation to ruling class, 238
Nazism, 41-43, 57-61, 102, 226-227, 233-243, 285-287, 297; capitalist character of, 236-237; and imperialism, 47; Marxist theory of, 46-47; relation to capitalism, 46-50, 60-61
Negroes, natural allies of workers, 151; potential enemies of capitalism, 151; reaction to their situation in U. S., 149-151. See also Assimilation, Lynching, Nationalism, Race, Race relations, Segregation, Slavery
Nenni Socialists (Italy), 317
Neoclassical economics, 253n, 254-257
Neumann, Franz, *Behemoth*, 233-241
New Deal, 41, 43, 54-57, 89, 111-114, 135, 158, 193, 195, 200, 213, 271, 340, 367-368
"New Economics," 210
New Fabian Essays (R. H. S. Crossman, ed.), 39
New Republic, The, 153, 244, 295
New Statesman and Nation, The, 291
New York, 131-132
New York Times, 133, 191
Nomadism, 35
Nurske, Ragnar, "The Schematic Representation of the Structure of Production" (*Review of Economic Studies*), 342n

O'CONNOR, HARVEY, *The Guggenheims*, 122; *Mellon's Millions*, 122; "Venezuela: A Study in Imperialism" (*Monthly Review*), 91-92
Olivier, Sydney, 318n, 320
Open Door policy, 88
Orthodox economics, 269-270; neglect of political factors, 312; scope of, 310. See also Classical economics, Neoclassical economics
Ostrovityanov, K. V., 231
Owen, Robert, 4

PADOVER, SAUL K., *Experiment in Germany*, 244-250
Paley Report, 90-92
Parmelee, Rexford C., and others, *The Distribution of Ownership in the 200 Largest Non-financial Corporations* (TNEC Monograph No. 29), 44, 44n, 45, 116
Parsons, Talcott, 16
Parti Socialiste Unitaire, 317
Patents, suppression of, 290
Patriotism, 297-299
Pease, E. R., *The History of the Fabian Society*, 319-320
Pecora investigation, 111
Petite bourgeoisie, 126
Philippines, 88
Pigou, A. C., *Economics of Welfare*, 263; *Socialism Versus Capitalism*, 263-266
Pittsburgh, 132
Plan Age, 263
Planned economy. See Socialism
Planning, 284; and British socialism, 328-329; international, 289; and Marxism, 329; need for in Western Europe, 70; prerequisites of, 288; theory of, 338
Point Four, 87-92
Political economy, from classical to vulgar, 60n; Fabian, 321-329
Popper, Karl, *The Open Society and Its Enemies*, 330n; "The Poverty of Historicism" (*Economica*), 330-337
Popular Front (French), 339-340
Postan, M. M., 30-31
"Poverty of Historicism, The" (Karl Popper, *Economica*), 330-337
Private Investment in a Controlled Economy: Germany, 1933-1939 (Samuel Lurie), 242-243
Private placement, 191
"Problem of Capitalist Accumulation, The" (E. D. Domar, *American Economic Review*), 358-360
Productivity, and incomes under socialism, 51
Profits, absent from circular flow, 277; and capital accumulation, 206; of corporations under Nazis, 49; and government expenditures, 115; importance of under capitalism, 350-351; and internal corporate financing, 118; relation to capital, 59-60; Schumpeter's theory of, 277-278, 282; share of national income, 214-215; in socialist society, 349; theory of, 321-322; in U. S. economy, 364-365, 369
Propensity to consume, 313-314
Psychological Warfare Division (PWD), 244, 246

RACE, 286n; "Bipartite Situation," 142; "Ruling-Class Situation," 142; sociologically defined, 140. See also Race relations
Race prejudice, 143, 147

INDEX

Race relations, caste theories of, 143-145; Cox's theory of, in U. S., 146-152; place of sex in, 148; as shaped by capitalism, 141-142; and violence, 148
Racism, 234-235
Railroads, growth in U. S., 344n; included in major interest groups, 165-167, 183; investment in, 155
Rasputin, Gregory, 135
Reconstruction Finance Corporation, 193
Regulatory commissions, 217-218
Rent, in circular flow, 277; share of national income, 214; theory of, 321-322
Report of the Federal Trade Commission on the Merger Movement (1948), 117
Republican Party, 137, 367
Reserve army of labor, 308
Resistance movements, 70
Review of Economic Statistics, 274
Review of Economics and Statistics, 274
Revisionism, 319-320; versus orthodox Marxism, 291-292
Revolution, international course of, 19-23. *See also* American Revolution, Chinese Revolution, French Revolution, Russian Revolution
Rhineland, 244
Ricardo, David, 253-254, 256n, 261, 263, 321; *Principles of Political Economy*, 256n
Road to Serfdom, The (F. A. Hayek), 283-290
Robinson, Joan, 93, 93n, 291, 293-294; *An Essay on Marxian Economics*, 262
Rochester, Anna, *Rulers of America*, 122
Rockefeller, John D., 155, 175
Rockefeller interest group, 168, 174-175, 179, 183, 185-186
Rockefeller Report, 90
Roman Empire, 35-36
Roosevelt, Franklin D., 55-56, 200
Rotary clubs, 132
Ruling class, attitude to government spending, 211-213; under capitalism, 59-61; determinants of ideology in U. S., 136-137; divisions and conflicts of in U. S., 137; fallacy of considering "managers" as, 63; general definition of, 58; methods of rule, 134-136; nature of, 57-63; in Nazi Germany, 237-238; nonexistence in USSR, 61-62; and trade barriers, 269-270; in U. S. South, 147-149. *See also* Class, Classes
Russia, 14, 18, 20-22, 85-86, 95; and managerial revolution, 41-42; relations with Germany before 1914, 99-101; relation to imperialism, 24. *See also* Soviet Union
Russian Revolution, 20-22, 61, 74; beginning of capitalism's final phase, 310

SACHSENHAUSEN, 245
St. Simon, Claude, 4
Sammlungspolitik, 100
San Francisco, 131-132
Saving, absent from circular flow, 278; capitalists' and workers' attitudes contrasted, 314; in relation to investment, 267-268, 300
Say's law of markets, 256, 256n, 258-259
Schiff, Jacob H., 163, 163n
Schlesinger, Arthur M., Jr., 202-204
Schumpeter, J. A., 274-282; *Business Cycles*, 275n; *Capitalism, Socialism and Democracy*, 17, 282n; *History of Economic Analysis*, 350n; "The Instability of Capitalism" (*Economic Journal*), 282n; *Theory of Economic Development*, 275n

Schwartz, Benjamin, *Chinese Communism and the Rise of Mao*, 74-76
Schwarzschild, Agnes, 93-94, 291
Science & Society, 39, 57, 253, 305, 357
Securities Act of 1933, 192
Securities and Exchange Commission, 44-45, 178n, 180n, 185, 186n, 192
Segregation, 147-148
SHAEF, 244, 246
Shaw, Bernard, 318, 318n, 320-322, 323n, 326, 328; editor, *Fabian Essays*, 317-329
Shell Oil Co., 91
Shiso no Kagaku, 362
Simple commodity production, 58
Simple reproduction, 293
Singer, H. W., "India's Five-Year Plan: A Modest Proposal" (*Far Eastern Survey*), 87n
Slavery, 147
Smaller War Plants Corporation, 116-117
Smith, Adam, 253, 263, 300; *The Wealth of Nations*, 54
Social Democracy, 71; as defender of capitalism, 57; theoretical foundation of, 317-319
Social Democratic Party (Germany), 101, 225-226, 248, 319-320
Social psychology, 311
Social science, in U. S., 139
Social security, as outlet for government spending, 212-213; as U. S. problem, 208, 216
Social systems, diversity of, 32-33
Socialism, 284-285; arguments against refuted, 287-289; assumes shape of a social movement, 4; becomes public issue, 4; as a bogy, 205: case for presented by Pigou, 264-265; not dependent on war, 210; economy analyzed, 348-350; first theoretical expression of, 4; and humanitarianism, 202-204; inevitability of, 11, 17-18, 73; and the law of value, 356-358; laws of, 209-210; a modern phenomenon, 4; nonexistence of in ancient and medieval times, 3; and racial exploitation, 151; relation to Western civilization, 34; road to, 11-14, 18-23; solution to the German problem, 226; solution to Western Europe's crisis, 70-71; solves problem of income distribution, 215-216; solves problem of monopoly, 216-218; solves problem of social security, 216; strategy for achieving, 324-326, 339-340; transformed by Marx and Engels, 5
"Socialism Is the Only Answer" (Monthly Review Pamphlet), 205
Socialism Versus Capitalism (Pigou), 263-266
Socialist parties, relations with Communists after World War II, 70-71; in France, 340; in Western Europe, 317
Sociology, 139
South Africa, 142
South America, 84
Soviet aggression, nightmare of, 72
Soviet-German Pact of 1939, 231
"Soviet imperialism," 105-106
Soviet Union, absence of ruling class in, 61-62; and Central Asian Republics, 289; character of social system, 50-54, 105; compared to Nazi Germany, 286-287; controversy among Soviet economists, 231; and democracy, 50-51; and dictatorship of the proletariat, 52; foreign policy, 53; and Germany and Japan, 297; and Great Russia, 289; and internationalism, 53-54; nationalism in,

298; policy toward Germany, 229-232; relation to imperialism, 105-106; treatment of nationalities in, 53-54. *See also* Russia

Sowohl als-Auch, foreign policy of, 99-101

Spengler, Oswald, 330

Splawn Report: Railroads, 161n, 165, 165n, 166-167, 169n, 173n

Stalin, Joseph, 75; *Economic Problems of Socialism in the USSR*, 352

Standard Oil Co. of New Jersey, 91, 175, 185

State, in Keynesian theory, 260; and National Socialism, 239-240; role under capitalism, 54-55, 63-64; role under Nazism, 47-49

State capitalism, 194-195

State Department, 229

Steffens, Lincoln, 198-200; *Autobiography*, 135, 198-199

Sternberg, Fritz, *Capitalism and Socialism on Trial*, 93-94, 103-107; *Der Imperialismus*, 94

Structure of the American Economy, The (National Resources Planning Board), 116, 158

Study of History, A (Toynbee), 30-38

Study of Monopoly Power (House Judiciary Committee), 216n, 217n

Sumner, William Graham, 121

Supreme Court, 202, 218

Surplus value, theory of, 308

Sweezy Maxine, *The Structure of the Nazi Economy*, 48n, 49n, 50n

Sweezy, Paul M., *Socialism*, 215n; *The Theory of Capitalist Development*, 259n, 280n, 327, 342n, 352-362

TAX STRUCTURE OF U. S., 271

Taylor, Fred M., "The Guidance of Production in a Socialist State," 338

Temporary National Economic Committee (TNEC), 44-45, 111, 113, 116, 192, 194, 271; Monograph No. 20, 113; Monograph No. 29, 44-45, 116; Monograph No. 30, 44

Tennessee Valley Authority (TVA), 219

Time preference, 278

TNEC. *See* Temporary National Economic Committee

Toynbee, Arnold J., 30-38, 330; *A Study of History*, 30-38

Trotsky, Leon, 40, 51n

Truman, Harry S, 88-90, 113; "Economic Report to Congress" (1950), 212n

Truman administration, 366

Turkey, 101

UNDERCONSUMPTION, AND CRISES, 353-355, 359-360

Underdeveloped countries. *See* Backward countries

Unemployment, 323n; in capitalism and socialism, 264; in Keynes and Marx, 260; in Marxian theory, 308-309; in 1949, 114; in 1930s, 113, 206-207; no problem under socialism, 210. *See also* Mass unemployment

UNESCO, 330

United Electrical Workers, unemployment estimate of, 114

United States, a class society, 123; emerges as leading power, 86; and managerial revolution, 41-42; occupation policy in Germany, 227, 247-248; reasons for failure to go socialist, 25-26; relations with backward countries, 88-92; relations with colonial empires, 89. *See also* American capitalism

USSR. *See* Russia, Soviet Union

Utilities, included in major interest groups, 165-166, 183

Utopian socialism, 4

Utopianism, 320

Utopians, 197-198

Uzlar-Pietri, Arturo, 92

VALUE, LAW OF, 327; under socialism, 356-358

Value, theory of, 307-308, 321-323

Vansittartism, 239

Varga, Eugen, 231

Veblen, Thorstein, 199-200, 225, 295-301; *The Nature of Peace*, 295-301; *The Theory of the Leisure Class*, 60n

Venezuela, 91-92

Violence, 204

WAGES, in Germany compared to Britain and U. S., 227; share of national income, 214-215

Waldorf-Astoria Peace Conference, 67

Wall Street, 118, 122, 131, 135, 155-157

Wallas, Graham, 318n, 320, 328

Ward, Lester, 121

Warner, W. Lloyd, 123, 127-129; with Meeker and Eells, *Social Class in America*, 123

Waste, as U. S. problem, 208, 219-220

Wealth, motive to accumulate, 279-280

Webb, Beatrice, 320

Webb, Sidney, 318n, 320, 324-325, 328-329

Weimar Republic, 98, 234

Welfare state, as alternative to Cold War, 211; nonexistence in U. S., 212n

Welfare State (NUEA Handbook), 205

Wells, H. G., *The Outline of History*, 16, 37-38

Western Europe, crisis of, 69-70; and need for planning, 70; possibility of socialism after World War II, 70; relations with other regions, 69-70

Wicksell, Knut, 255n

Wicksteed, Philip H., 321

Wilhelm II, 97-101

Wilson, John D., "The New Defense Facilities" (*Survey of Current Business*), 48n

Winstanley, Gerrard, 4

World War I, and American capitalism, 112

World War II, saved American capitalism, 207; turning point in history of imperialism, 85-86

Writings and Speeches of Eugene V. Debs, 202-204

YOSHIDA, Y., 352-355, 358, 360-361

Yugoslavia, 19